CLIVIAS

The wide variety of forms and colors of modern clivia flowers.

CLIVIAS

HAROLD KOOPOWITZ

with photographs by James Comstock
Foreword by Sir Peter Smithers

TIMBER PRESS
Portland · Cambridge

Mention of trademark, proprietary product, or vendor does not
constitute a guarantee or warranty of the product by the publisher
or authors and does not imply its approval to the exclusion
of other products or vendors.

Published in 2002 by

Timber Press, Inc.
The Haseltine Building
133 S.W. Second Avenue, Suite 450
Portland, Oregon 97204, U.S.A.

Timber Press
2 Station Road
Swavesey
Cambridge CB4 5QJ, U.K.

Printed in Singapore

Library of Congress Cataloging-in-Publication Data

Koopowitz, Harold.
    Clivias / Harold Koopowitz with photographs by James Comstock;
    foreword by Sir Peter Smithers.
        p. cm.
    Includes bibliographic references (p.)
    ISBN 0-88192-546-2
    1. Clivia. I. Title.

QK495.A484 K66 2002
584'.34—dc21

2002017987
CIP

This book is dedicated to my special friends:

JIM COMSTOCK,
who knows the true meaning of clivia obsession;

YVES AUBRY,
who knows a thing or two about birds;

HENDRIK VAN DER HOVEN,
who knows about all sorts of things;

NORITO HASEGAWA,
who knows an "obsession" is merely an understatement;

and last, but not least,

KAREN MUIR,
who really knows how to decorate!

In addition, this book is also dedicated to the memories of

FRED MEYER,
a true genius among the plant hybridizers of this world,

and

GENE CALKINS,
whose passion for clivias knew no limits.

Contents

FOREWORD

OR MOST of my long lifetime the clivias have been undistinguished occupants of north-facing windowsills, sitting in
saucers patiently surviving where few of the popular genera
would, possibly even blooming now and then. Until very recently
these were the indifferent plants sold by the nursery trade in retail
shops. But now Cinderella has begun to come into her own, and a
small but enthusiastic group of her admirers and breeders worldwide have brought her out from an undistinguished past to a lively
present and promising commercial future. This native of Southern
Africa has been extensively bred and greatly improved there, but it
has also been the subject of important developments in China,
Japan, and Australia as well as in California and Belgium. Now this
genus of four species and their very numerous derivatives has found
a monographer in Professor Harold Koopowitz, the distinguished
author of this book.

The world of horticulture ranges from the windowsill grower to
many diverse kinds of gardeners to those who are sufficiently serious and dedicated to need a basic knowledge of botany and nomenclature. On the other hand, academics in the field range from those
who are also expert cultivators to the pure botanists more familiar
with dried specimens in the herbarium than with living material in
the garden or greenhouse, and who probably never lifted a trowel in
their lives.

It is the good fortune of *Clivia* enthusiasts that Professor Koopowitz is right in the middle of this spectrum: a highly distinguished academic and an enthusiastic and experienced cultivator able to give authoritative advice on the handling of these rather specialized plants. Indeed, he needed to be both to have occupied with great distinction the position of Director of the Arboretum of the University of California at Irvine and be a moving spirit in the International Bulb Society over whose world conference he presided in February 1989. The result is this book, which is not only authoritative and accurate—as might be expected—but also replete with information about the culture and evolution of the modern *Clivia*, making it of great value to the grower and a pleasure to read. Now and again I detect the author's tongue in the academic cheek.

In the early monographs the process of coloured engraving lent reality to the written text. With modern photographic techniques this process is far advanced. But it is still the case that a fine image must exist in the eye of the photographer before it can become a telling illustration. And not only in the eye. At one of the exhibitions of my photography two women whom I did not know stood behind me, not knowing that I was the photographer, looking at a picture of a white tree peony bloom, a plant that I had cultivated with care and affection for many years. One of the women said to the other, "That picture was taken with love." I was startled to realize the truth of this. James Comstock is an enthusiastic admirer and cultivator of clivias, and his pictures in this book are his way of conveying to you his love for this beautiful living thing.

PETER SMITHERS
Vico Morcote

Acknowledgments

AN ENORMOUS NUMBER of people were willing to meet with me and to help educate me about clivias. To all of them I owe a debt of gratitude.

In California and the United States

Joe Solomone opened up his clivia range to Jim Comstock and me for several visits, and he was happy to sit patiently through my many questions. Likewise, Dave Conway made his collection available for our perusal and photography. Other Californians who were helpful include Hodge Amemiya, Randy Baldwin, Ron and Mary Chamberlain, Glynne Couvillion, Joe Dana, William Drysdale, Alan Meerow, Franklin Murphy, and Audry Teasdale. A special thanks goes to Jim Folsom and his staff at the Huntington Library and Botanical Gardens, especially Kathy Musial and Danielle Rudeen, who performed miracles and found me many of the older references and provided the reproductions of some of the older paintings. James Rose shared his plants as well as his enthusiasm.

In South Africa

Many people in South Africa opened both their homes and nurseries to us and went beyond merely being just friendly. In the Eastern Cape, Hendrik and Ellie van der Hoven shared their hospitality several times so we could study *Clivia nobilis* near Kei Mouth. In Grahamstown, Roy and Mary Lynne Lubke took us to see the *C. nobilis* that may have been close to the site where it was originally collected. Rodney Ellis drove us to Port St. Johns on a number of exciting trips to look for *C. miniata*. In KwaZulu-Natal, Sean Chubb and Greg Petit individually drove us to different localities to examine populations of *C. gardenii* and *C. miniata*. Avis Meresman and Danie Nel at the Cycad Centre were happy to talk to us and let us photograph a superb *C. gardenii*. In Mpumalanga, Angie and Roelie van Rooyen, together with Sieg and Linet Hamman, organized a hike and picnic so we could see *C. caulescens*. Henriette Stroh scheduled several days of activities, including meeting with various growers and hybridizers in Gauteng, and they drove us all over that province. Everyone I have mentioned also offered us the hospitality for which South Africa is justly famous.

Members of the Clivia Club took time out of their busy schedules to meet and discuss many different clivia topics with me. These ranged from breeding experiences to judging clivias at shows to the historical aspects of clivias in South Africa. Among these good people were James and Connie Abel, Des Andersen, Mick Dower, Graham Duncan, Tino Ferero, Koos Geldenhuys, Pat Gore, Ernie Hobbs, Jim Holmes, Wessel and Rudo Lötter, Frikkie Marais, Anna Meyer, Bing Wiese, Gert Wiese, and Elda de Witt. Through the miracle of e-mail, several others have been more than willing to help with some of my questions, and they include Mark Laing, Nick Primich, and Val Thurston.

In Europe
John Grimshaw was particularly helpful in providing photographs of *Cryptostephanus haemanthoides* and for taking pictures of Kees Sahin's collection. Mark Chase and Michael Faye offered their hospitality in London and facilitated my entry into the Herbarium at the Royal Botanic Gardens, Kew. Yves Aubry, who was with me at that time, helped to measure the herbarium specimens. Phillip Cribb was able to find me the one reference that seemed unobtainable in the United States.

In Australia and New Zealand
Several people were free with their knowledge, and these include Ken Smith, Keith Hammett, and Michael Styles. Thank you.

In Japan
Yoshikazu Nakamura was very generous in supplying me with many pictures, articles, and books on both Chinese and Japanese clivias, and I owe him a particular debt of gratitude. I am especially grateful for his bringing the paper on *Clivia* carotenoids to my attention.

Other Helpful People
There are others, too, who facilitated the writing of this book. Yu-Fu Liu and Yoshimitsu Sugiyama helped with their translation of the Chinese and Japanese literatures, respectively. Marilyn Howe found some of the chemical references that I had trouble locating. Several people read and commented on various drafts and versions of this book. They all made good suggestions, many of which I followed, and some of which I probably should have followed but did not. Neal Maillet of Timber Press gently prodded me toward using correct horticultural nomenclature despite my resistance. I would especially like to thank Lynn Bey-Roode for her editorial work and her meticulous and very careful attention to detail. Other friends who commented on early drafts included Hendrik van der Hoven, Jim Comstock, and Marc Hachadourian. However, I am solely responsible for any errors that remain, factual or otherwise.

INTRODUCTION

THE WORLD is filled with flowers. Some of them are regarded as special and given much attention, while others are considered rather ordinary and consigned to the backwaters of horticulture. There are also fashions in flowers and these change with time. This book is about clivias; they were immensely popular, sought after, and bred during the late nineteenth century. Then they languished, neglected in gardens and conservatories until, like a phoenix, they re-emerged a century later, even more popular than before and now amongst the most desirable of all connoisseur plants. Not only are the flowers spectacular, but clivias have also gathered about them an unusual devotion and an almost mystical allure. This mystique is illustrated by the following true history.

Elsie Grobler lived on a farm in the Transvaal in the late 1880s. Life was hard in those days, and although great distances made it difficult to travel, Elsie did get about in a covered wagon drawn by a team of oxen. After one trip into the adjacent Portuguese territory in the east, she returned with a plant to grow on her porch. This plant had strap-shaped leaves and bore trusses of orange flowers. It was *Clivia miniata*, a popular long-lived plant for the shady, protected verandas of that time. Where she obtained the plant from is not clear; that species does not occur naturally in modern Mozambique although it is found in adjacent Swaziland. It is possible that the route the ox wagon followed went through Swaziland. Perhaps Elsie bought the plant from someone along the way, but she was well versed in nature and it would not have been unusual for her to have collected the plant from the wild forests through which the wagon had passed. At any rate, on her return to the farm she planted the clivia in a half oil drum and it became one of her prized possessions. Visitors to the farm were anxious to buy or beg a piece of the plant but Elsie was reluctant to divide it. Before long people stopped asking. They called it Elsie's "Holy Plant" because she was so possessive of it. Actually she did not like to divide the plant because she thought it would take several years to recover before it started flowering again.

During the years 1899–1902 the country was in turmoil. It was the second Boer War and once again Britain was trying to annex the two Afrikaner Republics, determined to control the newly discovered gold fields. The South African farmers were difficult to subjugate. This was the first time that the British were faced with guerrilla warfare. The South African farmers (known as Boers) organized themselves into groups of commandos, wore khaki camouflage, and were very mobile and competent snipers. The British soldiers in their bright red uniforms still fought as blocks of well-disciplined troops, but that archaic system could not succeed against the Boer commandos. The women on the farms were essential for supplying resources that their menfolk needed. The only way that the British could succeed was to disrupt those lines of supply. Under Kitchener's command, the British resorted to a scorched earth policy. They set farms on fire and consigned women and children to concentration camps. Elsie saw her home set on fire, and, together with her children, was packed off to one of the prison camps. Life in the camp was grim; twenty thousand women and children died during the internment. But Elsie and her children survived, and at the end of the war in 1902 she was able to return to the farm. Among the blackened ruins of the veranda stood the half oil barrel, and in it the clivia plant was still alive.

The plant was as tough as Elsie. She had six children, two from her first husband and four from her second husband, and she later married a third man. All the children were keen gardeners and nature lovers having inherited their appreciation of plants from their mother. Among each child's wedding gifts was a division of the original clivia plant. It became a family heirloom.

Divisions of Elsie's clivia are still being handed down in the family, and some of her great-grandchildren now have pieces of the original plant. Henriette Stroh, a granddaughter, showed me her plant in flower. It bears clusters of starry, 2-inch (5-cm) flowers of a mid-orange color. The flower is peculiar in that each is supported on a bright orange ovary (the ovary is usually green in this species). Clivias as family heirlooms are not unusual, and I have found similar examples in many parts of the world from Scandinavia to Australia. I know of no other plants in Western culture that are used in this way.

There are few modern flowering plants that routinely change hands for hundreds or thousands of dollars per individual plant. Orchids are one such example. There is, however, only one group of plants where it is not unusual to pay as much as twenty dollars for a single seed or a thousand dollars for a choice division: the clivia. Fortunately, clivia plants and seeds are also available at much more reasonable prices, and growing their seed is so easy that anyone can aspire to produce exciting new and valuable varieties. Clivia growing and breeding is a newly emerging hobby taking on strongly international dimensions.

There is an additional mystique about the yellow-flowered forms of *Clivia*. From the time of their initial discovery they were considered special. Once very rare, they commanded exorbitant prices and were considered among the jewels of the plant world. Even today, exceptional clones still sell for thousands of dollars. But seed strains of yellow-flowered clivias are now available, which, while still pricey, are no longer the exclusive province of the very wealthy. Clivias are now within the reach of most gardeners. For the clivia connoisseur, yellow clivias are already passé, and the breeders are chasing more novel colors and forms. Pink- and pastel-colored clivias are currently fashionable and much sought after, while the mythical white clivia is only whispered about.

The special qualities of clivias were recognized in the Orient almost at the same time as they were in Europe. In Asia the term *lan* (Chinese) or *ran* (Japanese) is fixed to their name, and although these terms usually describe orchids, they can also refer to other "special" plants that are exulted above the ordinary. Niou et al. (1999) have described the clivia as "not a common grass, it is a treasured grass, like diamond but not a common stone, it is a precious stone." The Chinese have bred their clivias for leaves rather than for flowers, and some of the most rare and desirable forms are dwarf plants. Those with variegated leaves are more prized. The Asiatic clivias can command even higher prices than the yellow-flowered forms and at amounts that would cause an orchid collector's head to spin. A single seed from selected parents of Chinese clivias can cost a hundred dollars. Prices asked for exceptionally fine plants can be as high as U.S. $35,000. This is perhaps what one might expect from "living works of art," as one Chinese fancier has described them.

Clivia flowers are so large, colorful, and simple that they make an ideal introductory flower for botany classes. They are also very easy to breed, and even novices are usually successful at setting seeds. The seeds are very large, easy to handle, and equally easy to germinate. Growing clivias from seed gives one the chance to produce new colors and perhaps novel flower shapes, and this has attracted amateur gardeners to the plant. In occidental countries individual seeds are sold for several dollars per seed, and many hobbyists, particularly retired persons, see their hobby as providing a modest source of income. Others breed clivias for the creative experience of making something exceptional, either for their own personal enjoyment or to show off to their friends. I make a few crosses each year trying to make novel clivias, but only plant about fifty to one hundred seeds each season. Others who are more obsessed plant thousands of seeds from hundreds of crosses each year. There is room in the hobby for all types.

Clivia growing is an actively expanding hobby. The plants them-selves have become adapted to modern life. Preferring indirect light, they are ideal indoor plants. As homes have become smaller, so have the plants been bred for decreased size. They like to grow in shady places and they summer well outdoors in the narrow spaces between buildings, in shady alleys, and under trees where little else grows. They are ideal pot plants that like to be root bound, will suf-fer much abuse and neglect, and on top of that they are difficult to kill. In favorable climates they can be accommodated in the land-scape. One does not need to be a master gardener to grow clivias well. Add to these virtues their spectacular flowers and one has a plant that fits in well with the modern lifestyle. Europe produces nearly one million flowering potted clivias each year, and while the numbers in the United States are not as large, production and sales, particularly of the yellow clivias, are increasing. Similar patterns are emerging in Australia, China, and Japan. In South Africa—the home of the wild clivia species—interest is reaching epidemic pro-portions with numerous annual shows, emerging societies, and publications. Those involved with growing, collecting, and breed-ing clivias are often quite intense about their plants and their hobby; their interests sometimes border on the obsessive. This is not unusual, however, for gardeners who focus on specific plant groups usually want all the nuances and varieties available to them. However, the lengths that individuals will go to get a special clivia are sometimes surprising.

In part, the modern popularity of clivias is promoted by elec-tronic forms of communication. E-mail networks bring enthusiasts, situated thousands of miles apart and on different continents, together and into daily contact. They trade electronic pictures of their special flowers and discuss those plants and their culture in open forums. Many clivia breeders also advertise their plants and seeds on the World Wide Web. Seeds and pollen are moving across the world at a fast rate. Seeds are usually not subjected to those quar-antine and phytosanitary limitations that restrict movement of mature plants across international boundaries. Air travel has become so fast and inexpensive that some clivia growers think little of meeting in distant countries for international symposia and shows to discuss and appreciate these fascinating plants. Clivias are truly flowers for the twenty-first century.

Chapter One

WHAT IS IN A NAME?

PLANTS GET THEIR NAMES in a variety of ways. Their scientific names are latinized and are either very brief descriptions of the plant or memorials to specific people. Each scientific name (or Latin binomial) begins with a plant's genus name (here, *Clivia*), which is always capitalized, followed by the species name. The name *Clivia* is pronounced "klive-ee-ah" and it describes a genus of southern African plants belonging to the family Amaryllidaceae that are named in honor of Lady Charlotte Florentia Clive. *Clive* is a surname derived from the word cliff that refers to a sharp incline, and it is thought to have been assumed by a family in recognition of their residence on a steep slope. Some scientific names also include designations for varieties or subspecies. The genus name in *C. miniata* honors the British duchess Lady Clive, but the species name also describes the orange-red color of the flowers. (Translated from the Latin, *miniata* means "painted with red lead.") *Clivia gardenii* honors not only Lady Clive but also a British soldier, Major Robert J. Garden of the Forty-fifth Regiment stationed in what was called the Natal Colony in the 1800s; the name contains no reference to the character of the plant. As the centuries pass, the reasons why people are honored tend to get lost, as do their own personal histories. This is a shame because names are one of the important dimensions of a plant, and if one is to understand and appreciate a plant fully, it follows that the reasons for and politics

An engraving of Charlotte Florentia, duchess of Northumberland,
known as Lady Clive. By courtesy of the National Portrait Gallery, London.

behind its name are also important. Who Lady Clive was as a person, and how and why the *Clivia* name was almost stolen away from this extravagantly beautiful genus are not generally known, and yet it is an important part of the lore of this genus. (Readers are encouraged to consult this book's appendix for a capsule biography of this great woman's life.)

THE DISCOVERY OF CLIVIAS

The complete story of the several independent discoveries of *Clivia nobilis* and the race to name it is not well known. Clivia enthusiasts seem to be fascinated by the historical aspects of the discovery, and they are recounted here.

William J. Burchell arrived in Cape Town, South Africa, in 1810. He was a schoolteacher whose fiancée had fallen in love with and married another man on her journey to join Burchell. He remained a bachelor for the rest of his life. As with many other Englishmen, Burchell was fascinated by natural history, and South Africa was an excuse to indulge his interests and try to forget about his ex-fiancée. He decided to set out on a long safari of exploration. Burchell outfitted a covered wagon for his trip and together with six Hottentot guides and about twenty oxen set out to explore the country. Along the way he collected herbarium specimens of plants and made observations on animals. His name is commemorated in Burchell's zebra as well as in many plants, including *Burchellia bubalina*, the wild pomegranate, a conspicuous shrub that bears clusters of orange-red flowers. The expedition lasted for nearly four years. At first he proceeded north but then turned southeast, ending up in Grahamstown in what is now the Eastern Cape Province. From there he followed the coast back to Cape Town. Burchell found a plant that would eventually turn out to be not only a new genus and species, but would also be named for Lady Clive. Whether he found the plant in the forests just outside of Grahamstown or in the dune forests along the coast is not clear, for it still occurs in both forests. Today

Featherstone Kloof, a piece of remnant forest outside of
Grahamstown, South Africa.

Burchell's entire trek could probably be made leisurely in a few days,
but then it was an epic journey. In those days South Africa was a
wonderland for the botanically inclined, and it was easy to make
important discoveries. Burchell recorded that on a 1-mile (1.6-km)
hike near Cape Town he collected more than one hundred species
that were new to him. He returned to Great Britain after his journey
accompanied by thousands of herbarium specimens. He spent the
next decade writing up his data, arranging his specimens, and discussing them with other noted authorities of that time.

Along comes another player in the story. William Herbert was
one of those noted authorities whom Burchell consulted. He was
born in 1778, the son of the first earl of Carnavon, and Lady
Elizabeth, the eldest daughter of the earl of Egremont. He has
been described as having a brilliant mind. Educated at Oxford,

Clivia nobilis on the forest floor, Grahamstown, South Africa.

Herbert entered the ministry after a stint as a member of Parliament. He wrote many works of a religious nature as well as several botanical treatises. He seemed to have been fascinated by bulbous plants and wrote a monograph about *Crocus* as well as one on the amaryllis family. It is with the latter that his name is still associated, and his monograph about them published in 1837 is considered a classic. Herbert's name is commemorated in the Herbert Medal currently bestowed by the International Bulb Society for meritorious work with bulbous plants, and their publication is called *Herbertia* in his honor.

On his return to England, Burchell showed his plant specimens to Dean William Herbert, who was particularly interested in the bulbous specimens and other flowering monocotyledonous plants. Herbert examined the specimen collected near Grahamstown but mistook it at first for a plant of *Agapanthus*. There is considerable resemblance between the vegetative parts of the two plants, and dried specimens look especially similar. But Herbert soon realized that Burchell's specimen was novel and he wanted to acquire a living specimen. He persuaded Burchell to give him the exact locality of the collection and then managed to contact and persuade an army officer stationed in that region to bring a live plant back to him on his return to England. And so William Herbert took possession of a live specimen long before anyone else.

Herbert also relayed the exact locality information to a Mr. Tate, who traded in exotic plants. Tate was able to import a large number of the mysterious plants in 1828, but he also mistook them for the well-known *Agapanthus* and offered them for sale as such. As best we can surmise, clivias were purchased under the *Agapanthus* name from Tate by a Mr. Forrest, who managed the plant collections of Syon House, the Middlesex seat of the duke of Northumberland, and the residence of the third duke's wife, Lady Clive. Whether or not Forrest thought he had bought an *Agapanthus* plant is unclear, but it became clear both to him and Herbert that Burchell's plant was something very different when it bloomed for the first time (probably in 1827) at Syon House. Forrest had bought much more than an interesting plant; he also bought immortality for his employer's wife.

One can sense from his writings that Herbert was disappointed not to be the first to flower the plant. Herbert later wrote that his plant had been maintained in a stovehouse (a tropical conservatory of the Victorian era) at uniformly warm temperatures. He realized that had the plant been kept cooler, he might have been the first to see and name this genus.

There is another claimant for the title "*Clivia* Discoverer," and that is James Bowie. He was the son of a London seedsman, and while still a very young man was sent out exploring the world's plants on behalf of the Royal Botanic Gardens, Kew in England, which was already emerging as the premier botanical garden in the world. After a stint in South America, Bowie was sent to South Africa in 1816. By

The *Clivia nobilis* painting that Lindley used in his original description of the species. Picture courtesy of Huntington Library.

The *Imantophyllum aitoni* painting used by Hooker and copied from the painting Lindley had used. Picture courtesy of Huntington Library.

this time Burchell had already returned to England with his dried specimen of what would turn out to be *Clivia nobilis*. Bowie had to return to England shortly after 1820 when Kew suffered a budget cut after the death of its director, Sir Joseph Banks. It seems he returned to South Africa fairly soon because in 1823 he sent two plants of *C. nobilis* back to the new director, William Jackson Hooker. Bowie requested that the new species be named for a Mr. Aiton who was Bowie's patron at the time and who must have underwritten at least part of his expenses. Hooker, however, did not have the flowers that are essential for naming a new species. Herbert was actually growing the plant long before Bowie had discovered his specimens in South Africa, but Bowie has mistakenly gone down in history as the discoverer of *Clivia nobilis*.

Illustration of *Clivia gardenii* used by
Hooker in 1856. Picture courtesy of
Huntington Library.

John Lindley named the plant that had flowered in Lady Clive's collection *Clivia nobilis*, and it appeared that way in the Botanical Register. He made a play on words by stating that the name was a "compliment long due the noble family of Clive." It was touch and go as to what would be the plant's scientific name because Sir William Hooker had written a second description for the *Botanical Magazine*, a different journal. Normally the initial name published has preference, but in this case both descriptions were published on the same day in 1828! Hooker's plant had been collected by Bowie and it was named "*Imatophyllum aitoni*," the name published in the *Botanical Magazine*. Hooker had meant to call the genus *Imantophyllum*, but because of an error it was misspelled. He corrected it at a later time.

Clivia, however, became the name that was widely adopted, and this was probably in deference to the popularity of the great Lady Clive. By the time that Hooker again had a chance to name another species, approximately thirty years later, the name clivia was so entrenched that he did not hesitate to name it *Clivia gardeni*. By convention that name is currently spelled *C. gardenii*.

Some parts of the history are still murky. Both Lindley and Hooker knew that the original plant of *Clivia nobilis* had flowered in the duke of Northumberland's conservatory. Forrest had obtained permission from the duke to commission a painting of the flower, and when he informed Lindley that the plant was in flower, Lindley wrote that it was actually the second time the plant had flowered. He mentioned that the plant had flowered in July of the previous year, which would have been 1827. Forrest gave Lindley vital information about the plant for the species' description and allowed him to have a drawing prepared of the flower (as shown above). Subsequently, Forrest communicated with Hooker and allowed him to copy the commissioned painting. But Hooker stated that the plant had flowered the previous October, also in 1827. It is not unusual for *Clivia nobilis* to flower more than once a year, especially on a large plant that was adjusting to the Northern Hemisphere. One wonders if Forrest knew that Hooker also planned to name the species. Surely he would have realized that if Hooker published first, his employer's wife would have lost her chance at the name. This might have had an adverse effect on his livelihood! It is therefore more likely that Hooker used some sort of subterfuge to get his hands on the painting, perhaps stating that he merely wanted to publish the picture, not that he wanted to actually describe the species. Or maybe Forrest, not realizing the delays that can accrue during publication, knew that Lindley already had a three-month lead and so expected him to have publication priority.

For several decades there was confusion about which name to use. Some people used *Imantophyllum* while others used *Clivia*. It was not until 1864 that E. Regel clarified matters and designated Clivia as the proper name in a German journal *Gartenflora* giving the credit to Lindley because Lindley had actually written his description several months before Hooker.

NOT ALL NAMES ARE GOOD

The common name for *Clivia* in South Africa's Afrikaans language is *boslelie*, which translates into English as Forest lily, an apt epithet. The old name for the countryside around Grahamstown where *C. nobilis* was first found was Caffraria. The name was derived from Caffer or Kaffir, an Arabian word signifying unbeliever or infidel, and was used to refer to the black peoples who lived in the region. Outside of Africa *Clivia* became known as the Kaffir lily, and it is still marketed around the world and particularly in America and China under that name. In South Africa the word's meaning gradually changed and it became more and more defamatory until in recent times it became synonymous with the "n" word as used in the United States. Today no one in South Africa would refer to the plant by its American common name, but unaware of the name's derogatory significance, those in the American trade continue to use it. The name has also surfaced in English translations of recent Chinese books on clivias. It is about time that commercial nurseries in the United States and elsewhere stop the current practice. Clivia is a nice name, it is euphonious and not too long, easy to pronounce, and it commemorates an interesting lady. Although there is no need for a common name, Forest lily at least has neutral connotations.

KUNSHI-RAN

In Japan, where clivias are very popular as pot plants, they are called *kunshi-ran*. *Ran* means "special flower," and although it has been used for other plants too, it is used primarily for orchids today. *Kunshi* translates as "royal" or "majestic," so the entire name seems to mean a royal special flower. When I first encountered the name I thought it was very apt because a fine *Clivia miniata* in flower can be a spectacular plant worthy of being brought to the attention of a monarch. The name, however, appears to have been derived from the literal translation of the species name given to the first species described, *C. nobilis*, and the word "kunshi" refers to the noble house of Clive and not to a flower fit for a king. "Kunshi-ran" now appears to be the commonly accepted name for all clivias despite an attempt to apply the name "*ukezaki kunshi-ran*" (meaning the "upward facing royal Clivia" since the original species has pendent flowers) to *C. miniata*.

CLIVIA NAMES

As interest in clivias and especially in breeding them has proliferated, it has become increasingly important that people be able to identify specific plants. Some modern clivia plants change hands at a cost of tens of thousands of dollars. People need assurance that when they are discussing a plant of *Clivia miniata* 'Mellow Yellow', they are talking about the same individual plant. In other groups of plants such as daffodils (*Narcissus*) or *Dianthus*, there are thick volumes that list the names that have been given to every plant, and such names have to be registered. One can use these volumes to trace the ancestry of any particular daffodil. There are definite rules for naming orchids or roses, but until recently there were no generally accepted rules for clivias. A register of clivia names is currently being set up and will run under the aegis of the Clivia Club, an international group of clivia devotees headquartered in South Africa.

There is an international code for the different ways that desirable horticultural plants are named. Deciding on the kinds of names that should be used for *Clivia* will be among the most important activities of clivia groups in the immediate future. There appears to be much confusion concerning the way names were given to clivia plants in the past. Here we will try to sort out and elucidate some of the problems. Currently there are several different kinds of names in use that are applied to various clivia plants, and people have not clearly distinguished between them. As more people become involved with breeding these plants, it will become increasingly important to keep the record straight.

SPECIES NAMES

These are the names conferred upon different types of clivias found in wild populations. Fortunately, clivias belong to a small genus with only four currently recognized species (at least at the time of writing this account). There has been relatively little confusion between these names compared to that in many other much larger genera. The four *Clivia* species currently recognized are *Clivia caulescens*, *C. gardenii*, *C. miniata*, and *C. nobilis*.

GREX AND GROUP NAMES

Until recent changes in the *International Code of Nomenclature for Cultivated Plants*, "grex" names could be given to all of the progeny of a cross between two species. Any time that an exact cross was repeated, the same grex name applied. This was also true if different individuals of the same grex were mated. For example, *Clivia* Cyrtanthiflora was the grex name applied to the offspring of *C. miniata* × *C. nobilis*. Any *C. miniata* crossed with any *C. nobilis* had offspring that could be referred to as *C.* Cyrtanthiflora. It did not matter which was the pollen or pod parent. Crossing any *C.* Cyrtanthiflora with itself or with any other *C.* Cyrtanthiflora also still resulted in *C.* Cyrtanthiflora. However, if *C.* Cyrtanthiflora were backcrossed to either *C. miniata* or *C. nobilis*, a new grex name would be required.

Grex names are no longer allowed for plants such as clivias. They are reserved exclusively for orchids. However, the *Code* does allow grex names to be modified into cultivar-group names, with the word "Group" being added to the previous grex epithet. (The term *cultivar* is a contraction of *cultivated variety*.) Thus, *Clivia* Cyrtanthiflora is now more properly referred to as *Clivia* Cyrtanthiflora Group.

Note that when a grex name resulted from an artificial cross, the name was always capitalized and was not written in italics. If a cross is the result of a *naturally* occurring hybrid it would be written as *C.* ×*cyrtanthiflora* with an × before the epithet and the name italicized and written with a lower case first letter. Wild occurring *C.* ×*cyrtanthiflora* does not appear to have been officially described, but one herbarium specimen collected in 1902 near Butterworth, South Africa, looks like that natural hybrid. In order to be valid, names of naturally occurring hybrids must have been published together with the names of their parents. Although *Imantophyllum*

Cyrtanthiflorum (*Clivia* Cyrtanthiflora Group) was published in 1877, the publication described a man-made hybrid, not the natural cross. Thus, the use of the name *C. ×cyrtanthiflora*, which is frequently encountered, is not strictly allowed.

The use of *Clivia ×cyrtanthiflora* or *Clivia* Cyrtanthiflora Group for *Clivia* crosses involving any of the other species is not recommended, and new names are needed for these particular crosses. Early names that were latinized, usually during the nineteenth century, are normally retained. Hence, *C.* Cyrtanthiflora Group is still valid, but new group names or man-made hybrids are anglicized. Group names may not contain certain words such as "cross," "form," "grex," "hybrid," "strain," or "variety." Readers are referred to the *Code* for more detail.

Primary hybrids are the results of crosses between two different species. Crosses between primary hybrids and other parents are often called advanced hybrids. One such advanced hybrid between *Clivia* Cyrtanthiflora Group and *C. miniata* appears to have been made several times, and it deserves its own group name. These crosses are not to be included in *C.* Cyrtanthiflora Group.

The requirements for establishing a group are different from the naming of the old-style grex. Groups can be merely a recognizable assemblage of plants that have a resemblance—not all groups are merely grexes in new clothing. (Even horticultural selections from one species can be divided into groups.) The siblings of a cross can sometimes appear to be very similar to each other, and one may not want to bother to differentiate between them. In those cases, they can be given group names. This is what appears to have happened with some of the yellow clivias. Perhaps the most famous example is *Clivia* 'Watkin's Yellow', which really should be written or identified as *C.* Watkin's Yellow Group.

When a group name appears within the full name of a plant it is demarcated by parentheses or square brackets. The plant that was listed formerly as *Clivia* Cyrtanthiflora 'First in Love' is more properly referred to as *Clivia* [Cyrtanthiflora Group] 'First in Love'.

It should be recognized that even group names, like grex names, may outlive their usefulness in the face of generations of intensive plant breeding and increasing obscurity of parentage in hybrids. This is true of daffodils where the register now contains tens of thousands of names, but no grex names (Kington 1998). Roses are another case where cultivar names are used and grex names usually ignored. The new clivia register to be compiled will also contain cultivar names, may contain group names, and may not contain grex names. While grex and group names are helpful in understanding a species' contributions to breeding, they tend to lose their value after several generations. However, during that early period of identifying and naming plants, they are very important.

CULTIVAR NAMES

Within a genus, species, or group, desirable individuals may need to be singled out for special recognition. In that case they can be given cultivar names. Asexually propagated divisions (the products of tissue culture multiplication of the same individual) are genetic clones and thus share the same cultivar name. Sports or mutations that appear on or in a given cultivar during propagation are, in fact, genetically different and should be given new cultivar names. Seed strains that produce uniform plants such as many of the so-called F_1 flowers and vegetables can also be given cultivar names, but only if they are highly uniform for shape, size, and color patterns. Cultivar names are always written in roman script and can contain numerals or codes. They are always enclosed by single quotation marks. The first letter of each word is capitalized, and the epithet is embraced by single quotes. When it is clear that a selection has been taken from a plant of a "pure" species that is not the result of interspecific hybridization, the name should be written such as *Clivia miniata* 'Emmie Wittig's Pink'. Whenever a cultivar name is given to a plant of unclear parentage or hybrid origin, the genus name alone should be given, as with *Clivia* 'Orange Belle'. New cultivar names given to plants after 1959 cannot be latinized (for example, 'Purpurea').

Cultivar names will assume increasing importance as tissue culture multiplication of special plants becomes more commonplace. Cultivar names are not important for landscape plants but are very useful for show plants, important breeding plants, and other valuable and expensive plants.

STRAINS

Line breeding toward a certain end point often leads to relative genetic uniformity and similar looking plants. The term *strain* could also be used to identify these plants, and their naming would be similar to cultivar-group names. One might then write *Clivia miniata* New Dawn strain, which is the name that Jim Holmes has given to his yellow clivias where he has consistently weeded out any orange colors and now has an almost pure yellow breeding strain. Two other commonly used names are *C. miniata* Belgian strain and *C. miniata* Sahin's Twin strain. I suggest that the clivia fraternity find some consensus about whether to call these assemblages groups or strains since either word could be used. Strains and groups are seed grown and hence not genetically identical. And it is possible to derive new strains from older ones by further line breeding. It is worth noting that the *International Code of Nomenclature for Cultivated Plants* disallows the use of the word strain in cultivar names and cultivar group epithets, and the term strain is not recognized by horticultural taxonomists.

Within a group or strain, an exceptional clone can still be singled out for a cultivar name. Holmes bred such a plant from his *Clivia* New Dawn strain, and because it is very pale, he named it *C. miniata* 'Cape Snowflake'. One does not normally refer to the group or strain from which the particular cultivar is derived.

It may seem very complicated to name clivias but it really is not. We are actually fortunate in that we have many options in how to proceed with naming clivias. Cultivar names are most important for breeding purposes because they allow one to refer back to the exact parentage if one wants to repeat a cross. Group or strain names are most important for the commercial trade, both the general pot plant and landscape market, because they give general information on type, height, or color of plants despite clone variation that can occur within the group. If tissue culture becomes commonplace, then cultivar names such as *Clivia miniata* 'Vico Yellow' will assume more prominence, as they will let the purchaser know the exact nature of the cultivar being bought.

INTERNATIONAL REGISTERS

Authority to maintain registers varies depending on the group of plants. Many but not all registers are headquartered with the Royal Horticultural Society in Great Britain. To a large extent it depends where the major interest in such registers resides; one needs a committed group to run a register. The situation with a clivia register is complicated because much of clivia breeding has already taken place in China and Japan, where the alphabet scripts are different from those used in California, Europe, South Africa, and Australia, the other major centers of clivia breeding. With orchids, grex and cultivar names are always written in English, irrespective of the country where they are bred and grown. Whether or not clivia breeders in Asian countries are prepared to coordinate with the International clivia register remains to be demonstrated. The clivia register is to be administered by the Clivia Club. It needs to be pointed out that for the cultivar name to receive priority it needs to be published either with a written description or with a picture; electronic publishing does not count.

Chapter Two

CLIVIA AND CRYPTOSTEPHANUS:
THE SPECIES

CLIVIAS ARE monocotyledonous plants or monocots belonging to the family Amaryllidaceae. (Monocots, as distinguished from dicotyledonous plants, have one cotyledon or seed leaf at germination.) There are in excess of sixty genera in the family containing well over one thousand species. The genus *Clivia* shares several features with other horticulturally important members of the same family, which includes *Amaryllis, Hippeastrum*, and *Narcissus*. The main features of this family are the presence of six colored tepals (similar petals and sepals), six stamens, and an inferior trilocular (meaning there are three cavities) ovary. Flowers tend to be borne in clusters with the flowers all coming from a single point on the peduncle or flower stalk forming a distinctive inflorescence called an umbel. Most of the Amaryllidaceae have strap shaped leaves and form true bulbs. Although both *Clivia* and its closely related sister genus, *Crypto-stephanus*, do not form bulbs, they are usually identified and included in discussions or forums on bulbous plants (Meerow et al. 1999).

THE *CLIVIA* SPECIES

The genus *Clivia* is small and contains only four species. They are all evergreen herbs with leaves arranged in two ranks borne on a thick rhizome. The branching roots are thick with a thick outer covering called a velamen. Flowers may be carried on a stout peduncle that is usually flattened on one side. Several bracts (modified leaves) protect the developing umbel of flower buds but the bracts are of unequal size and the buds emerge from them while still quite young. The tepals are fused to form a short tube situated atop the ovary. The tube may be so short as to be almost nonexistent; sometimes it can be discerned by examining flowers after they have senesced and abscised from the ovary. Perianth parts may be straight or curved forming either narrow pendent tubes or flaring, funnel-shaped flowers. The sepals are narrower than the petals. The stamens are attached to the base of the perianth tube and have long filiform filaments bearing versatile anthers. The style is terete and slender, longer than the perianth, with a short terminal trifid stigma. The ovary locules contain a reduced set of ovules, often only five or six. Fruit is a colored berry when ripe. Seeds are fleshy, without a colored testa containing phytomelanin, and spherical, usually at least a centimeter in diameter.

Clivia miniata from *Flores des Serres*.
Photograph courtesy of Huntington Library.

The four *Clivia* species are *C. nobilis*, *C. miniata*, *C. gardenii*, and *C. caulescens* in order of their dates of recognition. However, I will deal with them alphabetically. Of these, the one that is most distinctively different and set apart from the others is *C. miniata*, which is also the most important of the species for horticulture.

All four species are often thought to be endemic to South Africa, but there are records of *C. miniata*, *C. gardenii*, and *C. caulescens* occurring in the small country of Swaziland that adjoins northeastern South Africa. Strictly speaking, therefore, the genus is endemic to Southern Africa.

Key to the Species of *Clivia*

1a. Plants with umbels containing mainly
erect florets with spreading flower segments . . . . *C. miniata*
1b. Plants with umbels containing pendent flowers 2
2a. Florets narrow and linear, inner tepals straight,
leaf tips blunt to obcordate . . . . *C. nobilis*
2b. Florets narrow and curved, inner petals recurved 3
3a. Plants primarily flower in the fall to winter
seasons. Stamens clearly exerted from the
floral tube . . . . *C. gardenii*
3b. Plants flower primarily in late spring to early
summer, rhizomes aerial and elongated. . . . . *C. caulescens*

Clivia caulescens R. A. Dyer

Named in 1943, *Clivia caulescens* was the fourth legitimate species to be named. At first glance the flowers appear to be very similar to those of both *C. gardenii* and *C. nobilis*, but the plants differ from those species in several important respects that justify placing it into its own taxon. The major feature that sets this species apart is its distinct thickened stem, about 2 inches (5 cm) wide, which often looks like a length of short green bamboo. The distance between nodes on the stem varies depending on how fast the plants have been grown. In some old populations, this stem can be over 3⅓ feet (1 m) long. Very long stems usually topple over, sometimes draping over rocks or other plants. This *C. caulescens* stem, however, is not unique to this species. Elongated stems occur in some forms of *C. gardenii*, particularly those grown in swampy conditions. In the northern part of its

Clivia caulescens.

range in the Soutpansberg, *C. caulescens* is said to be stemless, so not all members of the species actually produce stems.

Occasionally, all species can also produce elongated rhizomes that branch from the main stem and that wander a considerable distance underground before emerging to produce a new fan of leaves. The underground rhizomes are relatively narrow and have longer internodes than erect stems, but they indicate the potential to produce long supporting stems. Their main function appears to be to distance offsets from the main growth. One assumes that this may reduce competition for nutrients between the growths, and yet offsets can also be produced directly from buds at the base of the main growth.

Plants of *Clivia caulescens* are found in mountain forests in Mpumalanga (formerly the Eastern Transvaal) and Swaziland, where they are often perched on rocky crags. Here the climate tends to be damp and cool but frost-free. There is usually sufficient moisture so

Clivia caulescens growing as a lithophyte. Note the long stem.
God's Window, South Africa.

that rocks and trees have a covering of moss. The roots course through the well-decayed leaf mold and humus that cover the rocks, and they are further protected by a layer of moss.

Flowers of *Clivia caulescens* appear to be intermediate in size between those of *C. nobilis* and *C. gardenii*, but size measurements can be misleading because of the natural variation of flower size that occurs in nearly all wild populations. They can be produced in immense umbels with over fifty florets and look quite handsome when in flower. The umbel can extend over the height of the leaves, but often the inflorescence is carried at the height of the leaves. Pedicels supporting individual flowers are very thin and bend over under the weight of their burden. Usually the color is a red-salmon with contrasting green tips. Flowering occurs in late spring, usually between the months of September and November in their native South Africa. Umbels in cultivation may be produced at anytime of the year, but the peak flowering period is during the spring.

The leaves of this species have acute tips similar to those of *Clivia gardenii* but quite different from the blunted apexes seen on *C. nobilis* leaves. In addition, the leaves have smooth margins. They can be over 3.3 feet (1 m) long and are usually 2 inches (5 cm) wide.

Seedlings tend to have erect, pale green leaves. They grow fast, and if pushed with fertilizer and grown under optimal conditions, the seedlings can often be forced into flower within four years.

Clivia gardenii W. J. Hooker

Of the three species with pendent flowers, *Clivia gardenii* may turn out to be the most important for making modern hybrids. There are several reasons for this. In the first place, this is a very variable species both in plant size and flower color. There are quite dark forms, very pale forms, and a variety of shades in between. Secondly, unusual and rare color forms such as yellow or pink clones are known. Finally, and perhaps most importantly, the blooming season extends from the fall into the early winter, which is usually the dry

Clivia gardenii.

season in its native homeland. This season of bloom makes it possible to extend the flowering period with hybrids because many of them flower before the full flush of the *C. miniata* season.

Sir William Hooker named this species for Major Garden in 1856 after plants the major had sent to the Royal Botanic Gardens, Kew flowered. Hooker noted that although his specimen of *Clivia gardenii* had fewer flowers than *C. nobilis*, they were larger. He described the flowers as being very falcate (meaning they are curved to one side) and ranging in color from dull orange or brick red, both of which then merge into yellow and finally into green tepal tips. The tepal tips recurve, so giving the flower a quite

Clivia gardenii growing in the wild in KwaZulu-Natal, South Africa.

different look compared to that of *C. nobilis* with its straight, narrow tubular shape. The style and anthers extend beyond the mouth of the *C. gardenii* flower.

The species is known primarily as coming from KwaZulu-Natal, but it has also been recorded as being from Swaziland. As that country abuts northern KwaZulu-Natal, it is not surprising that it occurs there as well. *Clivia gardenii* is generally found at lower altitudes than *C. miniata*, but we have seen one locality where the two species coexist. No doubt other localities where they coexist also occur.

The leaves of *Clivia gardenii* can often be differentiated from the others because they have a paler midsection along the basal third of the leaf. The leaves are softer than those of *C. nobilis* and they have pointed tips. Leaf sheaths tend to enclose the base of the leaves to make a long neck before the leaves emerge. The leaf edges are not rough.

There is a variety of this species that is known informally as the "swamp clivia" that lives in shallow riverbeds and under boggy conditions. It is quite a large plant with a big head of flowers. The vegetative parts of the plant look quite different from other members of the species in that they produce thick rhizomes that rise out of the water and bear numerous though short aerial roots. There is some discussion that this might represent a fifth *Clivia* species because of its unusual growth habit. A preliminary investigation of the plant's chromosomes by Keith Hammett suggested that they might also differ from those of the more usual forms of *C. gardenii*. However, Sean Chubb found that seed-grown specimens of the swamp clivia produced normal-looking plants when grown under regular garden conditions. It is possible that the aerial stems and roots are merely an edaphic adaptation rather than a genetic one, and thus would be an insufficient reason for erecting a new species taxon.

Clivia miniata (Lindley) Regel
Clivia miniata (synonyms: *Imantophyllum miniatum* Hooker, *Himantophyllum miniatum* Koch, *C. citrina*, *C. kewensis*) was the second

A mixed population of *Clivia gardenii* and *C. miniata* in KwaZulu-Natal, South Africa.

species to be recognized and was so stunning that it received almost instant global recognition as one of the most desirable of all flowers. The Europeans and the Japanese acquired plants as soon as possible and they found that this species possessed many characteristics that made for the ideal pot plant. For example, it could survive in deep shade, could tolerate cool conditions provided it was frost free, liked being pot bound, had stunning flowers, and made decorative berries. What more could one want? Soon plants appeared at doorsteps and windowsills around the world.

Plants were placed on public display even before the species had been given a scientific name. Plant journals such as *The Gardeners' Chronicle* carried descriptions that made them appear even more desirable. The unique feature of this plant was the enormous truss of bright orange flowers, often a foot or more in diameter, held in an almost globular umbel on an erect inflorescence. There was considerable variation between different clones, from the intensity of the orange color to the shape of individual flowers to the extent of the contrasting yellow-cream throat. The flowers were perfectly complimented by the two ranks of slightly arching belt-shaped leaves. No wonder its popularity was almost instantaneous.

The flower shape was so different from *Clivia nobilis* that Lindley had problems placing it into the correct genus. He described it as *Vallota ? miniata*, the question mark denoting his uncertainty in placing it within that genus. He described it in 1854 as having leaves that looked like those of a clivia, but noted that the flowers more closely resembled the erect funnel-shaped blooms of *Vallota purpurea* (now called *Cyrtanthus elatus*). The epithet *miniata* refers to the red-lead color of the flowers. Lindley did not know what the rootstock of the plant might be and assumed that it was a bulb. Mr. J. Backhouse discussed Lindley's concerns in a later issue of *The Gardeners' Chronicle* and he pointed out that the seeds were similar to the spherical fleshy seeds of a crinum and were borne in a red berry. He noted that there was no bulb, and furthermore, that the plant had originated in Natal and not Caffraria. The plants had arrived at the nursery marked as "*Imatophyllum*" sp. (note the genus is misspelled), and Hooker (1854) did not take long to publish the species as *Imantophyllum ? miniatum* in *Curtis's Botanical Magazine*. He thought it was closer to *Clivia* than *Vallota* but was also unsure, as indicated by the query after the genus name. He used *Imantophyllum* instead of *Clivia*, at the same time acknowledging Lindley's claim for *Clivia* as *C. nobilis*. Hooker felt that this new plant might be different enough from *Clivia* to warrant a distinct genus name and decided to use *Imantophyllum* instead for this new flower. Koch later changed the name to *Himantophyllum miniatum*. It took Regel in 1864 to transfer the species back to the correct genus as *Clivia miniata*. He thought that the differences in perianth shape were insufficient to warrant different genus names, and as Lindley had actually written the description several months before Hooker, Lindley deserved precedence. Regel often gets sole authority for naming the species, but he himself had written the name as *Clivia miniata* Lindley. It really should be written as *Clivia miniata* (Lindley) Regel, giving recognition to Lindley for naming the species and to Regel for making the correct combination of genus and species epithet.

Clivia miniata was originally collected in Natal. Mistakenly, it was thought that the plants came from Caffraria, but later it was confirmed that they were from Natal. Its range does extend from Morgan's Bay in the south in the Eastern Cape Province, which could be considered part of Caffraria, through the Transkei and south of and up to northern KwaZulu-Natal. There is also a record of the species from Swaziland, but that record is without locality data, and the species' occurrence that far north has been questioned. In some areas, the populations exhibit much more variation in flower form and color than in others. In southern parts of its distribution, *C. miniata* overlaps with *C. nobilis*. And in the more northerly aspects of its range, *C. miniata* overlaps with *C. gardenii*. Interestingly, *C. miniata* normally is found on west-facing slopes, and both *C. gardenii* and *C. nobilis* are said to occur on east-facing slopes. Although each species prefers somewhat different habitats, there are some places where *C. miniata* and either *C. nobilis* or *C. gardenii* may occur as a mixed population. For conservation reasons, those specific localities are not disclosed.

Clivia miniata is always naturally an understory plant, but plants are sometimes found in sunny positions in the wild. Those plants appear to be the result of tree cutting by the locals. Such plants are often sunburned. We have seen *C. miniata* growing in a variety of different places. It may be perched atop large boulders or on rocky ledges with its roots growing through leaf mold. In other localities, it occurs on the well-draining slopes of mountain forest floors where the soil is enriched with decaying leaves.

Clivia miniata growing wild in KwaZulu-Natal, South Africa.

In wild forms the flowers tend to range in color from the very rare pure yellows to a range of pastel oranges through to quite bright and dark orange. Very dark red-orange flowers are rare, even in artificially bred cultivated clones, and their original occurrence does not appear to have been documented. Orange forms also have a contrasting cream-yellow throat that is variable in color and extent. Certainly, very dark, reddish colors do not seem to be known in the wild; if they do occur, they must be very rare. It is only in recent years that those colors have been introduced into South Africa's cultivated *Clivia miniata* from clivias cultivated in other countries.

Flower shapes in wild forms range from smallish, open, narrow tepal flowers to large, trumpet-shaped blooms with wide, overlapping floral parts. Usually the sepals are narrower than the petals. A range of flower shapes has either been deliberately bred or has appeared spontaneously among various hybridizers' seedlings. These variations in shape will be discussed at length in chapter 8. The number of florets in the umbel is quite variable with some of the better forms carrying thirty or more flowers. The umbel can be brush-shaped, globular, or somewhere in between those two extremes.

The leaves of wild forms of *Clivia miniata* tend to be relatively narrow compared to many of the cultivated varieties. We have measured leaves at over 72 inches (184 cm) long in some wild Transkei populations, but generally the leaves in nature are only about half as long. Leaf width is rarely over 2 inches (5 cm) in wild populations. Many strains of cultivated *C. miniata* have leaves that are considerably wider.

Clivia nobilis Lindley

This was the first species to be flowered in England and it is the type species for the entire genus. As the most southerly of the four species, it was the first to be discovered as settlers and explorers moved northwest from the Cape of Good Hope. *Clivia nobilis* (synonym: *Imantophyllum aitoni* Hooker) is the most widespread of the "tubular" species in cultivation, although many plants labeled as *C. nobilis* are in fact the hybrid *C.* Cyrtanthiflora Group. Although no other species is as showy as *C. miniata*, a well-grown plant of *C. nobilis* with its large umbels of narrow, pendent, tubular flowers in shades of orange with contrasting green tepal tips can be quite memorable.

Clivia nobilis is a fairly widespread species that generally hugs the coast of the Eastern Cape Province, with plants often growing within striking distance of the ocean spray. In some places its distribution extends nearly thirty miles inland. The species ranges from the small town of Port Alfred into the Transkei, but it peters out near the border of KwaZulu-Natal. In some parts of the range it coexists with *C. miniata*.

Clivia nobilis often grows in the understory of stabilized dune forests that flank the sandy beaches of the South African east coast.

Clivia nobilis growing at the Huntington Botanical Gardens.

It grows in association with the giant tree bird of paradise, *Strelitzia nicolai*. Plants are on the forest floor, which can be quite steep. They often form immense clumps, and many offsets—sometimes thirty or more—are not uncommon. The thick fleshy roots forage in soil that is almost pure sand and that seems to contain little obvious organic matter. While they appear to be growing in a dryer situation than the other species, they are subjected to frequent summer rains. The plants seem able to tide themselves over the occasional droughts and the dry winters. In a large population there is always one or two plants that have flower trusses, but the majority flower in late spring (September in South Africa).

This species usually has distinctive leaves that can be used to tell it apart from the others. Leaf tips are either notched or bluntly rounded, whereas the other species tend to have acute tips to their leaves. The margin edges of leaf blades are fairly rough to the

Clivia nobilis.

touch. For the first few seasons of growth, the seedlings tend to have their leaves reflexed and parallel to the ground. Seedling leaves are a deeper bottle green than those of other species, and their recumbent stance leads to easy identification. They also have a paler central stripe on the upper surface. Seedlings of *Clivia nobilis* are much slower growing than that of the other species, and this is probably reflected in slower growth of their hybrids too. As seedlings grow

Leaves of *Clivia nobilis* in the wild with the distinctive notch at the tips.

larger, the leaves assume a more upright stance, and in the adult condition, they tend to be quite erect.

James Comstock and I studied a population of *Clivia nobilis* in the dunes at a small seaside resort of Kei Mouth looking for color variants. Any differences in color were fairly subtle; most flowers were vermilion-orange with green tips. The extent of green coloring appeared to vary with the age of the flower, fading as the flower got older. But there were a few clones that seemed to have more and deeper green coloring than others, and these were particularly attractive. Very pale, pastel apricot flowers appeared to be growing in deeper shade, but the amount and depth of orange pigment was directly dependent on exposure to sunlight. The structure of the flowers is such that the tepals overlap to form a tube. The overlapped areas are a creamy white color, while the portions facing the outside are shades of orange. Plants growing in brighter areas were deeper orange in color. However, direct and intense sunlight or prolonged sun exposure results in bleaching and burning of the orange pigments. There are a few variants that do seem to be genetic. An almost pure yellow form was published in the *Clivia Yearbook* (1998), but such plants are very rare indeed.

Variation between *Clivia nobilis* clones appears to be primarily in the robustness of the flower inflorescence. Of course, this is also related to how well the plants are grown. There are, however, plants that consistently bear enormous heads of florets. We counted individual umbels with over fifty florets at Kei Mouth, while others growing close by had far less.

The flower of *Clivia nobilis* appears to be a narrow tube, but only the bases of the tepals are fused into a short ring. The sepals overlap the petals to make what appears to be a long, straight, narrow cylinder. In the other species with pendent flowers, the petal tips recurve to give the flower the shape of a narrow funnel and the individual flowers themselves are curved to one side to make a claw shaped tube. The stamens and style do not normally extend or protrude beyond the length of the tepals.

Clivia nobilis growing with *Dracaena hookeri* and *Strelitzia nicolai*.
Kei Mouth, South Africa.

Natural hybrids of clivias

Occurrences of natural hybrids between the various species are rare, although *Clivia miniata* overlaps with *C. nobilis* in the southern portion of its range and with *C. gardenii* further north. There is a wild-collected natural hybrid specimen in the herbarium at Rhodes University, Grahamstown, of a natural *C. ×cyrtanthiflora* that was collected in the Butterworth area of the Transkei in 1902, but it was never described in the literature. The grex was named after flowering a man-made hybrid in Europe. I have visited one site in KwaZulu-Natal where purported hybrids between *C. miniata* and *C. gardenii* are said to exist. My examination of those plants' vegetative characteristics suggested that they were intermediate between the two species, but unfortunately they were not in flower to confirm the diagnosis.

THE *CRYPTOSTEPHANUS* (WELWITSCH) SPECIES

This is a little-known genus that bears several similarities to *Clivia*. Plants are distributed from South Central Africa to East Africa, but are not in general cultivation. On both morphological as well as molecular grounds, *Cryptostephanus* appears to be a sister genus that shares a common evolutionary origin with *Clivia* (Meerow et al. 1999). Others have also recognized this close relationship, and although attempts at hybridizing the two genera have been undertaken, positive results have never been reported. This is an important project because if hybrids can be produced between the two taxa, then totally new colors and forms could be possible. Hybridizing by means of embryo rescue techniques may be feasible, and in order to promote efforts in that direction, it is worthwhile describing what is known of the few species in this genus.

Similarities between the genera *Clivia* and *Cryptostephanus* include multiple flowers comprised of a tubular perianth with short floral segments borne in an umbel subtended by several unequal spathe valves. In both, the inflorescence is born on a flattened, two-edged pedicel. Vegetatively, the plants appear similar. There is no bulb, and the leaves are borne in two ranks originating from the tip of a thick fleshy rhizome. Fruit is a globular berry containing spherical, fleshy seeds.

Differences between *Clivia* and *Cryptostephanus* include a whorl of twelve small, fleshy appendages inserted at the mouth of the tube that in *Cryptostephanus* create a poorly formed corona. In *Clivia* there are no coronal appendages. Another difference, found in the *Cryptostephanus*, is the presence of a capitate globular stigma that may be hidden within the floral tube; in some species it is at a lower level than that of the stamens. The clivia stigma, by contrast, is usually slender with three terminal branchlets, and it is exerted either well beyond the stamens at the mouth of the floral tube or at their level. *Cryptostephanus* species bear their stamens in two series, and the stamens consist of short filaments attached to the floral tube. The seeds of *Cryptostephanus* are covered with a testa containing a pale brown pigment, phytomelanin. Phytomelanin normally produces a dark black color in the seed coats of many amaryllid species, but it is absent from clivia seeds. It is interesting that the phytomelanin in *Cryptostephanus* appears to be intermediate in coloration and concentration when compared to other amaryllids that have intense black pigmentation, and yet its relative *Clivia* has no pigmentation.

Five species were originally named to the genus *Cryptostephanus*, three of which are currently recognized. Two of the original five species (*Cryptostephanus herrei* and *C. merenskyanus*) have been transferred to *Cyrtanthus herrei*.

Key to the Species of *Cryptostephanus*

1a. Corona of 6 segments . . . . *C. densiflorus*
1b. Corona of 12 segments 2
2a. Flowers pale, white to pastel pink. . . . . *C. vansonii*
2b. Flowers darkly pigmented, purple to black . . . . *C. haemanthoides*

Cryptostephanus densiflorus Welwitsch

Originally collected in Angola, *Cryptostephanus densiflorus* Welwitsch was the founding species for the genus. This is a much smaller plant than the other two species and it possesses glaucous leaves, usually 12 inches (31 cm) long and only ½ inch (1.25 cm) wide. The plant bears six to eight leaves. The peduncle is shorter than the leaves. I examined the type and one other specimen that were housed at Kew and found that those species had thirteen and six florets in the umbels respectively. Baker (1888) described the umbel as "dense, twenty- to thirty- flowered." Individual flowers are about ½ inch (1.25 cm) long and ⅕ inch (0.5 cm) wide. He also remarked on the flowers being dark purple, but the description on the herbarium sheet of the smaller (not the type) specimen is "three dark red sepals, petals bright pink." In this species the stamens are all at the same level and the style is capitate. There are only six coronal segments (other species have twelve), and the tips of the petals do not open out significantly.

The two specimens were collected at an altitude of 4921 feet (1500 m) and 4333 feet (1321 m) from an open forest, with Baker remarking that the species was not very common. The type specimen was based on a plant collected near Lopolla in Angola in the mountains of Huilla. It is not known if this species is deciduous like that of the other glaucous species, *Cryptostephanus haemanthoides*, or if it is evergreen like *Cryptostephanus vansonii*. The species flowers in late spring.

There are no real cultivation guidelines for *Cryptostephanus densiflorus*. As far as I am aware, *C. densiflorus* has never been in cultivation, even though its coloring makes that species very desirable. Unfortunately, the political turmoil in its country of origin precludes its introduction for the foreseeable future.

Cryptostephanus haemanthoides Pax

Perhaps the best known of the species—and the most spectacular—is *Cryptostephanus haemanthoides*. If it can be bred with *Clivia*, it might generate a totally new set of colors. Despite this possibility, only in recent times have a very few plants of the species been brought into cultivation. All parts of this plant are much larger than the other two species, and it can bear dense umbels with over 150 almost black flowers.

Cryptostephanus haemanthoides was collected in 1877 by Hildebrandt and was the second of the species to be described. The plants are glaucous and have about five pairs of blue-gray leaves, which, like the other species of *Cryptostephanus* and *Clivia*, are arranged in two opposite ranks. Leaves are about 30 inches (75 cm) long and 1¾ inches (4.5 cm) wide. Several herbarium specimens at Kew had leaves that were only 12 to 16 inches (31 to 40 cm) long. The leaves can twist, are more spreading, and are not as neatly arranged as those of *Cryptostephanus vansonii*. The roots are fleshy and gray-white in color suggesting that they may also be covered with a velamen-like layer, similar to the condition in clivias.

Cryptostephanus haemanthoides appears to be a more xeric species that is exposed to greater sunlight, and it has been described as occurring among grass and rocks or in very dry semidesert with scattered thornbush scrub. It is also known to grow in open forest woodlands. Plants may occur in the shade under bushes or in more exposed situations. The species is known from one area of Kenya and it is said to be widespread in Tanzania. It has been collected from altitudes ranging from 2050 feet (625 m) to nearly 5000 feet (1524 m). Plants are deciduous and lose their leaves during the dry winter season. During that time they must subsist on resources stored in the fleshy roots and rhizome. Some of the roots are ½ inch (1.25 cm) in diameter and the rhizome may be 2 inches (5 cm) in width. In the specimens I have seen, only about 4 inches (10 cm) of the rhizome tip stays alive and the older portions degenerate. Although plants are said to occur in clumps, it is not known if such clumps are derived from branching rhizomes or from seeds that do not stray far from the mother plant.

Flowers are about 1¼ inches (3.1 cm) long with the tube being ¾ inch (2 cm) wide. Stamens are exerted and attached to the mouth of

Cryptostephanus haemanthoides. Tanzania. Photograph courtesy of John Grimshaw.

Flowers of *Cryptostephanus haemanthoide*s. Tanzania.
Photograph courtesy of John Grimshaw.

the tube. The style is also exerted and bears a small capitate stigma. Flower color has been described as dark red to blackish purple, but descriptions on herbarium specimens cover a range of interesting colors (Cribb 1979). Some of these descriptions are as follows: brown petals with white tips and white stamens, very dark crimson with yellow stamens, dark purplish like a black tulip with yellow-cream anthers, deep purple, crimson-purple, velvet brown, chocolate brown, black, indigo, and so on. The corona is of twelve separate lobes and often a contrasting cream-white color.

This species flowers in the summer after the onset of the rains that generally occur from February to March, but they can start flowering before that in late December if the rains have already started. Inflorescences of *Cryptostephanus haemanthoides* can be very large, and they seem to carry a considerable number of flowers at all stages of development. While some specimens can carry as few as thirty-five flowers in the umbel, others may have as many as two hundred. The fruit is a small red spherical berry.

As with *Cryptostephanus densiflorus*, there are no real cultivation guidelines for *C. haemanthoides*. Hybridizers are only now experimenting with this species and trying to learn to grow it. If one were fortunate enough to get a plant of *C. haemanthoides*, one might be tempted to grow it under more intense light with somewhat drier conditions than *C. vansonii*. I have found, however, that *Cryptostephanus* leaves can burn like those of a clivia plant. It may be possible to bring those plants into flower if they are dried out during the winter and spring months, but as they have no bulbs for storage, one should monitor the plants carefully to make sure they are not damaged by excessive dryness. Rates of desiccation in pots are much faster than those in the open ground because there is usually some moisture in the ground available to the plant.

Cryptostephanus vansonii Verdoorn

While still rare, this is the most common species in cultivation and the easiest to obtain by the persistent collector. It was named for a Mr. Van Son who flowered a plant in his garden near Pretoria, South Africa, and the species was described in 1943. This species of *Cryptostephanus* occurs as a forest floor plant at higher altitudes in the Bvumba and southern Chimanimani Mountains of eastern Zimbabwe, but it might also occur in neighboring areas of Mozambique. I saw it growing in leaf litter on top of large boulders in the Bvumba. The plant looks very much like a slender leafed clivia, but although it produces offsets, it does not seem to make the robust clumps common in clivias. In the original description, the leaves were described as being 24 inches (62 cm) long and ranging from 3/4 to 2 inches (2 to 5 cm) wide. The two clones that I grow have leaves that are narrower, 1/2 to 1 inch (1.25 to 2.5 cm) wide and only about 18 inches (45 cm) long. The type specimen had a peduncle 8 inches (20 cm) long, but my plants tend to have inflorescences about

15 inches (38 cm) tall, which can extend during fruit development. Peduncle height, however, appears to be dependent on light intensity, and in some seasons flower stems have been only 7¾ inches (20 cm) tall. Other plants I have seen also appear to be less robust than the original description.

The flowers in *Cryptostephanus vansonii* range from white through to a clear, baby-ribbon pink. But most of the forms in cultivation are white with a pinkish tinge. The corona can be white, yellow, pink, or apricot, but while it is sometimes of different color to the tepals, the structure is so small that it does not contribute in an obvious way to the overall color of the flowers. Gordon McNeil (1963) described one clone as opening white and "fading to a violet mauve." In my pink clone, the floral tube including the ovary is short, about ⅙ inch (0.4 cm) long, and the limb is about ½ inch (1.25 cm) long. Tepal limbs are spreading. The type specimen had about thirty flowers, and that corresponds well to the flowers I have grown. In both the developing and freshly opened flowers, the globular ovary is the same color as the petal tubes, but as the flower ages the ovary swells and greens up. Plants are self-fertile. Flowers do not all open at once as they do in clivias but appear to develop randomly, usually with several flowers open at a time. This extends the time that the plants are in bloom, and the season for a single umbel can be as long as two months. This species normally flowers in the summer but flowers may be produced at any time of the year. The seed heads form a spherical berry fruit ⅜ to ¾ inch (1 to 2 cm) in diameter that matures to a bright orange-red when ripe. Seeds are a tan-brown color and are generally rounder and smaller than clivia seed.

Several clivia breeders see this species as a possible route to making a clear white clivia hybrid. Successful attempts—if any exist—have not been publicized. Because the parents are self-fertile, breeders would have to use flowers emasculated in the bud to ensure that stray self-pollination does not occur. (See further comments in chapter 6 concerning intergeneric hybrids.) The chromosome number of *Cryptostephanus vansonii* was counted at twenty-four (Gouws

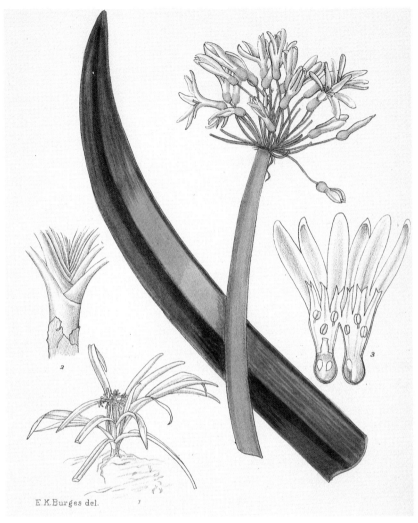

Cryptostephanus vansonii. From Flowering Plants of South Africa, t.885.
Picture courtesy of Huntington Library.

1949). This contrasts with those of the *Clivia* species, all of which possess a chromosome number $2n = 22$ (Ran et al. 1998). This means that if breeders succeed in making intergeneric hybrids between

Pink form of *Cryptostephanus vansonii.*

these two species, they will likely encounter sterility problems for future breeding unless the hybrids can be converted to polyploids.

Cryptostephanus vansonii is relatively easy to grow and flower, and it seems to flourish under the same conditions that clivias enjoy. Plants grow well in a 1-gallon (4½-liter) pot with a well-draining, light friable mix containing leaf mold and some sharp sand. I have seen plants survive—although not flourish—in a heavy clay mix. I grow mine under the same lighting and feeding regimes that I use for clivias. Plants can go for several years without repotting but do seem to appreciate fresh mixes. They will grow outside under southern Californian coastal conditions and will produce somewhat darker pink flowers if exposed to more light. Leaves will burn under intense sunlight, however.

Cyrtanthus herrei (Leighton) R. A. Dyer

This is a magnificent plant that was initially mistaken for a species of *Cryptostephanus* because the flowers also bear coronal segments. In particular, they superficially resemble *C. haemanthoides* since they have glaucous leaves. Unlike species of *Cryptostephanus*, however, *Cyrtanthus herrei* (synonyms: *Cryptostephanus ? herrei* Leighton, *Cryptostephanus merenskyanus* Dinter ex Schulze) produces bulbs and has flattened seeds. Individual blooms tend to be much larger than those of the *Cryptostephanus* species. Leighton, who described it originally, was not really sure that it was a plant of *Cryptostephanus*. Dyer later placed it into *Cyrtanthus* and called the coronal lobes a "false corona," but to me they do seem very similar to the coronal lobes of *Cryptostephanus*. This species locality is South Africa, and it is also found in southern Namibia. The Namibian forms were separately described as *Cryptostephanus merenskyanus* but have since been reduced to synonomy with *Cyrthanthus herrei*.

Pests are few but *Cyrtanthus herrei* is susceptible to mealy bug and the various fungi that plague so many amaryllids. A systemic insecticide is useful because even drenches may not reach insects hidden between the leaf bases. Seeds can be started and grown under the same conditions that clivias require. Germination is usually slower, and it will take several years for *C. herrei* seeds to reach flowering maturity.

Chapter Three

THE BIOLOGY OF A
CLIVIA PLANT

THIS SECTION is for those hobbyists who want to gain an understanding of their plants that exceeds the normal information needed to be a plant grower. A knowledge of what makes up the body of a plant and its biology lets one understand and anticipate the plant's needs, and one becomes a better grower. I find that many "intense" hobbyists cannot get enough information about their favorite plants, but the natural history and biology of plants is often omitted from horticultural books. That is a pity. All the parts of the plant have gone through a design filter called natural selection and are the result of millions of years of evolution. All parts are adaptations to ensure survival and reproduction for the continuance of the next generation. They need to be of adequate design so that they can function, but there is usually variation among individual plants. Variation is due to both inherited genetic information and the ways that those genes are expressed depending on the environment. Such variation is important, and it allows wild populations to adjust to alterations in the environment. Modifications in a population's variations are expressed as evolution—changes in form and physiology.

A wild clivia plant is designed to survive in nature, a sometimes hostile environment. Its success in doing so is measured by the number of offspring it produces over its lifetime and in the number of those offspring that are also able to reproduce. In order to do this the plant must be able to balance its own needs to grow and maintain itself against the long-term needs that are required to flower and produce seeds. Like nearly everything in the world, there are costs, and in the plant world the costs are in units of energy and certain inorganic elements. The energy comes from sunlight and is stored in the chemical bonds making up carbohydrate molecules. The elements are things like potassium, phosphorus, calcium, iron, and many others. Some of the elements may be in short supply, and the plant will have to partition carefully what can be expended in making and provisioning the seeds from what it needs itself to survive. While producing flowers is important for reproduction, the plant needs to balance those costs as well so that it can also provision the seeds. A successful gardener's job is to make it as easy as possible for the plant to carry out its tasks and to build an adequate store of energy and elements. The better this is done, the greater the flowering performance of the plant.

There is more to know when becoming a better plant grower. In understanding the natural history of the plant and the signals it receives from the environment, one facilitates and encourages optimum performance. It is not surprising that one can often coax plants grown in captivity to achieve a far greater performance they are ever able to achieve in the wild or in nature.

LEAVES

Usually the first thing one notices when looking at a clivia plant are the leaves. They are long and strap- or belt-shaped, often considerably longer than wide. They only occur in two ranks and are engineered so that they stay upright for much of their length. The leaves typically form a relatively stiff structure that may arch over if it becomes very long. How do the leaves stay upright? In part they are buttressed at their base with a clasping sheath that, together with the other sheaths, helps to hold the base of the leaf in place. The sheath totally encircles the stem of the plant at its base, but then it is sculpted to join the narrower leaf. At the junction of the sheath and the leaf is a layer of tissue that continues to divide. As in most other monocotyledonous plants, clivia leaves increase in length by cell division from this intercalary meristem. The intercalary meristem continues to divide for most of the life of the leaf, and thus the leaf will continue to elongate, although the rate of growth may slow down as the leaf gets older.

Inside each leaf are a large number of parallel veins. These perform two different functions, one that provides a conduit for water and nutrients, the other that is primarily mechanical. The veins contain cells with thickened walls that help add to the rigidity of the entire leaf. In a wide leaf the number of these veins can be considerable.

The primary function of the leaf is to photosynthesize, but it is also a storehouse for water and sugars produced by photosynthesis. The organelles (tiny subcellular organs) that carry on the important work of photosynthesis are called chloroplasts. They capture the energy in photons of light and make it available to the plant in chemical bonds that in turn can be stored in sugar molecules. Over the millions of years of evolutionary time, clivia plants have become adapted to living on forest floors, which have relatively low light levels. In order to capture the sparse light efficiently, they are able to produce enormous numbers of these chloroplasts. Leaves from plants grown under extremely low light conditions are a very dark bottle green, while those growing under higher light conditions need less chloroplasts and are a much paler green.

The chloroplast-bearing cells in clivias are arranged in a very characteristic way in the leaf. There are five to six layers of more or less cuboidal cells under the dorsal (top) surface of the leaf that are loaded with choloroplasts and a few similar layers of cells along the undersurface. The cells in the middle of the leaf are larger, more irregular in shape, and have few to no chloroplasts. This central layer is primarily for storage of water and photosynthate, the products produced by photosynthesis elsewhere in the leaf. If a plant receives adequate water, the central layer will help make the leaf plump and turgid, but under water stress, these cells loose their fluid and the leaf will shrink and become thinner. One can learn to gauge if one's plants get enough water by feeling their leaves. If their leaves are thin despite frequent watering, there are either too few roots or rot problems in the roots that prevent the leaves from getting sufficient water.

The leaves are covered with a single layer of elongated cells that make up the epithelium. The function of the epithelium is protective. These cells secrete a waxy layer called the cuticle that is presumed to be water insoluble and gas proof, but in reality the cuticle does allow gases, water, and small chemicals to pass across it. It slows the loss of water and makes it more difficult for herbivorous insects to attack the leaf. The cuticle and epithelium are transparent and allow light through to the chlorophyll-bearing cells. The plant must breathe, and the epithelium of the undersurface of the leaf has many small pores called stomates that can be opened and closed to allow oxygen and carbon dioxide to pass freely into and out of the leaf. Stomates can also be closed to restrict the loss of water. The upper surface of clivia leaves has no stomates, a condition common to many plants.

The base of the leaves in seedlings is often heavily pigmented with a purple coloration. This disappears as plants mature. Perhaps the color's function is to help camouflage the seedlings while they are young.

ROOTS

Roots in clivias are thick, fleshy, and branching. They forage widely, though usually in the surface layers of the soil where they grow. The roots may be as thick as ³/₈ inch (1 cm), and even newly germinated seedlings produce quite thick roots. The microscopic structure of clivia roots is somewhat different from other plants, and in some

A young plant of *Clivia miniata*. Note the thick fleshy roots, the leaves arranged in two ranks, and the shortened stem.

respects they resemble the aerial roots of orchids. Instead of a single layer of cells forming the epithelium of the root, there are some six or seven layers. In orchids that layer is called a velamen, and the same term has been used for clivias. The velamen is thought to help the orchid root absorb water and nutrients. Normally, roots use fine extensions called root hairs to absorb water and nutrients but those structures are too fragile for aerial roots and would lose too much water via evaporation. In clivia roots, however, the outermost epithelial layer of cells does produce a thicket of very long root hairs. Each root hair is an extension from a single epithelial cell and can measure several millimeters long. They give the growing root a velvety texture.

Rather surprisingly, the thick roots of clivia seedlings make it very difficult for the roots to penetrate the soil, especially as they start to develop before a substantial plantlet is produced. A seedling typically has one large root and one to a few small leaves. The roots lengthen by cells dividing just behind the tip. The force needed to lift the seed and leaves is less than that needed to push the root into the soil, and as a result the growing root tip lifts the entire seedling into the air. This is a vexing problem for hybridizers because no matter what soil mix they use for germinating seeds, the roots keep pushing the baby plants out of the soil. Seedlings may need to be replanted several times until they take hold. Once several roots have formed, they tend to act as anchors working against each other and hold the plant in position.

In the center of the root is a narrow cylinder of conducting tissue called the stele. It contains xylem for carrying water and dissolved inorganic minerals to other parts of the plant, stems, leaves, and flowers. It also has phloem that distributes organic molecules (derived either directly from photosynthetic tissues or storage products) that originated from photosynthesis but that will be stored for later use in other parts of the plant.

Much of the root is storage tissue, where water and organic molecules can be sequestered until needed. A strong healthy root system not only lets the plant forage for resources, but it also provides a major storage site that the plant depends upon during lean times.

STEMS

Clivias produce three kinds of stems. The first are the stems that bear and support the leaves; the second are underground rhizomes that produce adventitious plants and move them some distance from the mother plant; and the third are the stalks that hold the flowers.

The diameter of a clivia's main leaf-bearing stem depends on both the individual plant and its age. Like most other monocotyledonous plants, clivias do not have real secondary thickening. The vascular tissue is in the form of separate bundles interspersed through a background of pith cells. The vascular bundles carry nutrients and water while the pith is used primarily for storage and support. In the species *Clivia caulescens*, the stem can be quite long, reaching lengths of several meters in very old plants. Forms of *C. gardenii* that grow in boggy conditions also produce stems of considerable length. The stem length in these species is the result of wide internodes that elongate between the leaf bases. (Nodes are the sites of origin of the leaves.) Underground clivia rhizomes also have long internodes but the stems tend to be narrower in diameter than other stems. The nodes on the rhizomes bear reduced, scale-like leaves. At the base of each leaf is a bud that could develop into either a flower stem or another shoot. The offshoots in older plants may come directly from either the base of the stem or the underground rhizomes.

The third type of stem is called the peduncle. It is the inflorescence stalk that supports the head of flowers. The smaller stalks supporting each individual flower at the tip of the peduncle are referred to as pedicels. Each pedicel is equivalent to a side branch emerging from the peduncle. Side branches are usually subtended by leaves or similar structures derived from leaves. Each subtending clivia leaf is reduced to a bract. The type of inflorescence in clivias is called an umbel; possessing an umbel is among the main characteristics of the family Amaryllidaceae to which clivias belong. In an umbel, all of the pedicels emerge from the peduncle at more or less the same point.

The peduncle has other functions besides supporting the flowers. It has to provide a strong perch for the birds that will act as pollinators, and it must also support the weight of other, heavier birds that will eventually collect the ripe berries containing seeds. Two different kinds of birds are involved: small sunbirds that do much of the pollinating, and larger louries that carry out the seed dissemination. The peduncle is flattened so that it provides two narrow ridges on its sides, and these ridges often possess strengthening cells. Without these adaptations, it would be quite difficult for either group of birds to grip onto the peduncle to carry out their jobs. In fact, a very wide, rounded peduncle would be almost impossible for the birds to grip.

The peduncle is also important because it displays the flower head. *Clivia* enthusiasts like a peduncle that is tall enough to lift the flowers above the leaves. The length of the stalk is under two controls, one of which is genetic, the other environmental. Some plants never make tall flower stems. This is particularly true of nearly all dwarf clivias from Chinese and Japanese breeding, where the flower stem is always very short and the flowers often hidden between the leaves. It does not seem possible to get their peduncles to extend very far. One might guess that the factor that makes for dwarfism (very short internodes and reduced cell division resulting in shorter leaves) also works at the level of peduncle production. But there are dwarfs of other *Clivia* strains that bear taller peduncles that do display their flowers nicely. There has been much discussion and guesswork about environmental factors that control peduncle length, and most enthusiasts agree that the plants need a cool fall and winter to make adequate flower stems. If those seasons are unusually warm, peduncle length may be reduced. The response to temperature is probably clonal and hence gene dependent, but some clones do make good stems no matter what temperatures they are exposed to. For modern Belgian clivias, plants need two months where the day temperatures are kept below 50°F (10°C).

There is variation in clivia pedicels. Except for *Clivia miniata*, the pedicels are thin, rounded in cross-section, and quite flexible, and the flower weight makes them droop. Thus, the other species have pendent flowers. In *C. miniata*, the pedicels tend to be erect and rigid, much thicker than those of the other species, and angular in cross-section. A modified leaf or bract subtends each pedicel in the inflorescence. In other amaryllids the bracts can be large enough that they protect the developing flower buds, but in clivias they tend to be reduced and papery. They form an insignificant part of the inflorescence and are vestigial, rather like the appendix is in people.

FLOWERS

The main function of the flowers is reproduction. They contain the sexual organs. When seeds (new individuals) are produced, new genetic combinations—the result of combining the genes from pollen with those of ovules—are made. This combination is the source of the variation among individuals. Variation is important for the survival of wild populations, and it is especially important in plant breeding where rare and unusual combinations of genes can lead to the development of new types or forms of clivias.

Flowers are comprised of two whorls (rings) of parts called tepals. The outer whorl has three sepals and the inner has three petals. The sepals and petals are usually similarly colored. The two whorls alternate with each other but are fused into a ring at their base. Often the term tepals is used when there is no need to differentiate between the two whorls and when they both are petaloid. On the death of the flower, the entire structure falls away as a single unit, leaving the ovary still on the pedicel. If there was no pollination, then the ovary itself may break off later at a special abscission site between the ovary and pedicel. If some of the flowers were pollinated, all of the pedicels and their ovaries may remain green, irrespective of whether they were pollinated or not. Presumably, photosynthesis in the ovaries can help contribute toward provisioning the growing seeds.

The structure of clivia flowers is typical of flowers that are bird or butterfly pollinated. Both those pollinators tend to prefer orange to red. The flowers of the pendent clivia are typical of sunbird-pollinated flowers. The sunbirds are the Old World counterparts of the New World hummingbirds, but they usually perch instead of hover. Val Thurston has observed the olive sunbird pollinating *Clivia gardenii* in her Natal garden. The flowers have long tubular shapes that accommodate the long and typically curved bills of the sunbirds and that offer nectar as a reward. Flowers from other genera that share sunbird pollinators are often strikingly similar to clivia flowers in both shape and coloration. Two examples are *Cyrtanthus obliquus* and *Aloe ciliaris*. The latter is a vining aloe that often shares the same ecosystem as *Clivia nobilis*. What pollinates *Clivia miniata* is still a bit of a mystery, but their erect shape and open nature suggests that butterflies are a good guess. Very few pollination systems are exclusive in terms of their pollinators, and there is no reason why the pendent flowers could not also be pollinated by butterflies. Large bees might be attracted to the yellow or white throats of any of the species, especially those of *Clivia miniata*. Thurston has seen bees and large flies on the anthers of *Clivia miniata* in her garden, but whether or not those are the normal pollinators in the wild is still to be determined. With any luck, some enterprising student or naturalist will one day make some observations on *C. miniata* pollinators in the forests of Natal.

COLOR

The colors of wild clivia flowers appear to run the gamut from orange to pink to red. The throats are usually a contrasting white with yellow, green, or yellow and green markings, and the tepal tips in the pendent species most often have green pigments. In plants such as daffodils, the yellow, orange, pink, and red pigments are all based on carotenoids. But in clivias, rather surprisingly, the orange, reds, and pinks are anthocyanins (water-soluble flavonoid color pigments), while only the yellows come from carotenoids. *Clivia* flower coloration is achieved through an outer layer of cells containing the orange-red pigments overlaying a thick base of several cell layers that contribute either white or yellow colors. In *Clivia miniata*, the outer layer is usually only one cell layer thick, but in *C. caulescens* it can be two or three cell layers. In the latter case, the cells with deeper orange pigments may also contain chloroplasts. The disposition of pigments in the other two species is not known.

Clivia pigments fall into three types: water-soluble anthocyanins, which are orange-red and usually found

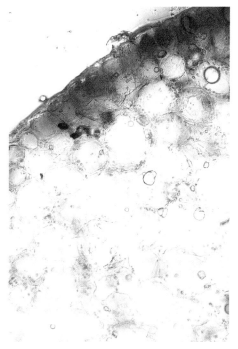

Section through a petal of an orange *Clivia miniata*. Note the anthocyanin-containing cells in the epithelium and the green chloroplasts in the underlying cells.

in the vacuoles of the epithelial cells making up the surface of the tepals; lipid- (fat-) soluble carotenoids; and green chlorophylls. The lipid-soluble carotenoids and green chlorophylls are packaged into small organelles called plastids. Chloroplasts are plastids that contain chlorophyll. Plastids tend to be found in deeper tissues of the tepals. The plastids in flowers and yellow berries contain only the yellow pigments, in which case they are usually referred to as chromoplasts. Slight differences in the molecular structure of the various anthocyanins or carotenoids can affect the ultimate color of the flower.

Production of flower color will be discussed in detail in chapter 6, but I want to point out that at least two anthocyanins occur in the tepals of the same flowers. Whether or not they occur in the same cells or in different cells is not clear at this time. The proportions of these pigments in a flower can vary from plant to plant, and the amount of the pigments in a flower also vary depending on ambient conditions. A certain level of sunlight seems necessary to produce very dark red flowers, but too intense sunlight will also bleach the pigments and burn the flowers. One needs to find a balance between enough and too much light exposure, and unfortunately this seems best discovered by trial and error. With regards to yellow or green pigments, the depth of color depends on how many plastids or chromoplasts occur in the deeper tissues of the flower. Chlorophyll can be bleached by sunlight, so dark green colors will be retained for longer in deeper shade conditions.

REPRODUCTIVE COSTS

There are three things that the inflorescence must do. It needs to attract and reward its pollinators; it must grow and protect the new seeds; and it must help to disperse the new offspring. The plant must balance the costs of all three activities against what is also needed to maintain itself. Biologists who study this balancing act talk in terms of reproductive costs. The currency for such costs may be energy units from stored carbohydrates, as well as rare nutrients such as inorganic chemicals like phosphate that are needed to make all of the DNA for the pollen, eggs, and developing embryos. Production of an inflorescence is not a trivial matter. In some plants, the weight of a season's inflorescence is over a tenth of the biomass of the entire plant. In plants that bear multiple flower stems, it can exceed that weight. The time between planting a seed and first flowering for clivias is usually the time needed to build up sufficient reserves so that they can be expended during reproduction without the mother plant dying. In the wild that may take many years.

If a plant is too successful at reproduction, it might exhaust itself, and reproduction the following season can be compromised. In some cases, a weak plant that indulges in maximum reproductive effort might simply expire after reproduction. *Clivia* seedlings will not flower until they have at least six pairs of large mature leaves— how fast that is achieved depends on cultural conditions. Some varieties will require additional pairs of leaves. There is a dwarf Belgian seed strain where between 10 to 20 percent of the plants will flower in the second year, and over

Section through the erect flower of *Clivia miniata*.

90 percent will flower in the third year, provided they are grown correctly (de Coster 1998). Many of the other varieties grow more slowly, especially those that produce large standard-sized plants, and it can take five or more years for some of those to produce sufficient leaves.

Not all flowers get pollinated in the wild. When clivias are hand pollinated in cultivation, they can produce very heavy loads of seed, but flowering or flower quality may be reduced during the following season. In the wild it would not matter if the plant skips a season following a good seed set, but in a garden or greenhouse it is different. Plant breeders need to consider the cost effects of a missed flowering season if a plant is to be used repeatedly for seed production or if a special plant needs to be grown for show.

Clivias show considerable economy in the construction of their flowers. In *Clivia miniata* the tepals are thick but not solid.

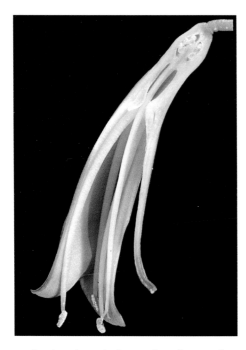

Section through the pendent flower of *Clivia caulescens*. Note the nectar cavity produced by the base of the stamens.

Individual cells have a complex shape rather like a piece of a three-dimensional jigsaw puzzle. Only the ends of cells abut against each other, leaving plenty of air spaces between them. The number of cells needed to build the tepal is thus reduced, as is the amount of material that needs to be discarded after pollination or death of the flower. This cell shape not only creates an efficient way of reducing the costs of building the flower, but it also allows for the turgidity and rigidity needed to support the pollinators. In the pendent-flowered clivia, the flower itself does not need to support the weight of the pollinator.

The stamens are generally positioned with their anthers near the mouth of the flower. Each anther has a long filament attached near the base of a tepal, and because the anthers are versatile, they are attached near the center and can move in several directions. The style, like the filament, is also long and filiform with a trifid stigma that usually protrudes beyond the anthers. In *Clivia gardenii* both the stamens and stigmas project further out than other species. Most clivias are receptive to their own pollen, and as the pollen is very light, dry, and friable, there is always the possibility of self-pollination due to wind pollination. Jostling or moving the plant can result in self-pollination, especially those with pendent flowers. Because there are so many flowers in an inflorescence, and because

flowers are often at different developmental stages, animal pollinators can effectively self-pollinate a plant as they explore a number of
flowers in the same umbel. Thus, self-pollination must be quite frequent even in the wild.

As a reward for their visitors, the flowers produce nectar. *Clivia*
nectar tastes sweet and probably contains several sugars. The nectar
is produced at the base of the tepals; it is possible that the stamen
filaments also secrete some or all of the nectar. In the species with
pendent flowers, special provision must be made to prevent nectar
from falling out of the flowers. There is a bend near the base of each
filament of *Clivia caulescens* that forms a strut that extends toward
the style before proceeding out of the flower. The six struts in turn
form a basket that helps retain the globule of nectar. The pollinator
must push its beak or proboscis between the filament bases in order
to access the nectar.

FRUITS AND SEEDS

Following pollination, the ovary situated below each flower swells.
Unlike many other amaryllids, fruit maturation can take a long time,
often over a year. Usually fruits are ripe just before or during the following season's flower production. The fruit is a soft berry, and when
it it is ripe, the ovary changes color. Berry colors often differ from
those of the flowers; in fact, there is more variation in berry color than
in flower color. In part this is because the flavonoid pigment in the
berry is different from the two flavones (anthocyanins) found in the
flowers. Berries can be bright pink, purple, cerise, brown, yellow,
orange, or red, and some remain green, never seeming to change color.

The fruits are likely to be eaten by forest birds, in particular a
rather magnificent bird called the Knysna lourie (*Tauraco corythaix*). It
is also possible that primates—baboons, vervet, and Samango mon-
keys—as well as a variety of rodents feed on the berries and help distribute the seeds. The fleshy pericarp of the ovary is usually eaten but
the seeds are apparently unpalatable and so are dropped. I think the

Brightly colored fruits of *Clivia miniata* are attractive to birds.

ripe berry flesh is tasteless, but maybe I and other humans lack the correct kind of taste buds. Since the ripe flesh is often glutinous, the sticky seeds can be deposited on branches and rocks and stay where they are placed. If conditions are just right, seeds that are deposited high up in trees can lead to the rare instances of epiphytism. Those conditions include a deep moss layer, or better yet, a crotch between two branches where detritus, dead leaves, and dust have accumulated to provide some soil for the germinating seeds. I have seen epiphytic examples of three *Clivia* species in various forests of South Africa.

Clivia seeds are more or less spherical and can be quite big, over ³/₈ inch (1 cm) in diameter or even larger in some cases. The seed coat is quite thin and not pigmented, unlike in *Cryptostephanus* where seeds can be light to dark brown. *Clivia* seeds are a creamy fawn color and short-lived. If a large number of seeds are produced within a single fruit, they press against each other as they develop and will have flattened rather than spherical sides. There are two anatomical features that can be discerned from the outside of the seeds. There is a scar where the seed was attached to the placenta of the parent ovary that indicates where nourishment was conveyed to the developing seed. On the opposite side from the scar there is usually a small darkened and raised point. This is the place through which the initial root and then the seedling plant will emerge. A seed contains enough reserves to allow the new plant to produce at least one substantial root and about two leaves, each about 2 inches (5 cm) long. This is true even of seedlings produced from variegated plants that are achlorotic and do not have any functional chloroplasts.

ECOLOGY AND CONSERVATION OF *CLIVIA*

Clivias are all forest species and as such are adapted to the shade of forest floors. Forest floors may be rocky or sandy, but there is usually a soil covering of leaves or mosses, sometimes both. Clivias are adapted to a fertile humus soil environment. In many parts of the world people grow their plants in rich organic composts that they seem to appreciate. With one exception (the swamp populations of *Clivia gardenii* in KwaZulu-Natal), the plants prefer a well-drained environment; their roots are generally shallow on hard slopes and only slightly deeper in the very porous, sandy soils of coastal dune forests.

Like many other amaryllids, clivia plants are loaded with toxic chemicals, and there are few natural predators and pests in the wild. In South Africa, however, one moth caterpillar is a serious pest to cultivated clivias. It seems not only to tolerate the natural toxins but, from all accounts, to positively relish a diet of clivia plants. This moth is the dreaded lily borer (*Brithys pancratii*), and serious growers in South Africa need to carry out a strict preventative program. The lily borer is said to extend into southern Europe; fortunately, this kind of lepidopteran is not known in other parts of the world.

While many plant toxins are dangerous if consumed, they may have medicinal values when used properly. The Zulu peoples have a rich tradition of herbal medicines called "muti" in which clivias feature strongly. All *Clivia* species are protected plants in all regions of South Africa where they grow, but the harvesting of clivias for pharmacological purposes is considered a right for the native peoples in KwaZulu-Natal, and considerable quantities are used for those reasons. Clivias contain alkaloids that have names such as lycorine (originally described from the plant *Lycoris*) and hippeastrine from (*Hippeastrum*) and clivimine and clivonine (named for their occurrence in clivia leaves). Roots also contain these compounds although in minute amounts. There are at least nine different alkaloids that were discovered first in *Clivia*. (Lycorine has been found to have antiviral properties.) The ethnological uses for clivias fall into two categories, medicine and magic, and although I offer some information on both, readers who wish to know more are referred to Hutchings (1996).

Although their effectiveness has not been clearly demonstrated, *Clivia miniata* root infusions are prescribed to combat snakebite. They are to be drunk and also applied directly to the bite wounds. Perhaps the more important use for *Clivia miniata* is to facilitate childbirth. Leaf extracts have an effect on the uterus muscles, so weak leaf concoctions are taken during the last three months of pregnancy, and stronger concentrations are used to induce labor (Hutchings 1996). Where Zulu herbalists have collected *C. miniata* plants, there is always a mound of leaves to be found. This is a curious phenomenon because snakebite is relatively rare, whereas pregnancy is common. I would have thought more of the leaves would have been collected.

Other species of *Clivia* do not feature heavily in folk medicine. Ethnobotanists usually confuse the *Clivia* species, and what is generally identified as *C. nobilis* is more likely *C. gardenii*. Unlike *C. gardenii*, *C. nobilis* does not grow in KwaZulu-Natal, but the two species were confused by the early ethnobotanists. Strong concentrations of *C. nobilis* (more likely *C. gardenii*) are said to merely be mildly emetic, meaning they induce vomiting. There is a 1939 reference that the Zulu sprinkled *C. nobilis* concoctions around a person as a protective charm. The use of herbs for protective charms is important in Zulu

Clivia miniata leaves lying on the ground after the stems had been collected for "muti." KwaZulu-Natal, South Africa.

herbal medicines. The following uses as they were relayed to me should perhaps be taken with a grain of salt. Thunderstorms are common in South Africa, and lightning causes a number of deaths. The Zulu people have several different botanical charms to ward off lightning strikes. For example, the succulent plant *Haworthia limifolia* is often placed on the roof of a house in areas that are subject to thunderstorms. According to an old African muti woman (a herbalist), another defense requires that a young man hold a clivia rhizome in one hand while urine is poured over the rhizome (it is not clear whose urine it used). The young man then slams the rhizome hard with his other fist, and lightning is guaranteed not to strike the person after that.

The Xhosa people of the Eastern Cape also use clivia plants for similar medicinal and magic purposes (Batten and Bokelmann 1966). I came across the next recipe from a reliable lawyer (though I don't think he actually lost any cases because of this enchantment). The charm is prepared as follows. Leaves are stripped off the rhizome of a plant of *C. miniata* and the bare stem is then divided into four lengthwise. The rhizome sections are dried. This is said to create a powerful protective charm, especially when taken into courts of law.

In nearly all the regions in KwaZulu-Natal where I examined natural populations of *Clivia miniata* I found piles of chopped leaves and holes where plants had been dug up. *Clivia nobilis* seems to be safe in the Eastern Cape, where the Xhosa do not use it, but *C. miniata* is used there and so is threatened. Clivias may take up to five years to reach flowering size, and thus they are expensive once they are mature and ready to be sold. There is considerable demand for the plants for landscaping; in South Africa, the growing Clivia Club has helped to popularize the plants, and there is even more demand by the general public. The Clivia Club stresses that seed is easy to germinate, and if one wants good quality flowers one needs to breed them. The demand for plants for landscaping are different from the needs of producing show plants because exceptional flower quality is not important for landscaping, whereas mature plants are. Plants stolen from the wild are mature and usually found in clumps that can be divided into a few plants, and except for transportation costs, they are essentially free. The landscaper's profit margins are therefore quite high. It is almost impossible to pinpoint a plant as being wild collected once it has been established because of the long history of this plant in cultivation. There are reports of entire localities in the Transkei in the Eastern Cape that have been stripped of *C. miniata*. An additional threat is deforestation that continues in the Transkei region, and the species is thus also being deprived of its habitat. With regards to the other species, none has flowers as showy as *C. miniata*, and there is less pressure on those plants for landscaping.

Each species consists of many populations, and the numbers of individuals in the wild must be in the order of hundreds of thousands, if not millions. Nevertheless, as populations get reduced in size and number, the gene pool of the species is eroded, and valuable variation is lost. Separate populations, even of the same species, are hardly ever equivalent in either size or number. Some populations are fairly uniform and may have undistinguished plants or flowers, while other populations can be quite variable containing many different clones, all of which are highly desirable. Gardening demands constant innovation and the production of new varieties and types of plants, and rare genetic mutations are often only found by examining large populations of individuals. We do not know what will be fashionable in the future, but genetic erosion reduces the possibilities and directions of breeding endeavors to create new varieties. Plant pirating on a large scale affects the future options of all gardeners.

Modest harvesting of pollen or some seeds does not affect the integrity of a wild population. And, happily, most clivias grow in clumps so that carefully taking a division or side-shoot does not really affect the gene pool. Digging up large numbers of plants in the hope of making a pretty landscape is unconscionable and must be condemned; it diminishes our future potential enjoyment of these wonderful plants and it interferes with their future evolution.

There are various threats to the future well-being of *Clivia*. Both the muti trade and the plant's desirability as an ornamental plant threaten *C. miniata*. The other species are threatened by land conversion in the form of deforestation either for firewood or to clear forests for farmland. South Africa does have many forest reserves where populations should be safe, but we can expect continual erosion of other unprotected wild populations. None of the species is, however, in danger of extinction either in the wild or in captivity, but genetic erosion is a real threat. Some populations have greater floral diversity than others, and if those are plundered without regard to the population's integrity, enormous damage can result.

EPIPHYTISM

Clivias have thick roots covered with a velamen-like layer, so it is not surprising to come across epiphytic examples of clivias growing high in tree branches like orchids. I have seen epiphytic individuals of three of the four *Clivia* species, *C. gardenii*, *C. miniata*, and *C. nobilis*. All of the epiphytic plants shared a common feature in terms of where they were growing, either perched in the crotch between branches where humus had accumulated or tucked into cavities made by lianas or the roots of strangler figs. Unlike many orchids, the epiphytic clivias do require a modicum of a leaf litter or humus layer in which to bury their roots. In a sense they are merely opportunists making the most of the fortuitous disposition of a seed in the right place.

Chapter Four

CULTIVATING
AND GROWING CLIVIAS

CLIVIAS IN THE LANDSCAPE

CLIVIAS ARE TOUGH PLANTS that, once their minimum requirements have been met, seem able to thrive on neglect. They have three major needs. First, clivias need minimum temperatures that are above freezing. They do not tolerate frost or snow on their leaves, but will survive temperatures that go down to a few degrees above freezing. Where they are exposed to subfreezing winters, they will need to be taken indoors at those times of the year. Second, clivias should be cultivated in a shady situation. Although plants will survive if they are exposed to direct sunlight in either the early morning or late afternoon, both the leaves and the flowers will get bleached, and their magnificent umbels will have a reduced longevity. Finally, in order to flower well and produce strong tall peduncles to support the umbels, clivias must be exposed to a drop in evening temperatures for about two months in the fall. Although they can tolerate very tropical temperatures and high humidity, they will not flower well under those conditions. If one is fortunate to live in a climate that provides these three requirements, then clivias are superb additions to the landscape. They are also ideal for those difficult shady conditions for which so few other flowering plants are available. Their broad, strap-shaped leaves lend themselves to tropical effects. Clivias succeed well in U.S. hardiness zones 10 and 9, where the temperatures hardly ever drop below freezing for significant lengths of time. They will also survive in a slightly colder garden provided that they are given extra protection against direct frost exposure and prolonged freezing temperatures. Clivias should be summered outdoors in the shade.

CHOOSING A SITE

There are three prime ways of using clivias in the landscape. They can be planted directly into the soil, placed in permanent planters such as large window boxes, or used in large movable containers as special focal points.

In southern California, clivias are popularly planted close or next to the walls of houses. In such positions they are allowed to clump up and become permanent plants in the landscape, and they are expected to remain in their positions for decades with relatively little maintenance. Clivias in larger gardens or public parks of southern California tend to be sited in mixed plantings and usually in the shade of trees, whereas in South Africa they are often planted *en masse* under the shade of trees. Plants are expensive enough that one rarely finds large beds of clivias, except in the landscape of wealthy patrons. If a few plants are to be positioned next to a house, choose a northern to eastern aspect as this will offer some protection from the intense summer and fall sun. A southern or eastern aspect is the better exposure for plants in the Southern Hemisphere. However, in the absence of sufficient protection, even plants in optimum situations may show signs of sunburn.

A few clumps against the wall of a house make a very pleasant display when the plants are in flower. They provide a pleasing leaf texture to combine with other tropical foliage, and they look particularly fine when mixed with ferns that also appreciate a shady, moist

Clivias in the landscape at the Huntington Botanical Gardens,
San Marino, California.

position. Shrubs in California are often planted against the walls of a house, and as they mature, empty areas beneath their shade are formed. These areas are ideal for filling with clivias and other shade-loving perennials. Unfortunately, one often sees three to six plants lined up in a single row as a foundation planting. Such an arrangement is rarely successful because the plants, which are usually seed grown, flower at different times during the season, and the display ends up being sporadic and disjointed. Straight rows of plants are better produced from equal-sized divisions of the same plant.

In U.S. hardiness zone 8 (and possibly 7), clivias should be planted against walls as that will add a modicum of protection during the coldest part of the year because of the heat they retain and radiate during the winter. Walls of a heated building such as a home will be more effective than those of a small outbuildings like a garage or shed.

Small children might be attracted to the berries whilst they are unripe and green as well as when they are ripe and varied in color. The red berry pulp is not tasty and is probably not poisonous, but unripe berries may not be edible, and the large seeds within the fruit may contain toxins. Plants, therefore, should not be situated where they are readily accessible to small children. I have not heard of any poison problems in California, where clivias are common plants in the landscape, but it is better to be safe than sorry.

CLIVIAS UNDER TREES

Their shallow roots make clivias excellent subjects for planting directly in the shade of large trees. It is easy to feed and care for the root systems of clivias without the plants having to compete with the tree for nutrition and depth of soil.

One needs to examine potential clivia sites critically. The sun changes the angle of its arc during its yearly cycle, and the shade cast by the tree will also change. During the summer, the sun moves in a northwesterly arc, and as fall approaches, it moves in a more southwesterly arc. (In the Southern Hemisphere the directions will be

Clivias under the trees at Anna Meyer's home, Gauteng Province, South Africa.

reversed.) I have seen plantings that flourished until the summer when the late afternoon sun was angled in a way that it blasted the leaves under the trees. Also, if the tree has a high canopy, it may admit burning light when the sun is at certain angles. The landscape architect must study the site very carefully, something that does not often happen anymore when the architect sits and designs the landscape with the aid of a computer. I have seen plantings succeed on one side of a square while a similar planting no more than twenty feet away and under a similar tree got burned because the architect did not take the sun's movements into account. This extra effort to site the plants properly may sound like a great deal of trouble, but the result of a good planting can be so spectacular that it is worth the extra effort. One should, of course, be extra careful when pruning or thinning the branches of trees protecting a bed of clivias.

Deciduous trees are not good subjects under which to grow clivias. Not only will the plants' leaves suffer sunburn during the winter season, but because they flower in the springtime—often before the shade trees' leaves emerge—the flowers will also sustain weather damage that includes both bleaching from the sun and bruising from pelting rain. A dense evergreen canopy, by contrast, offers some protection from those harsher elements.

COMMERCIAL LANDSCAPES

Plants used in commercial landscapes are typically tough and resilient, require no pampering, have great disease resistance, and can exist with a minimum of attention. Clivias are ideal for commercial landscape projects, and when used in the right climatic zones, are frequently the sole survivors years after the other perennial plants have withered and disappeared. Commercial landscapes often have much hardscaping with planters where there are wall overhangs and with stairwells that provide abundant shade, and of the handful of suitable candidates for these positions, clivias are among the very few that also offer spectacular flowers. Even if the modest light requirements needed to promote flowering cannot be met, the plants can still be grown to vegetative perfection. The long, dark leaves can be used to full advantage under these limiting conditions; the flowers and berries are then a secondary bonus. In those situations of low light, the flower quality of clivias is of little importance, and plants with lower quality flowers can be used.

CLIVIAS IN BEDS

The nuances and variations found among individual clivia plants demand that flowerbeds should be positioned with viewer accessibility in mind. Too often the particular plant one would like to examine is so far away that the plant simply cannot be well appreciated, and in a large established bed of clivias in full bloom, one often cannot invade the bed to get near the target flower. Gentle hillside slopes make for easier examination, as do beds that are not too wide. Formal plantings of long narrow beds are more accessible to the appreciative plant person, and if there is a short narrow hedge of box or similar shrub at the front of the bed, it will not only protect the smaller plants from encroaching enthusiasts, but will also offset and contrast the clivia leaves for those times when the plants are not in flower.

Bed preparation is relatively easy because the site does not have to be deeply dug as clivias' roots normally rummage at or just below the surface soil. There is, however, one proviso: the site needs to be well draining. Cold and wet conditions promote rot, especially in the winter, and good drainage goes a long way toward preventing trouble. Incorporating sharp sand or gravel or raising the bed a few inches above the surrounding areas will help alleviate problems. If the bed is soggy and in a persistently damp situation, one might need to install a French (agricultural) drain or some other feature that directs excess water away from the site. A French drain can be a trench dug about 18 to 24 inches (45 to 62 cm) below the surface, and it should be partially filled with coarse gravel and a layer of finer

Clivias in a stone planter. Anna Meyer's home, Gauteng Province, South Africa.

gravel on top of that. The size of the gravel is not too important, but it should all be more or less the same size otherwise smaller pieces will fill in the spaces between the larger stones and tend to block drainage channels. The trench should slope downward away from the center of the bed and extend beyond the bed. It should be filled with about 9 inches (23 cm) of gravel, which should in turn be covered with a topsoil of coarse, sandy loam mixed with appreciable quantities of organic matter. The latter could be partially decomposed bark or leaf mold. Clivias are known for their ability to withstand drought conditions, but in a well-drained site the plants will benefit from copious watering and will respond accordingly. Although clivias succeed when they are pot-bound plants, they have

A bed of clivias in South Africa. Anna Meyer's home, Gauteng Province, South Africa.

wide-ranging roots in a garden situation, and this needs to be taken into account when designing a bed.

A well-installed bed of clivias can be expected to last for thirty years or even longer. Unlike clivias in the wild that experience a continuous rain of leaf litter, the soil in a garden will become exhausted over time. Beds will appreciate a topdressing of composted leaf mold or bark in the early fall before they commence their winter spurt of growth, and a slow-release, well-balanced fertilizer such as 20:20:20 can also be added to give a boost to flower production the following spring. The plants will tolerate considerable neglect and still flower, but the quality and size of umbels will be superior if they are given a modicum of attention.

SELECTION OF PLANTS

In a large display bed, high quality plants will be lost among the general glitter of the flowering season. It is better to use the finer clones for focal points in a mixed landscape backed by other types of foliage or as single plants in a container. Failing that, the better plants should be brought to the front of the bed where their flowers can be appreciated. Because clivias come in such a variety of vegetative sizes, one should be aware that combining plants from two different strains may result in a very uneven landscape effect. If plants from more than one strain must be brought together, it would be better to mingle the various types of plants evenly throughout the bed otherwise the effect may be one of discontinuities and, ultimately, disharmony. During the first flowering season, one should examine the bed with regards to flower timing and quality. Plants can then be staked for later removal or moved while in flower. The landscaping will suffer during the season they are moved, but as one is building such a long-term, permanent display, one season's disruption is a worthy inconvenience.

Useful sources of plants for a bed display are seedlings from one's own breeding program. While one might want to grow the best flowers in containers, the better quality plants could be used for bedding displays, provided one has the right location in the garden.

Some clivias are not good candidates for the garden. Those include variegated clivias, whose leaves are usually too delicate to withstand the vagaries of garden life, and the very smallest dwarfs and miniatures, which are too precious and cannot compete with their more vigorous and rambunctious neighbors, and so eventually get lost. Besides, these dwarfs and miniatures are special collector's plants that are best grown in containers where they can get suitable attention.

PLANTING CLIVIAS IN THE OPEN GROUND

Clivias sold for landscape purposes are usually planted in 1- to 5-gallon (4½- to 23-liter) pots. Most of the roots of a container-grown plant tend to circle as close to the outside of the pot as possible. If there is a well-aerated soil mix in the container, then the roots may be distributed through out the mix. Clivias produce shallow roots, and if a plant is transferred from a container to a flowerbed, there is no need to dig a hole as deep as the container. Roots that are situated deeply in heavy soil may die. Dig a hole that is wider than it is deep, and also wide enough to accommodate the roots that should be planted no more than a few inches deep. After removing the plant from the pot, uncoil the roots and spread them evenly in the hole. Pot-bound plants may have extensive tangles of roots that are difficult to handle, and in that case, the roots can be cut short. Take a large clean knife and slice across the root ball, cutting it in half. Do not use the same implement to cut or trim another plant because that is a sure way of spreading viral, bacterial, or fungal diseases. The plant's cut roots should be exposed to the air in a shady place for a day or two until the cut surfaces get a chance to dry. The plant can then be replanted after spreading the roots and discarding any loose and broken-off pieces.

A mulch of dried leaf litter, small bark nuggets, or chipped branches spread around the plants to cover the root area will help control weeds, conserve water, and provide the organic matter that clivias appreciate. Before the mulch is spread, scatter a long-term (nine-month) slow-release, encapsulated, granular fertilizer (such as Osmocote* 18-6-12) on the soil surface around the root area. Remember that the root tips are probably foraging some distance from the base of the clump, and granules deposited against the base may not provide nutrients where the root tips are feeding. You could apply as much as 1 to 2 tablespoons of granules spread in a ring about 6 to 18 inches (15 to 45 cm) from the base of the plant, depending on the size of the clump. Mulch can be spread directly

---

* Mention of trademark, proprietary product, or vendor does not constitute a guarantee or warranty of the product by the publisher or author and does not imply its approval to the exclusion of other products or vendors.

on top of the granules, and it should be renewed at least once a year at the same time that plants are refed. Rates at which fertilizer is made available to the plants will depend on temperatures and pattern of irrigation.

Clivias are sometimes gross feeders that welcome large amounts of fertilizer. One of my friends in East London, South Africa, spreads one cup of well-rotted chicken manure around the base of each plant. His plants have optimum climatic conditions, and he routinely flowers seedlings within two to three years. Plants in active growth will respond more favorably to food than those that are merely biding their time. In China, waste products produced during the manufacture of soybean curd (tofu) become organic fertilizers that are recommended for clivias. Several Chinese trees are also said to provide leaves that make excellent compost.

COMPANION PLANTS

There are many suitable shade-preferring plants that can be incorporated in clivia plantings to help soften them and provide interest when they are not in flower. Cycads, palms, and tree ferns make a suitable backdrop against which to display clivias. Among the palms are *Archontophoenix, Howea, Raphis,* and the dwarf *Phoenix roebelenii.* Small plants for the foreground include *Bergenia, Heuchera, Impatiens, Liriope, Ophiopogon, Soleirolia soleirolii, Tulbaghia simmerlei,* and the various trailing campanulas. For a dramatic tropical effect try *Strelitzia nicolai* and *Draceana hookeriana,* both of which grow alongside clivias in nature. *Cordyline stricta* or *Fatsia japonica* are other plants that provide tropical foliage. Abutilons, camellias, fuchsias, and *Brunfelsia pauciflora* are flowering shrubs that also appreciate similar conditions and can add color after the clivias have finished their display. Cane-stem begonias and the taller nandina cultivars make nice accent plants. Be careful placing all these companion plants so that they do not grow to obscure the clivias.

CONTAINERS IN THE GARDEN

A large clump of clivias in an appropriate container can form a stunning display if the container matches or compliments the landscape. Conditions for successful growing in containers are similar to those for plants placed directly in the garden. The most important needs are the correct amount of sunlight, soil aeration, and adequate drainage. The latter two parameters are interconnected.

Clivias have a reputation for performing well when they are pot bound. When pot bound the roots are probably able to drain the containers efficiently and prevent soggy anaerobic souring of the soil. It is generally recommended that the container size be only slightly larger than the size of the existing root ball, but if you want to use large permanent containers, you may have to dig up an old clump of clivias from the garden since it is difficult to obtain large enough plants. Planting three or more plants into a large container is usually not satisfactory unless they are the same clone; the display provided by several plants differing in leaf characteristics, umbel height, and flower type could give an unbalanced picture. At a minimum the plants should match for leaf width and length. To extend the length of the floral display, you could select plants for early season, midseason, and late season flowering, provided that each variety is not too dissimilar in size. Dissimilarities in flower shape will not be so jarring as the plants perform in sequence as the season proceeds. However, the display will not be as spectacular as when a single large clump with many simultaneously flowering umbels is presented.

Pot depth is relatively unimportant because of clivias' shallow roots, but there must be enough width to accommodate the plant comfortably. If a deep container is needed for land- or hardscape purposes, then part of the depth of the pot can be filled with broken crocks, Styrofoam chunks, or gravel (first make sure that there is sufficient drainage at the bottom of the pot). The so-called Styrofoam peanuts are excellent for drainage and plant roots seem to like them, but one should avoid concave Styrofoam chips or other shapes with indentations where water can accumulate. Many large containers have only a single small hole at the bottom, which is inadequate. Either enlarge the hole or drill additional drainage holes using a suitable tool. Ceramic, concrete, or clay containers are suitable, and wooden half barrels or kegs can complement a rustic landscape. It is a good idea to drill additional drainage holes in wooden barrels near the base of the vertical staves. Clivias are so long-lived that they will probably outlive a wooden container or even an inadequately fired clay pot.

Clivias will succeed in a variety of soil types provided they are well drained and have sufficient organic matter. Many of the currently available soil mixes used in pots have little sand or inorganic matter incorporated into them, and after a year or two, the soil level in the container will start to drop, and the plants will sink down in the pot, spoiling the effect. To maintain the soil level, at least half of the volume of potting soil should be gravel, pumice, coarse sand, or small chunks of lava rock about 3/8 inch (1 cm) in diameter. Any one of those components can be incorporated into the planting mix as they all help with drainage. If there are no inert constituents, you will find yourself having to replant the clivia plant every two or three years, and handling a large, old, well-established clump is no trivial matter. The weight of leaves, rhizomes, and roots can be more than a single individual can manage. The amount of inert material in the soil mix is less important for special plants grown in smaller containers (up to 5-gallon [23-liter] pots). As these smaller specimens can be easily repotted when needed, the level of the plant in the pot is less important for display, unless the plant is to be entered in a competitive show.

CLIVIAS IN THE HOME

Clivias make splendid houseplants. Their preference for subdued lighting, tolerance of dry conditions in both air and soil, wide temperature endurance, and longevity clearly earmark them as remarkable indoor plants. They will survive both abuse and neglect far better than most other plants. However, with a modicum of attention to supply their modest needs they will grow luxuriously and reward the grower with a fine flower display.

Although clivias will grow and often flourish in abysmally dark situations, they will do better if you give them adequate light. They will also bloom better if they get some light exposure. How much is enough light? The simple rule for both indirect or reflected sunlight is that if there is enough light to throw a sharp-edged shadow of your hand when you hold it 1 foot (30 cm) above the plant, the light is too bright. North- or south-facing windows tend to provide good light, but you should monitor the sun's position during the year as it will change and you may find unexpected scorch marks on the leaves. You can protect the leaves from the sun by using lace curtains or moving the plants out of the sun's range. Remember that variegated leaves are even more susceptible to sunburn than normal leaves. If the leaves on your plant are pale apple- or yellow-green, they are probably getting too much light. If they are an intensely dark bottle green, they may not be getting enough light. Some varieties naturally have leaves with paler banding patterns, so do not confuse those with sunburned leaves. However, these banded clivias are rare, and it is unlikely that you would pick up one of these specimens at the local nursery.

As far as temperature is concerned, plants should be protected from both central heating and cooling systems. They must be moved away from the direct blasts of either dry, hot air or cold air. Temperatures in which you feel comfortable are good for clivias, the only proviso being that in the fall they need a drop in night temperatures in order to flower. Place them on a porch or against a cold window to achieve the correct ambient temperatures; as long as the plants do not freeze they will relish the cool temperatures. Several months of cold fall temperatures should insure a good floral display the following spring.

What I have said about potting, containers, and media elsewhere in this chapter also holds for plants in the house, but note that plants tend to dry out faster indoors especially if there is central heating. The main pests on indoor clivias are mealybugs. If you have only a few plants, the pests can be controlled using cotton buds soaked in rubbing alcohol to dab the pests. Inspect the undersides of leaves and occasionally part the central growing leaves. Mealybugs give away their presence because their white bodies look like wooly patches against the dark green leaves. If the infestation is particularly bad, use a proprietary brand insecticide offered for houseplants.

Dust will accumulate on clivia leaves, and it is a good idea to sponge the leaves every few months as this will make for a more attractive plant. Do not use any of the proprietary brands of "leaf shine" because these agents actually attract more dust. To polish the leaves, use a soft cloth or paper towel with a little milk on it.

MAINTAINING A COLLECTION

For those who are not fortunate enough to be able to plant clivias in the landscape, collections of plants in containers that are under protection can be easily grown. In fact, it is usually better to grow selected plants in containers where they can be more easily cared for and are more available to close scrutiny. Potted plants can be brought indoors so that their leaves and flowers are better appreciated at close quarters, and plants rotated through the home can provide year-round interest. Pollination is also more easily controlled indoors. For these reasons, clivia enthusiasts grow collections of special potted plants even in climates where the plants could be situated in the landscape.

HOUSING THE COLLECTION

There are several alternatives for where plants that are not established in the landscape may be grown. In inclement climates, these range from windowsills and doorsteps to cellars under lights to greenhouses. In more favorable climates, such as in Mediterranean and subtropical areas, plants can be accommodated on porches or in shade houses. During the summer months and into early fall, all plants will appreciate going out-of-doors, provided there is sufficient shade. Very large, standard clivias occupy a great deal of room, so it is difficult to accommodate many in an indoors situation. However, you can grow large numbers of seedling or the smaller dwarves inside.

A shade structure with benches that bring the plants closer to eye-level makes a very satisfactory arrangement in subtropical conditions. If you garden in a Mediterranean-like climate, you will need to provide some sort of roofing to keep the rain off the plants when they are in flower. In summer rainfall regions, shade cloth makes an adequate roof. The density of shade cloth used in construction varies depending on ambient and geographical conditions. In regions with very bright sunlight, such as Southern Africa, you may need to use cloth densities that occlude 85 percent of the sunlight. In foggy places such as San Francisco, 65 percent shade cloth could be sufficient. The color of the shade cloth does not seem important; either black or dark green shade cloth is the most popular. Some people suggest, however, that white shade cloth might be more effective at protecting plants that are grown under marginal conditions from frosts.

You could set plants on the ground, on benches, or on shelves inside the shade structure. Clivias tolerate such low light conditions that they can often be accommodated in several layers of shelves of plants. Shelves should be arranged near the outer walls of the shade house so that supplemental light can enter the shelf from the side. Care must be taken so that the shelf drains excess water to the outer side of the structure; water draining on the plants from pots above them can be a disaster waiting to happen because diseases will spread like wildfire in those situations.

Freestanding benches or shelves can be isolated from slugs and snails by placing the legs of the stand in containers of water or oil.

You could also wrap naked copper wire around the leg since mollusks will not cross bare copper if there is sufficient wire to make a wide enough barrier. There is a flat copper tape for this purpose that comes with an adhesive edge to facilitate sticking it to each leg of the stand. These barriers do require some maintenance; the copper barrier normally needs to be replaced after a year because it can dry out, and oil barriers often get covered with detritus that create a bridge that the mollusks will use to gain access to your plants. Also remember that if you introduce a new plant to the shelf that contains resident mollusks or their eggs, you will be introducing a pest that is then confined to your growing area since it cannot crawl off the bench. Take care not to introduce those marauders accidentally because they can do considerable damage.

CONTAINERS

Clivias are usually not fussy about their containers. I have seen them growing in ceramic pots, clay pots, wooden barrels, plastic pots, and even plastic bags. Their main need is adequate drainage. In climates that have high humidity, use wood or clay pots, which evaporate moisture through their walls; for drier conditions, ceramic or plastic are acceptable. If you must use plastic pots or bags in high humidity regions, make additional holes in the bottom of the container or even along the sides of the container. Some of the deeper plastic orchid pots made in Asia are ideal for dwarf varieties of clivia, which come with holes already made along the sides and at the base. (These should be thought of as aeration pores rather than drainage holes.) Since there are large numbers of holes in the pots, you should cover them with pieces of plastic mosquito screening such as that used for insect screens to prevent the mix from falling out. You can use a cylinder of screen where the aeration holes are made in the side of the container. These screens will also help deter many insect pests.

As clivias in the wild have roots that grow close to the soil's surface, one might expect them to enjoy shallow receptacles such as azalea pots or bulb pans. However, they appear to adapt readily to containers of most shapes, provided they are given adequate soil mixes. Young seedlings do germinate and grow fairly well in very shallow flats or pans, and it may be convenient for you to use those.

One major concern when selecting containers is that they should not be too large. Clivias—provided they are fed—seem to grow quite well when they are pot bound. The roots can be gently coiled to fit comfortably into the pot, but there must be room for additional root growth and eventually for several suckers.

POTTING SOILS

Clivias seem to succeed in a wide variety of potting soils as long as three criteria are met. These are excellent drainage, excellent aeration, and good organic matter. Usually the first two conditions can be met in the same way. The medium in which the plant grows needs to have sufficient material so that it drains freely, and at the same time there also needs to be a component that retains moisture so that the potting soil does not dry out too rapidly. On the other hand, if it retains too much moisture, the medium will not be well aerated, and that leads to a variety of problems. Drainage can be achieved by adding coarse, washed river sand or washed construction sand. The latter is often available in hardware stores, where it is available for mixing with cement. Gravel made from pumice is a good, lightweight additive if it is available. Synthetic particulate matter such as ground Styrofoam, perlite, or granular rock wool are also possible additives that will increase drainage and the desired aeration. Additives that increase water retention include sphagnum peat, small sized bark, coconut coir, humus, and other similar products. If the proportions of bark are too high, soggy bark will exclude air and cause anaerobic conditions that result in root loss. A 10 to 20 percent volume of Douglas fir bark makes a very good mix, and humus will form naturally from the bark. Bacteria and fungi break down rotting vegetation to humus, which is made up of a variety of organic molecules, and over time those are further broken down by microorganisms into their original components, CO_2 and H_2O. Garden compost is a good source of humus, and bark will be readily broken down to humus if the correct temperature and water conditions are available. As mulches and compost get changed into humus and then back into CO_2 and H_2O, they loose volume. In a garden bed this process is not too problematic because you can always add a layer of new mulch. However, as the soil volume in containers shrinks, the plant is drawn down to the bottom of the pot, and merely adding more components to the top of the pot can lead to trouble as the crown will get buried. It is better to repot the entire plant, placing new soil at the bottom of the pot and the plant on top of that. If you use a potting soil with a very high percentage of organic matter, you may need to repot very frequently. This can become a major chore when large plants in big containers or many smaller plants are involved. As clivias can go for many years without repotting, it is worthwhile adding an appreciable amount of inert material to the potting soil.

If you are adding particles such as pumice gravel or bark to the soil mix to improve drainage, it is a good idea to screen the particles so that they are all more or less the same diameter. Mixed sized gravel packs much more tightly than gravel of similar dimensions. In uniform-sized mixes much more airspace is retained. If the mix is primarily organic (bark, for example), it will tend to compress and exclude air spaces as it decays.

Peat and humus are important additives to the soil as their weak, negative electric charges attract and hold positively charged elements, such as potassium and magnesium, that are essential for plant growth. These positive elements will later be made available to the plant's roots. Clay particles are also negatively charged, and a small amount of powdered clay added to the mix could be beneficial. Soils rich in humus can hold appreciably more water than inorganic soils because a shell of water molecules congregates around the humus particles. Not all of this water is available to the plant, but some is. Although clay particles also attract and hold a shell of water molecules that in turn help retain water in the mix, too much clay will tend to compact the mix and exclude air. There are also artificial gel beads that can be added to the mix that swell up and hold onto considerable amounts of water that will be made available to the plant's roots.

Clivias seem to tolerate a wide range of pH. Many commercial potting mixes have a pH as low as 5. In southern California, the plants do well in basic clay soils where the pH can reach 7.5. Some commercial growers recommend a pH of 6.

Clivias will actually survive without any soil. James and Connie Able, growers in South Africa, mounted a clivia plant on a board with just a little moss under the crown. The plant was watered frequently and fed with a mild fertilizer. It survived and even flowered in that condition, although its root growth was diminished. Plants in pots require less attention and would probably produce better quality flowers. Other growers have reported situations where they have potted their plants in totally organic mixes that eventually dissipated, leaving a plant with the pot filled primarily with roots and no medium. Such plants will continue to grow and flower very well if they get adequate moisture and occasional food. Epiphytic clivias in the wild are occasionally reported as growing in the crotch of a branch or in a cavity where detritus has accumulated. Clivias, therefore, are not fussy about their growing medium as long as it is well draining.

LIGHT

Clivias dislike direct sunlight, although they can tolerate a certain amount of direct sunlight in the very early morning or late afternoon. Remember, if there is enough light to cast a direct shadow on the leaves, it is too bright. Even short exposures to the noon sun can burn leaves and bleach flowers. On the other hand, if the plants are grown in deep shade, their flowers will not develop to their full potential in terms of color. If a plant gets badly burned it will

Leaves damaged by sunburn.

usually recover if placed in the shade, although it may take nearly a year before it looks good again.

WATERING

Although clivias are usually found in the wild in forest understories where moisture is usually freely available, they are able to endure prolonged droughts and seem able to tolerate infrequent irrigation. However, if they are to be grown to perfection, they need adequate moisture. Watering a large collection by hand can be tedious, and commercial nurseries and wholesale producers of clivias usually resort to drip irrigation whereby each pot has its own permanent spaghetti tube supplied with a drip outlet. Large numbers of pots can then be watered simultaneously, even automatically using a timer. Individual pot irrigation is to be preferred over sprinklers for several reasons. Sprinklers wet the entire plant and can splash diseases from plant to plant. Water from overhead sprinklers may not reach the plants that fall in the "rain shadow" of other plants, especially as a collection matures and pots become crowded; this is true even if the sprinklers are on for a long time. Finally, sprinklers are a problem when plants are in flower as excess water will collect in and spoil the blooms, which in turn destroys pollen viability. If one must use sprinklers, then the plants need adequate air movement.

Clivias are able to tolerate a wide range of high salt concentrations. In southern California, which has hard water and a salinity that on occasion has approached 700 ppm, clivia plants seem to tolerate those values without any problems. Little is known about the extremes and limits of clivia's salt tolerance. *Clivia nobilis* sometimes grows in the wild within the reach of ocean salt spray, but other species are confined to moist inland forests. If you have to irrigate with well or borehole water and are having problems with the plants' growth or appearance, you may find it useful to test the water's properties. White incrustations on the soil surface of the pot or around the drainage holes indicate excessive salt buildup, and plants should be repotted in fresh mix. Salt buildup can be avoided by occasionally flushing the pots with rainwater.

If plants are on a drip system, dust will accumulate on the leaves. Plants will look better is they are occasionally hosed down, but either pick a day when the relative humidity is low so that the plants will be dry before nightfall or increase air circulation following their shower.

FEEDING

As with other things, clivias are quite accommodating with regards feeding. Since some of their feeding preferences have been discussed in the section on clivia in the landscape, I will not repeat anything here. In North America, inorganic, water-soluble fertilizers are used, and they can range from foliage applications to slow-release granules placed in each pot. Although clivias are quite easygoing plants, they do respond well to good care.

REPOTTING

Clivias can be repotted at any time, even when they are in flower, provided you are careful not to damage the roots or expose the naked plants to very dry conditions. The best time to repot is at the end of summer and before the fall growth spurt when flower umbels are developing. Also at this time berries will be set and unlikely to abort because of transplant shock, but you should probably not transplant or divide a plant that is carrying berries because the peduncle is brittle and berries are easily knocked or broken off.

When a healthy plant is to be repotted it should be knocked out of the pot. Usually the pot is so full of roots that it is a difficult task to get the plant out. Resist the temptation to grab the plant by its neck and yank since that is rarely successful and the plant may get severely damaged. Likewise, once the plant is out of the pot, lift it by the ball of roots and not the leaves. If the container is made of clay, soaking the plant thoroughly the day before transplanting may help loosen the roots. It is often advisable to break a ceramic or clay pot if you are having difficulty removing the plant. Plastic pots can be cut with secateurs or tin-snips to release the plant. Using a hose with a fairly strong spray, you can wash the soil off the roots. Trim away dead roots. If offsets are large enough, they may be cut away using a sterile blade, but do not tear the offset free. Remember not to use the same blade on different plants as that will spread disease. A stainless steel knife, soaked for twenty minutes in household bleach, is an effective, sterilized instrument. If you are repotting several plants, have a number of knives soaking in the disinfectant to expedite matters. Alternatively, you can dip the blade into alcohol and then flame it with a propane torch or burner. It is important that the blade get red hot; one quick swipe through the flame is not enough to sterilize it.

Do not be tempted to remove very small offsets or trim away and shorten too much root. While the plants are tough and can survive being brutalized, too much cutting will set them back substantially, and it can take several years to recover from an abusive gardener. Offsets that are removed when too small will take years to establish themselves and regain flowering abilities. It is better to wait the extra year or two that the offset needs to build up sufficient reserves before you cut it off. Patience will save you many additional years of waiting for the offshoot to recover enough to reach flowering size.

Clivia divisions should have their cut surfaces dusted with powdered sulfur or other commercial fungicides, and the rhizomes should be allowed to dry for a few days in a shady spot. Damaged leaves can also be trimmed back at this time. Note that the sap in the leaves is under pressure and it exudes out of cut surfaces, and since some people are allergic to the sap, it makes good sense to avoid it. The thick, viscous sap dries after a few hours in the air, and the leaves are then easier to handle. If divisions are laid aside to dry, be careful that they are not in physical contact with divisions from different cultivars as an exchange of pathogens could then occur.

Gently twist the roots to fit into the new, slightly larger pot and work fresh compost between the root mass. Be careful not to injure the plant. Soil should be barely damp and firmed but not compacted. Plants should not be watered for several days to give the plant the chance to heal any cuts and bruises. Then water the plant thoroughly until liquid flows out of the bottom of the container.

COLLECTION COMPONENTS

Even as modern gardens are getting smaller, so must the plants that can be accommodated in them. Very few people now have the facilities where unlimited expanses of shade cloth can be erected. This means that it is important to be very selective about the plants that make up a collection. It is a gardening truism that a poor specimen takes up as much space and attention as a fine specimen. Should you specialize in just one type of clivia such as yellows, variegated, or dwarfs? Of course the answer depends on the individual, but there are some good points to be made about specialization in collections.

Focussed collections usually involve plants that have similar care needs. For example, the shading required for variegated clivias is a little different from standards since the leaves of variegated plants are more sensitive to both sunburn and chemicals. Similarly, dwarves require less feeding than standard varieties. People who have restricted collections also tend to be more aware of what are the very choice plants, and whether or not they possess those types. The gardener's or the collection's reputation (if that is of concern) is easier to forge when interests are confined to a subset of the type. The old adage "jack of all trades, master of none" also holds for plant collections.

PEST MANAGEMENT

For the most part, clivias are pest free, but you should nevertheless encourage an environment that is disease and pest free. You can go a long way toward achieving this by maintaining a weed-free collection. You will need to not only weed the pots but also the floors beneath the benches. One particularly pernicious and cosmopolitan weed is oxalis, and it is particularly important to weed containers before oxalis sets seed capsules. If you are vigilant, you will be able to keep oxalis under control. Other weeds will also occur, depending on the geographical area.

Some parts of the world have specific and different problem pests depending on the country. Regulations concerning applications of phytochemicals vary so much from region to region, and sometimes even between counties, shire, or districts within a state or province that I am reluctant to recommend specific brand names or pesticides. If you need specific advice on combating a particular pest, you can usually get advice from local area agricultural authorities or plant nurseries. Local clivia hobbyists usually have good advice that is specific for your area and they will know the more common pests you might encounter. Nevertheless, clivias are for the most part trouble free and long-lived.

Routine preventative spraying used to be the easiest way to preclude attacks by insects and other pests. While this regular procedure still occurs in large nurseries, home gardeners are now encouraged to take a more environmentally friendly approach, and that usually means only spraying with insecticides following evidence of the pests' presence or actual damage.

In Southern Africa, clivia growers battle with the dreaded lily borer, also known as the lily leaf miner. This is the caterpillar of the noctuid moth *Brithys pancratii* that lays eggs on the underside of clivia or other amaryllid leaves. The front half of the adult moth's body is a dark brown, and the abdomen and rear wings are white, though sometimes the posterior edges of the rear wings can be brown. Most amaryllids contain high concentrations of poisonous alkaloids to deter predators, but these caterpillars have evolved ways of tolerating the chemicals. After hatching, the caterpillars penetrate and work their ways into the leaves, eating as they tunnel. They have a voracious appetite as they work their way down toward the base of the leaf and then invade and destroy the growing tip of the plant. Often they are only noticed after the damage has been done, and by then it is too late to save the shoot. The leaves may appear to be untouched only to fall apart when the plant is handled. While the caterpillars and infected leaves can be removed by hand, regular application of pesticides is a more effective deterrent. Graham Duncan, the famous bulb man at the National Botanical Institute at Kirstenbosch, recommends carbaryl (a chemical found in Karbaspray or Karbadust) be used as a prophylactic (Duncan 1999). Pyrethroid insecticides applied weekly also help to keep this pest under control. If you do not use chemical means to protect the plants, you should inspect them regularly. The lily borer seems to be a specific African problem, although they do also occur in Southern Europe. There are also some caterpillars in Australia with similar habits to the lily borer that feed on amaryllids.

Perhaps the most pervasive of clivia insect pests are mealybugs, called wooly aphids in some parts of the world. They find their way to the clivia plant in either of two ways. The young larvae are so light that they can be wafted to the plant on air currents, or they may be deliberately carried from plant to plant by ants that actively farm them. The ants milk the mealybugs for the plant juices the mealybugs have been drinking, so if you control ants you will go a long way toward controlling mealybugs. Mealybugs secrete themselves between the bases of leaves and use their mouthparts to pierce the leaves. Later, when the leaves mature, there will be small, discolored patches on them where they were bitten into. The mature insects are usually on the undersides of leaves, or they are occasionally wandering slowly about. Infected plants are those with white deposits on the leaves. The insects can be dealt with by dabbing individuals with ethanol, but that is ineffective for the young mealybugs that stay hidden in the interstices between leaves. Mealybugs tend to prefer dry conditions. Unless the infestation is particularly heavy, mealybugs are not noticeable without close inspection. The most effective treatment is to drench the plant with systemic insecticides.

A lily borer caterpillar feeding within the peduncle of a clivia plant.

Scale insects are protected with a hard carapace and usually need specific chemicals that can penetrate the shell. It may take several applications of insecticide to get them under control, and you should use agents that are specifically prescribed for use on scale insects. Again, systemic insecticides seem to work better. Fortunately, I have found that scale infestations are relatively rare in southern California and easily controllable if caught early.

In recent years, the so-called giant white fly (*Aleurodicus dugesii*) has invaded southern California. These bugs prefer hard leaves and are not averse to setting up colonies on clivias. Spraying with general insecticides that contain acephate (such as Orthene) controls them relatively easily. Fortunately, clivias are not among the preferred plants for the giant white fly, and these insects appear to be a relatively minor component of the pest spectrum. They make the plant look untidy, but we have not yet seen plants succumb to the pest.

Aphids can damage flower buds and they may also transmit diseases. More pernicious are the tiny insects, called thrips, that infect flower buds and damage the flowers by feeding on the surface layers of the epithelium, scarring the petals and leaving white or yellow patches in what would normally be orange portions. Applications of a good systemic insecticide as the flower buds appear go a long way toward avoiding this problem. Thrips tend to be ubiquitous, and unfortunately, only a few are needed to disfigure a clivia flower. In South Africa thrips may damage the leaves, but it is rare to find thrips on leaves in southern California even though there may be severe thrip damage to flowers. Floral thrips often feed on clivia flowers that are still at the bud stage. They move between the tepals and into the central cavity of the flower where they eat the inner surface of the tepals. Areas of tepal that are grazed become a finely mottled white color that disfigures the flowers. Floral thrips can be controlled by spraying the flower buds with a general insecticide, but be careful that the insecticide itself or its carrier chemical does not damage the flower buds.

Slugs and snails appear to be a universal garden problem, and this is especially so in southern California, where these pests can devastate a planting of flowers. Both slugs and snails are primarily evening feeders. They do relatively little damage to leaves of adult plants but will destroy seedlings. Both mollusks like to climb up into the umbel and nibble on young buds or even at petal edges of mature flowers. Even though they are usually inactive during the day, snails tend to remain resting within the flowers only to become active again after the sun sets. Slugs will leave the umbel during the daytime. Good mulch provides excellent hiding places for a variety of pests including slugs and snails. In midwinter, start applying various snail baits to attract and decimate the mollusk population. If midwinter coincides with the rainy season, you may need to set up a regular schedule to renew applications of the bait. Applications should not be confined to the clivia bed but should also be spread in surrounding parts of the landscape. Baits should be administered evenly over the soil surface in pots or other containers.

Even though you can pick snails off the plants when you see them, it is best to take preventative measures and apply slug and snail baits as soon as the first buds appear. Reapply the baits during the flowering season. Some baits are mixed with bran that pets may find attractive, so take care when you distribute them. Southern California has had some success in recent years in reducing the European snail population by using other snail species that feed on their eggs. Unfortunately, they seem to have no effect on the slug population.

In general, problems with plants in large containers are easier to handle than those in beds because it is usually easier to access those in pots, and because they are higher off the ground, they are easier to examine and treat.

FUNGAL PROBLEMS AND ROT

There are a number of fungal and bacterial problems that attack clivia plants, but few of them have been studied in much detail, suggesting again that these are not serious clivia problems. Different diseases appear in disparate parts of the world. There is also a differential susceptibility to most of these diseases that is clone dependent; some plants appear to be more affected than others. You should remove and destroy susceptible plants from the planting unless they are particularly fine forms. The susceptible plants will look ratty, and this will destroy the integrity of the display. While treating the diseased plants with fungicides may clear up the infection for a while, they will probably succumb again at a later date, and it can take routine preventative spraying to keep the problem at bay. Adjacent plants do not often get infected.

I have come across a number of cases of rot, but they have nearly always proved easy to treat and often clear up on their own without specific treatment other than keeping the plant somewhat drier than usual. Clivias are amazingly resilient, and even young seedlings that have lost their apical growing points to rot have later made lateral shoots and recovered. However, in areas of high temperatures and summer rainfall, soft bacterial rots may become a problem. Mark Laing (2000) has isolated *Erwinia carotovora*, one of the organisms that can cause rot in plants, from clivias. The symptoms start as a yellowing of some bottom leaves. Investigations will reveal a brownish watery lesion. As the disease progresses, the entire base of the plant may rot and fall away. The bacterium is infectious and can be spread by a variety of agents ranging from cutting instruments to flies and other animal vectors; even rainwater can splash the bacterium from plant to plant. As soon as you notice an infection, remove and isolate the plant. If the plant is important you can try to save it, otherwise it is easier to simply destroy it. Unpot the plants you do try to save and cut away all of the infected tissue. Use a clean instrument for each cut because the blade itself will infect clean tissue after it has been in contact with the bacterium. Seventy percent ethanol, 10 percent household bleach, or 3 percent hydrogen peroxide are adequate disinfectants. The cuts must be made to remove all traces of discoloration from the rhizome and leaves. Laing recommends that the cut surface be dusted with powdered sulfur or copper oxychloride. You can leave it to dry for a day or two before planting it into sharp, clean sand until the plant appears to have recovered.

This litany of pests and diseases is not complete. Each geographic region has different problems, be they beetles that nibble the flowers or rot that destroys the crown. Local plant enthusiasts usually tend to know their native problems and how best to treat or combat them. But remember, clivias are easy and not in the least temperamental provided their three basic necessities are provided.

VIRUS DISEASES

Virus is the bane of most monocot plant collectors. Relatively little is known about virus diseases in *Clivia*, but several different symptoms are seen. Many beginners tend to confuse virus diseases with leaf variegation, but the two are easily separated. Normal variegation is seen as longitudinal striping in the leaves, and these stripes extend along the entire leaf length. The stripes may be thick or thin, and their extension for nearly the entire length of the leaf discloses their benevolent nature. Viral markings are usually visible as faint streaks of pale green or greenish yellow against the darker green background of the leaf. The streaks are relatively short or irregularly shaped. They may be difficult to discern if the leaf is partially sunburned or grown in bright light. The virus may even produce a rather ill defined, ring-shaped, yellowish mark. Obviously infected plants are relatively rare, and unless the virused plant is an exceptional clone, it should be destroyed.

Biting insects such as aphids often transmit viruses, but there may be other agents as well. Gardeners working with cultivated plants also transmit viruses when infected sap is transferred to a clean plant on clippers or spades during trimming or dividing operations. In addition, pollinating a clean plant with pollen from a virus-infected plant can also transmit the virus.

The rarity of viral infection is probably due to many clivias in the trade being seed grown rather than divisions of mature plants. In most plants the viral particles are excluded from rapidly dividing tissue such as that found in apical meristems or seed embryos. Only after the new tissue has matured can it become infected by the spread of the virus from diseased portions into the healthy tissue. Viruses are either excluded from developing seeds or else any infected seedlings die soon after germination. Seed can therefore be used to clean up an infected stock or a special strain of clivias. Traditionally, infected plants are used as the maternal plant for making seed. If pollen from an infected plant is used, there is the possibility that viral particles will be transported, along with the pollen grains, and infect the ovary tissue of the mother plant. The disease can spread from there over the entire plant. Therefore, if you use two plants to make a cross and one is infected, do not use the clean plant to carry the fruits.

CONVERSING WITH CLIVIAS

Should you talk to your plants? Of course. Why not? (But remember the neighbors will think you are strange.) Regular and frequent talking to your plant forces you to focus on it, and you will become cognizant of changes occurring in your collection. Pest infestations will be spotted sooner, as will build up of salts in the pot and other potential problems. You will also see the flower buds emerge and the new leaves grow, and you will actually start to appreciate that your plant is a living being. If you are too embarrassed to talk to your clivia plant, then perhaps you could sing under your breath. After all, plants are said to respond to music too. As you get too many plants to give each individual attention, it is a good idea to give them a little appreciation time. Stroll among them, perhaps a glass of wine in hand, and peruse what you have achieved and collected. Do this frequently, not so much to drink wine, but rather to enjoy your plants and assess their state of well-being. Nipping problems in the bud or not finding any problems at all will increase your well-being too.

Chapter Five

UNDERSTANDING
CLIVIA COLORS

THE TYPE COLOR in wild *Clivia miniata* is a clear, mid-orange, whereas that of the other species is predominantly orange but with other, additional shadings and green tepal tips. Occasional mutants include those with creamy yellow colors. There is intense interest among clivia hybridizers and growers around the world in extending the color range. Currently, their efforts are directed at producing clean white, rich yellow, clear pink, deep red, and even mauve colors. Despite claims to the contrary, there are few clivia clones where these colors have already been achieved, but breeders are very active in pursuing them. From among the hundreds of thousands of new seedlings that flower each year, hybridizers have hopes that the desired shades will soon be achieved. Perhaps new colors will even emerge.

Biologists are getting to the point where much about the physical color in these plants is understood in detail so that they know what needs to be achieved to widen the color range. There is also some understanding of the mechanisms of breeding in clivias, not due to any rigorous scientific breeding experiments but rather to the accumulated experiences of many breeders working with different clones over the past several decades. The long generation times—often more than five years—is partly responsible for discouraging scientists from investigating the genetic basis of clivia color. Most scientists are forced to work with organisms that have short generation times. However, the insight gained from traditional horticultural breeding can be just as sound.

In this section I discuss the ways that colors in clivia flowers are actually made. I will discuss *Clivia miniata* first, and make some additional comments about the other species at a later time. Some of the discussion is of primary interest to those who are trying to breed better clivias, but it may have little relevance to the windowsill grower. Nevertheless, I have found that many clivia enthusiasts are absolutely fascinated by this topic. I have included references to sources where those thirsty for greater depth may find additional information.

Until the late twentieth century, much of the clivia breeding was done by the seat of one's pants. People have spent much energy trying to explain their results in clivia breeding using rudimentary Mendelian genetics. This method has often been without much success because it means thinking in terms of simple dominant and recessive genetic controls for color pigmentation. Understanding the physiological basis of pigment production would make the whole process of breeding for color clearer, although it would still be quite complex.

If you examine a normal *Clivia miniata* flower, your first impression is that it is an orange flower. Closer examination reveals that the outsides of the tepals are usually orange from their tips to the base, but the inside the flower normally has a throat of contrasting color. Although the throat is variable, it is usually white with a central linear smudge of yellow. In a few cases the yellow is replaced with green. The extent of the throat pattern is very variable; at some extremes the orange is reduced to a mere picotee edge of orange. That pattern is very desirable but unfortunately also very rare. Other rare flowers are those where the throat is large and clear white or solid, bright yellow.

When flower buds are first noticeable, they are entirely a creamy yellow color. As the flower stem elongates and the buds

Colors of modern standard clivias.

become exposed to light, the beginnings of orange pigmentation on the outside become visible. The amount of pigmentation appears to be related to the amount of light that the flower is exposed to. This is true especially of the dark red-orange flowers, which, if developed indoors, may only be a smooth and very nice, clear, pastel orange. Where tepals overlap and if they do not separate in the matured flower, the covered portion generally stays a creamy white. Thus, if you dissect the flower from among the pendent species with narrow tubular flowers, you will notice that most of the inner petals are creamy and their inner surfaces equally pale.

FLOWER PIGMENTS

Color in the flowers is based on chemicals called pigments that absorb light of certain colors and reflect light of others. Light of mixed colors is white, and the white portions reflect all light colors. In flowers, white can be achieved in one of several ways. There may be white pigment containing bodies called leucoplasts, but they have received very little scientific attention and it is not known if they occur in clivia flowers. A white flavone pigment occurs in many flowers, such as those of *Narcissus*, but does not appear to occur in *Clivia*. Another way of producing white is through having tiny air spaces between the cells that make up the tepals. These are like little air bubbles and reflect any light that impinges on them. The situation is rather like the well-known occurrence seen when making meringue. Egg albumen is a colorless liquid that, when beaten to make meringue, becomes filled with tiny air bubbles. These bubbles reflect the light making the meringue appear white. This same phenomenon—air bubbles producing white color—is fairly common in many flowers, and clivia tepals contain large amounts of airspace. White color then is usually due to the physical make-up of the flower and not specific white pigments.

Flower pigments are either water-soluble flavones or lipid-soluble (oil-soluble) carotenoids, and both types usually occur within the same flower. The two kinds of pigments may be distributed within the same cell or occur in different cells and in different parts of an individual flower. There are several different kinds of water-soluble pigments in *Clivia* that might be confined to different cells or occur all in the same cell. The actual situation in *Clivia* is not clear because analyses are made of pigments using entire flowers and not single cells. The water-soluble pigments are found in the large, central, fluid-filled cavity called the vacuole that is bounded by a membrane. This cavity occupies most of the volume of the cell, leaving only a small rim of cytoplasm, and cells with vacuoles that are filled with pigment look as if the entire volume of the cell is colored.

Oil-soluble pigments, on the other hand, are confined to small organelles called plastids, and they are scattered in the cytoplasm of the cell that surrounds the vacuole. This group of pigments is either attached to the membranes within the plastids or contained within oil droplets in the plastids. The plastids have their own chromosomes and are believed to have been derived from bacteria-like organisms that became incorporated into early primitive cells and now maintain a symbiotic relationship with those cells. There are, however, nuclear genes that can, but do not always, control the expression of genes in the plastids.

ANTHOCYANINS

Water-soluble pigments in clivias are a family of flavonoid chemicals called anthocyanins. There are quite a few different anthocyanins and they may be expressed in different parts of the plant. Usually these pigments are found in the epithelium and outer layers of the tepals, the epithelium of ripe berries, and at the base of the leaf in seedlings and young plants. Anthocyanins come in a variety of different colors. In clivias they are typically seen as pink, orange, or red pigments, but the actual color of the anthocyanin depends on a number of different factors that will be discussed below. There are several groups of anthocyanins, usually and originally named after the flowers from which they were first isolated. Among these are cyanidins, delphinidins, pelargonidins, petuinidins, and peonidins; they differ slightly from each other in their intimate chemical structure.

In all, there appear to be more than five families of anthocyanin pigments, and there is even a white flavonoid called leucoxanthin, but it does not appear to occur in *Clivia*. In petunia, which is among the better understood flowers in terms of color pigments, at least thirty-five genes are involved with the production of flower color (Holton and Cornish 1995).

Robert Griesbach at the U.S. Department of Agriculture and I have analyzed the anthocyanin makeup in a number of different clivias, and I have summarized our findings below. Normally, other chemicals called co-factors can change the peak color of the pigment. There may be more than ten co-factors in a single clivia flower. In addition, the color can also be drastically affected by the pH (concentration of hydrogen ions) in the vacuole. The anthocyanin, however, is considered the major player that determines flower color.

Clivia miniata

Within normal-colored clivia flowers, there are at least two different pelargonidins, pelargonidin-3-glucoside (P-3-G) and pelargonidin-3-rutinoside (P-3-R). The latter has an additional rhamnose (a simple 6 carbon sugar) attached to it. Both of these pigments occur in the same flower and probably within the same cell vacuoles. The pigments in the berries and leaf bases are cyanidins. In normal orange clivias, the major pigment present is P-3-G, but in the redder clivias, such as Flame™, we find not only more P-3-G, but also more P-3-R. Increased color intensity also comes from additional cell layers beneath the usual pigmented surface. In fact, we found proportionally much more P-3-R and a smaller amount of P-3-G in a pastel-colored clivia called 'Morning Light' from Jim Comstock's breeding.

Clivia nobilis

This species appears to have both pelargonidins and cyanidins in both the fruits and flowers. There seems to be a wider array of other pigments in smaller quantities as well.

Clivia caulescens
The situation in *C. Caulescens* is similar to that in *C. nobilis* with both pelargonidins and cyanidins occurring in both fruits and flowers.

Clivia gardenii
This species has not been available for pigment analysis, which is a pity because there appears to be more color variation in this species than in either *C. nobilis* or *C. Caulescens*.

Our analysis of anthocyanin makeup points to the usefulness of incorporating the various species into the *Clivia miniata* bloodlines as a way of widening the color spectrum and introducing other pigments.

ANTHOCYANIN SYNTHESIS

The first step in the synthesis of anthocyanin is the formation of chalcone from the combination of two simpler molecules. The reaction is controlled by an enzyme chalcone synthase. Another two enzymes convert this hydroxychalcone into dihydrokaempferol, the basic common molecule that can be converted into a wide variety of end products depending on which additional enzymes are present. The next enzyme converts the kaempferol into leucopelargonidin, a colorless pigment. The next conversion results in pelargonidin-3-glucoside. In all, a minimum of five enzymes are needed in this pathway. An additional step converts the pelargonidin-3-glucoside into pelargonidin-3-rutinoside. The different proportions we find between these two anthocyanins in a single flower may be due to the amount of that last enzyme in the chain. Pelargonidin-3-glucoside appears to be responsible for the orange coloring and pelargonidin-3-rutinoside for the red shades.

The cyanidin found in clivia berries shares the beginnings of the chain of reactions in the synthesis of anthocyanin, going from chalcone to dihydrokaempferol through a parallel set of reactions to cyanidin. In all, seven enzymes are needed to make Cyanidine-3-rutinoside, the anthocyanin in clivia berries and flowers, but only

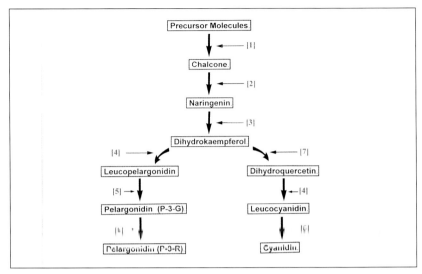

Anthocyanin pathways. This is a simplified anthocyanin pathway that ends in
pelargonidin and cyanidin. Each number represents a specific enzyme
(1 through 7) that catalyses the reaction to the next step. Only one additional
enzyme (enzyme 7) is needed to make cyanidin instead of P-3-G. Enzyme 6 is
unique to the P-3-R step. (Based on Holton and Cornish 1995.)

the first three steps share common enzymes with the pelargonidin
pathway. Above is a diagram of a simplified pathway that leads to the
various anthocyanins.

Enzymes are proteins, and at least one gene is usually required
to make one enzyme. It therefore takes at least six genes to produce
the enzymes needed to make cyanidine and five genes to build
pelargonidin-3-glucoside. These two different pathways share the
first three genes and two of the later ones. The idea of a single gene
determining flower color—as is taught in high school Mendelian
genetics—is a great oversimplification.

YELLOW CLIVIAS

All cells in a plant contain a copy of the entire genome (genetic information) of that individual. Every time a plant cell divides, the DNA

that makes up its genes needs to be replicated to make a new copy. Mistakes made during this process are called mutations, and they can result in changes in the shape of the enzymes that they code. If the change is too severe, then the enzyme may not be functional. Depending on where in the chain of chemical reactions it must work, the changed or non-functioning enzyme could block the synthesis of the anthocyanin end product entirely or even change the nature of the end product. It is these mutations in yellow clivias that block the formation of anthocyanin. Without the anthocyanin, we see only the carotenoid pigments, and hence we see yellow-colored clivias.

As there are a number of places in the anthocyanin pathway where anthocyanins can be blocked, it follows that mutations in any of those genes can affect pigment production. However, nuclear genes in plants occur as pairs called alleles, with one allele on each chromosome. One allele is inherited from each parent. If there is a mutation in one gene, the other allele can compensate for it. It follows that both parents must have had the same mutation if their offspring is to make a yellow *Clivia* specimen. However, two yellow clivias mated together might each have mutations for different enzyme steps, and in such a case they can compensate for each other and produce offspring capable of making anthocyanins or orange colors. This has confused many of the clivia breeders who come to refer to true breeding yellows, intimating that there are others that do not breed yellows.

When breeding yellow clivias, breeders need to know the backgrounds of both the parents (for example, page 132) in order to be sure of getting yellow flowers in the next generation. Clivias with the same mutant gene on both chromosomes (parent A) have yellow flowers. Mutations in any other genes would also yield yellow flowers provided that the mutation was found on both chromosomes (parent B). However, mating two yellow clivias with different mutant genes allows the full complement of genes to be expressed, and orange flowers will result. If this orange-flowered seedling is backcrossed to either parent A or B, 50 percent of them will be

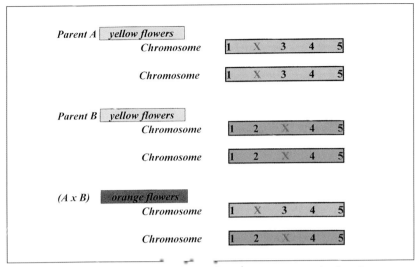

Inheritance of yellow coloring in clivias. Numbers represent the first five genes for the pelargonidin pathway. Mutant genes (the red xs) code for enzymes that do not work; they block the ultimate production of pelargonidin. Clivias with the same mutant gene on both chromosomes (parent A) have yellow flowers, as do clivias with mutations in any other genes on both chromosomes (parent B).

yellow seedlings. As there are a number of other places where mutations can block the pathway, it is not possible to decide on compatible parents merely by looking at the color of the flowers.

There are flowers that are essentially yellow but may have a blush of anthocyanin. Breeders are not absolutely certain how these come about, but it might be explained as follows. The specific enzyme that a gene encodes catalyzes each step in the anthocyanin pathway. In the absence of the enzyme, the chemical reaction may still proceed spontaneously but at a very much slower rate, and small amounts of anthocyanin could be produced. There are also pattern genes that determine which part of the flower is allowed to express the various genes. Thus, in a picotee flower (one that has a distinct petal margin of contrasting color) with orange edges, the anthocyanin genes may be turned on only in the appropriate part of the flower. In other words, the plant may contain the full set of genetic instructions for making good anthocyanin, but those instructions are activated only in specific places. Another possible explanation of how an all yellow flower is created is that something could have happened to the pattern gene so that the anthocyanin genes, while present, simply do not get turned on at all.

Several breeders have yellow flowers that they claim can produce orange offspring. When breeders then discard all of the orange flowering plants, they achieve higher and higher percentages of yellows in each succeeding generation. This suggests that the ancestral stock involved mutations at several different sites. The pathways to make anthocyanins are branched, and within a single plant, several different anthocyanins are produced. If these were not blocked basally but rather toward the ends of the branches, then the breeder would need to do selfing and line breeding to produce homozygous lines. Pure breeding yellows can actually be accomplished within a few generations.

As most yellow clivias also make yellow berries, the cyanidin pathways—much like the anthocyanin pathways—are also blocked. As there are no known cases of orange flowers with yellow berries on the same plant, the mutations must occur before the production of dihydrokaempferol, the common link before the divergence of the two pigments. As any of three different enzymes are involved with pigment synthesis before cyanidin and pelargonidin synthesis diverge, there is the possibility of several different mutations in those genes being responsible for yellow flowers. Cyanidin coloring on seedling leaf bases is, conveniently, also blocked, so it is easy to separate potentially yellow flowering seedlings from the normal wild type upon germination. Unless the yellow clivias have blockages in the same genes, they will not be compatible, and when mated together will produce orange-colored offspring. The reason is that any individual plant contains two sets of nuclear genes, one set inherited from each parent. If the mutation was in only one member of the pair of genes (the other gene of the pair is therefore normal), the gene could still function, producing enough enzyme to compensate for the other nonfunctional gene. To get yellow flowers, both genes for a particular step must be nonfunctional. Mutations at any of the first three steps discussed above lead to yellow clivias. If two yellow parents have mutations for different enzymes, their off-spring would have to be orange, but the anthocyanin blocks can re-emerge in their grandchildren if the orange children are mated to the correct parents. *Clivia* breeders have tried to distinguish between the various yellow clivias and sometimes use the term *par yellow* to indicate noncompatible strains.

CAROTENOIDS

Carotenoids provide the yellow coloring in clivias. In conjunction with the anthocyanins, they help to brighten the colors of flowers and berries. Usually the carotenoids are in the deeper tissues of the tepals and not in the surface layers. These occur in plastids where they appear in the cell cytoplasm as yellow granules. Plastids are thought to be derived from symbiotic microorganisms. Green plastids are called chloroplasts. Carotenoids are also found in chloroplasts, where they are an integral part of the membranes in those organelles and where they play a vital role during photosynthesis. Water is split during photosynthesis leaving a highly reactive single oxygen atom (called a free radical) that has so much energy it can damage parts of the cell. Carotenoids are able to absorb some of this energy and protect the chloroplast apparatus from damage. Plants unable to make carotenoids are so damaged by these high-energy radicals that they are unable to survive the seedling stage. Carotenoids are also able to capture the energy from sunlight and can pass it on to the chlorophyll molecule for use during photosynthesis.

In flowers or ripe berries, the carotenoids may be sequestered in tiny oil droplets within the plastid, but the genes underlying the synthesis of carotenoids are actually located in the nucleus and not in the plastid. Although the plastid itself has its own circular chromosome, that chromosome is located within the organelle.

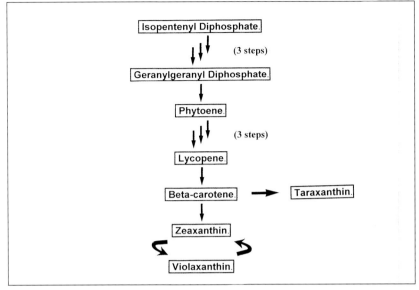

Pathway for the major carotenoid pigments found in clivias. Lycopene is the first colored product produced and is pinkish. The three major carotenoids in both yellow and orange flowers are all yellow carotenoids; taraxanthin and violaxanthin can be interconverted to each other as indicated by the curved arrows.
(This plate based on Bartley and Scolnik 1995.)

Reproduction of plastid chromosomes is independent of cell nuclear division, and mature plastids bud off new plastids that each contain their own circular DNA. The organelles are only inherited through the mother plant, whereas the enzymes and other proteins needed to produce carotenoids are produced in the cytoplasm of the cell and then imported into the plastid where the carotenoid is synthesized. The clivia egg cell is usually provided with several proplastids (undifferentiated plastids), but they are excluded from the sperm cells. Clivia plants inherit only their plastid genes from the mother plant, a fact that becomes important again when we examine how variegated clivia plants are produced (see chapter 11).

Like anthocyanins, carotenoids are synthesized by a string of reactions mediated by enzymes. Scientists know these chemical pathways in fair detail. Carotenoids are built up from a 5-carbon compound called IPP (isopentenyl pyrophosphate). IPP is used to build a molecule containing 20-carbon atoms called GGPP (geranylgeranyl pyrophosphate). Two molecules of GGPP are fused to form phytoene, which is actually the first step in the pathway that is committed to carotenoid synthesis. Two enzymes next remove hydrogen ions and convert the phytoene into a molecule called lycopene. Lycopene is the first compound that is colored (often pinkish) and is a pigment in fruits such as tomatoes and peppers. At this point the molecule is a long chain of thirty-two carbon atoms with an additional eight carbons attached on side branches. The ends of the branches are then cyclized into a terminal ring of six carbons on each end of the molecule. Additionally, two enzymes appear to be needed to convert lycopene into α-carotene. This alpha-carotein is an important yellow pigment that protects chlorophyll molecules during photosynthesis. Other carotenoids can also be produced, and each step in the process produces a different shade of orange, pink, or yellow. The three major carotenoids found in both yellow and orange clivia flowers are all yellow carotenoids and are beta-carotene, taraxanthin, and violaxanthin. The latter two can be interconverted to each other. Pure white or pure pink clivias would have the carotenoid pathway blocked either just before or just after lycopene.

Drs. Matsuno and Hirao (1980) investigated the carotenoid components in two different, wild-collected orange clivias, an orange cultivated hybrid, and a yellow clivia plant. They found that in all four cases the flowers contained seven different carotenoids. Most of the yellow pigment was the carotenoid called lutein 5,6-epoxide (also known as taraxanthin) and it accounted for between 61 and 70 percent of the pigment, depending on the clone examined. This carotenoid is quite common in many other yellow flowers, such as dandelions, and it occurs in small amounts in nearly all chloroplasts. The second highest component was beta-carotene, which varied from 9 to 13 percent. Taraxanthin is derived from beta-carotene. Another carotenoid that occurred in quantities between

4 and 11 percent was violaxanthin, a compound that is closely related to taraxanthin. Matsuno and Hirao found that there was more violaxanthin in the yellow clivia plant and the least in the cultivated orange clivia plant. Other carotenoids occurred in smaller amounts. The four clones varied one from another in the exact proportion of each of the yellow pigments that they contained. An enormous number of different carotenoids are known in nature—approximately six hundred—and hence they represent another possible base from which to breed new colors and tones, particularly colors such as amber, cream, or even stronger yellows and golds in the yellow clivias.

Most yellow clivias tend to be rather pale. Instead of trying to breed more intense yellow colors in the flowers by changing the pigment, breeders could increase the numbers of chromoplasts in the cells and also perhaps the concentration of carotene produced within them. Normal line breeding, which involves selecting parents that appear to be the most intense, will achieve a more intense yellow. In some flowers, it is important to know which are the pod and pollen parents with regards to certain inheritable traits, but we do not know enough about color inheritance in *Clivia* to decide if this is important here. Carotenoids are sequestered in the plastids (which are inherited through the maternal parent), so there could be genes in the plastid that determine how the pigment is packaged, even if the genes controlling production of the carotenoid are nuclear. It might be useful to try using the most intensely colored parent as the pod parent.

In other kinds of plants the flower buds are green, and after anthesis (flower opening), the chloroplasts loose their chlorophyll, exposing the carotenoids; the deeper green the bud, the more intense the yellow in the mature flower. Developing flower buds of *Clivia* are usually creamy yellow and not green, but green flowers are known to exist. Some of the orange flowers also have chloroplasts that give them either green throats or, if the chloroplasts are distributed throughout the flower, a brown cast to the entire flower. In

The wide range of colors seen in clivia fruits depends on the mixture of chlorophyll, anthocyanin, and carotenoids, as well as on their underlying genes in the mother plant. Small variations can change the color of the fruit.

the latter case the flower is a brownish red color. If green casts can be incorporated into yellow flowers, breeders might be able to intensify the colors. The ideal end point would be a golden-yellow flower like a daffodil, but most breeders are still some distance from that goal.

WHITE CLIVIAS

There have been many reports of pure white clivias. Those that I have actually chased down have all been disappointing. Most have been the result of over-exposed film or poor quality color copying, and many flowers have been old and sunburned. In a few cases, people have just called cream-colored flowers white. Growers are so eager to have snow-white clivias that they are happy to believe any suggestions that that goal has been achieved. A few have even been named based on poor photography. There are persistent rumors of clivias with white flowers in the wild. White clivias should be possible, but no one has achieved that objective yet. One report from South Africa sounds promising but until I have seen the flower in person, I am reserving judgment.

There are at least three explanations of how a white clivia plant could be achieved. In the first case, there could be a blockage in the carotene pathway caused by mutant enzymes so that plastids cannot make alpha-carotene. This case is like anthocyanin production being blocked. However, the chloroplasts must be able to make alpha-carotene since a plant that cannot make alpha-carotene would not survive. The second possibility involves proplastids having normal carotenoid genes that do not develop into chromoplasts in the flower because they are not turned on. Producing white clivias this way is possible because some clivia flowers do have large white patches in their throats where there is no yellow pigment. Getting to white is a matter of selecting for larger and larger white patches, a function that is presumably under the control of nuclear genes that regulate pattern in the flowers. The third way of producing white flowers might involve chromoplasts that make carotenoids that are unstable and bleached by sunlight. Some narcissus plants with unstable carotenoids have flower parts that open creamy yellow but are then bleached white by sunlight so that they mature to a clean white. In some slipper orchids, too, there are inherited factors that cause disintegration of the chloroplasts and chromoplasts in the flower parts shortly after the flower opens, and this may be the reason why some of the cream-colored clivias fade to white as they age. Orange flowers that later mature to pink (see the section on pink clivias) also possess the desired genes.

Line breeding for paler yellow clivias to achieve white in clivias is analogous to the situation in daylilies (*Hemerocallis*). Daylily breeders have also been pursuing white dreams by mating the palest, creamy yellow flowers, and yet they still have not been able to achieve a good, snow-white flower. Breeding among yellow clivias simply seems to make for paler and paler creams, just as it does with daylilies. These pale flowers are very nice in their own right although they will probably not lead to snow-white colors. We probably need a more devious route to get to a pure white clivia flower, but achieving white is possible.

PINK CLIVIAS

Pink colors are often found in clivia flowers. They tend to be blotches of pink color, often with an orange central stripe or an orange to red picotee edge to the tepals, and they are sometimes called pink striped flowers. The flowers open orange and then mature to pink. To make a pink clivia plant you need to get rid of the carotenoid-bearing chromoplasts. If the yellow carotenoids are removed, a pinker flower will result, provided the anthocyanin is pink. Sunlight bleaching or some developmental factor as suggested earlier in this chapter will cause the obvious pink coloration.

I have only once seen a pure, baby-ribbon pink *Clivia* specimen in a flowering of *C. miniata* 'Emmie Wittig's Pink' in South Africa. A flowering on a division of the same clone by a different grower, however, produced flowers of a peach color. Those flowers had just opened, and if allowed time to mature might not have remained peach. If one could achieve pure white clivias, then it should be relatively easy to make clean pink clivias as well. In the same vein, pink clivias could be a route toward white clivias if one were to select the palest pink parents. Some of the whitest daylilies have been achieved by using the palest daylilies from pink lines in the breeding programs.

PEACH AND APRICOT COLORS

The so-called peach-colored clivias are pale, creamy yellow flowers overlaid with a flush of pastel pink. They are lovely, ethereal flowers and very much in demand. They have not been analyzed in detail. In the *Clivia miniata* 'Morning Light' clone where the pigments were analyzed, there was much less total anthocyanin than in normal wild type orange flowers, but the amount of pelargonidin-3-glucoside was also quite reduced. If, as I believe, pelargonidin-3-glucoside is responsible for the orange color and pelargonidin-3-rutinoside for red colors, then the peach flowers are due to a diffuse overlay of the red pigment over the pale, creamy base.

OTHER *CLIVIA* SPECIES

Clivia caulescens and *C. nobilis* appear to have a reduced amount of pelargonidin-3-rutinoside, similar to that found in normal orange *C. miniata*. Darker and redder forms of *C. gardenii* do occur, and it is possible that they are richer sources of pelargonidin-3-rutinoside for breeding purposes. Certainly, I have certainly seen some hybrids derived from *C. gardenii* with quite rich, red colors. A main purpose of breeding with these species is not only to change the shapes of individual clivia flowers but also to change the distribution of color patterns available. The usefulness of the pendent species is particularly obvious as more complex hybrids incorporate and assort the tubular species' genes into the *C. miniata* genome.

NEW COLORS

Will it be possible to make clivias in other colors? What about lilac and purple? And will we ever see blue clivias? After all, delphinidin is merely due to a subtle change in the anthocyanins and their vacuolar environment. The color ranges seen in other anthocyanin-based flowers such as petunias and pelargoniums make it seem possible to extend the color range in clivias. If breeders could get the flowers to express the fruit color genes that are currently only expressed in the berries, they will have come a very long way to achieving new colors. Our understanding of the molecular expression of genes is advancing at a tremendous pace, and it may eventually be possible to engineer any new color. But that is probably still some distance off in the future. The current allure of *Clivia* has a great deal to do with their bright orange flowers, and there is little incentive to invest the amount of money needed to carry out genetic engineering. Traditional breeding, however, is still a powerful tool and can be employed by the average plant enthusiast in a back yard or greenhouse. With the enormous numbers of seedlings being made and flowered globally, there is a good chance that interesting new colors and combinations may emerge spontaneously.

I have seen three clivias that have mauve-purple tones. It is not unusual for clivia colors to change and fade as the flowers age, so lavender, lilac, and mauve colors sometimes develop. However, the plants I examined display strong mauve-purple tints when the flowers are freshly opened. Maybe these plants will be the road to purple or even blue clivias in the future. With all the colors available and all the breeding currently going on, clivias are assured of a multicolored, rainbowed future.

Chapter Six

Hybridizing and Growing
Clivias from Seed

C LIVIAS CAN BE expensive plants. It is not unusual to pay U.S. $50 for a single, five-year-old plant yet to throw its maiden flower. If you purchase a plant via mail order, you may have to pay additional postage and packing charges. Yellow clivias can still cost hundreds of dollars per plant, and select clones of any kind typically cost many hundreds of dollars. Rumors of people in the Orient paying thousands for a particularly fine variegated specimen are not uncommon. In 1999 the asking price in China for an exceptional plant was close to U.S. $30,000. Of course, there are also more affordable varieties. It is relatively easy to grow clivias from seed. If you are a good grower, you might even flower the plants in less than five years. One strain actually produces some flowers from seed in the second year, with nearly 90 percent of the plants flowering in their third year. Clivia seed is large and easy to handle, and even if a single seed costs a dollar or somewhat more, it is certainly an economical way of building up a collection. A single plant can produce fifty or more seeds in a season, so if you already have plants that flower and make your own seeds, you will be well on your way to acquiring a collection without spending a lot of money.

There are two different goals for making seed. In the first case, you might want to produce additional plants for pot plant decoration

A developing flower bud in a clivia seedling holds the hopes and dreams of the plant breeder.

or landscaping. Growing plants from seed is an economical way of doing this since the prices for seed range from a quarter to several dollars per seed, depending on the type. A number of people sell clivia seed or seedlings; most are amateurs whose seed sales bring in extra pocket money or help toward the purchase of special stud plants.

The second reason for hybridizing is to create new kinds of flowers. The challenge of producing new kinds of plants intrigues many growers. It is, in a way, an artistic endeavor much like sculpting or painting, but gardeners use live plants to reach their goals. As Comstock says, a gardener's artistic medium is the genetic material of the parent plants. In some respects, flower breeding is where the sciences and arts intersect. Understanding the biology of a plant can facilitate hybridizing with it, but the ultimate success or failure of the effort involves an esthetic evaluation and a creative imagination about how the plant might be used to achieve further goals. Breeding can be a lifetime effort of working with generations of plants toward a specific goal. For example, some people are currently working toward creating a good, snow-white flower, a dwarf yellow, or a clear pink standard variety. Such goals are limited only by one's imagination. Of course, there is also the possibility that a seed will produce an entirely new and desirable flower purely by chance, and perhaps this appeals to the gambling instinct in many people.

Hybridizing is easy and yet it gives your hobby a special twist that raises you above the common gardener. I have met clivia hybridizers from all walks of life and they seem to sink into an easy camaraderie when they meet each other, even when they are from different parts of the globe and can barely speak each other's tongue. Breeding new varieties of flowers adds a totally different dimension to the gardening experience and fortunately requires very little in the way of special skills.

STRUCTURE OF A CLIVIA FLOWER

Hybridizing is usually aimed at improving flowers. In *Clivia*, however, the leaves are sometimes more important than the flowers, particularly where variegated and dwarf plants are concerned. Nevertheless, all deliberate breeding involves the flowers, so I will provide a few details about the structure and function of the various components of clivia flowers. The flowers are so large and the parts so easy to see that clivias make a superb plant for novice plant breeders.

The tepals function as attractants for the pollinators, advertising their presence from afar. Within the ring of tepals is a whorl of stamens, one attached to the base of each petal or sepal. The stamens are made up of a slender stalk called the filament that carries at its tip a sac called the anther. Each anther is divided longitudinally into four compartments. The pollen is made in those compartments, and when ripe, each sac opens with a longitudinal slit and the sac itself shrivels. The pollen remains as a loose dusty mass on the end of the filament. Usually the pollen sacs dehisce or split soon after the flower opens, but because not all the stamens dehisce at the same time, there may be several days between the first and last anther ripening.

In the center of the flower is a structure called the pistil. It bears a three-chambered ovary that lies under the petals, making clivia a plant with an inferior ovary. The ovary bears the ovules, each of which contains an egg cell that might develop into an embryonic plant if that egg gets fertilized. A slender stalk (known as the style) extends down the center of the flower and generally protrudes beyond the petals. Toward its tip, the style divides into three stigmatic branches, each of which bears a strip of tissue that is slightly sticky and able to trap pollen that comes into contact with it. The stigmatic surface usually becomes receptive after all of the stamens have dehisced. Pollen applied before that time may still be able to pollinate the flower provided it can stick on. A lot of pollen often gets lost, however.

If conditions are good following pollination, a small tube will germinate out of each pollen grain and make its way through the style and into the ovary, where it will search out an egg cell. Within the pollen tube, two sperm cells will be produced, one that eventually fertilizes the egg, the other that fuses with a polyploid nucleus in a cell behind the egg. People often confuse pollen with sperm but pollen is not the equivalent of sperm. Each pollen grain actually represents a small microscopic individual plantlet that is temporarily parasitic on the mother plant and able to produce sperm if it finds a suitable egg.

There are two fertilization events, one involving the egg that will result in the new embryo, and the other the making of a mass of polyploid tissue called the endosperm. Endosperm is a food store for the seed and young plantlet after germination, and it actually makes up the greater volume of the seed. This "double" fertilization appears to be a feature of all flowering plants. Hybrids between distantly related species often fail, not because an embryo cannot be formed, but rather because endosperm is not made. This endosperm failure may be the reason why it is difficult to make hybrids between *Clivia* and other genera such as *Cryptostephanus* and *Amaryllis*.

It takes one pollen grain to make a seed, but under normal conditions hundreds of pollen grains are deposited during pollination. Normally, the ovary can only produce a few seed. Ovaries with as many as twenty seed are known, but that is unusual; one to five seed is a normal yield for a clivia ovary. There is competition between the pollen grains for the few available eggs, and the pollination situation can be further complicated by mechanisms the mother plant has for rejecting pollen of certain types. Details of these "pollen-tube wars" are not known, although they would make for a fascinating story. What happens in the ovary may give some insight into why some crosses are successful and others are not.

HYBRIDIZING GOALS

Possible directions
One reason for embarking on a hybridizing program—other than merely increasing the number of plants you possess—is to try to create new and better clivias. Among the many possibilities are

attempts to try and refine or improve upon the flowers of an already existing type. For example, one might try to perfect yellow- and orange-flowered types. Another possibility might involve striving to create a totally new kind of flower. Those still needing considerable work include greens, pinks, blushes, picotees, and dark reds. There are also several shapes that need a lot of work, such as doubles, spiders, and iris forms.

Flower shapes

Wild clivias have flower parts based on multiples of three. The perianth or corolla is formed from three sepals and three petals that are fused together at their bases. The perianth parts are relatively similar to each other in shape and coloration, and thus one can also refer to all six segments collectively as tepals. There are six stamens, and the central style supports a stigma with three lobes. This is the basic plan that natural selection has produced. The wild types are shaped by and adapted to their pollinators. However, there is much variation in size and shape of the wild species, which suggests that the pollinators are relatively undiscerning. A variety of subtle variations on the basic plan still get pollinated in the wild. Over the millennia, a large number of genetic mutations and variations related to flower shape have been maintained or added to the gene pool. The large number of genetic mutations is advantageous of breeders because rare combinations of genes surface among the seedlings that can then be incorporated into breeding programs. Hybridizers, who are generally much more demanding and discerning than natural pollinators, are able to recognize and select subtle nuances that can then either be incorporated into or exaggerated to create new kinds of flowers. Sometimes characteristics can be bred out too. Among the variations are the following:

TRUMPET SHAPED. This is a basic flower shape, which appears to be conical in longitudinal section. The tepals are more or less overlapping. Tepals can be pointed or rounded. Better forms have broad and overlapping flower parts.

BUGLE SHAPED. This is based on the trumpet shape, but the tips of the tepals reflex. The proportion of tepal that reflexes varies with the individual plants. Tepal tips are usually pointed in this group. In some of the best plants, fully half of the tepal reflexes to contribute toward a spherical surface for the umbel.

TULIP SHAPED. The tepal tips are both rounded and incurved to produce a typical tulip shape. Most of the florets tend to be arranged in an upward facing cluster, almost like a large brush.

IRIS SHAPED. The inner petals are incurved and the outer three sepals reflex to give a typical bearded iris shape. This shape is quite rare; I have only ever seen two plants with florets of this shape, one in South Africa and the other in California.

SPIDER SHAPED. These flowers have rather narrow tepals that are widely spreading, and in extreme cases, the tepals may even recurve. Some forms with very narrow petals do not open widely but instead form fluted florets that are merely poor trumpets.

MULTIPETALLED. Clivia growers use this term when there are more than the normal number of six tepals. Some strains routinely have four sepals together with four petals, and their flowers also have eight stamens. The result still has the appearance of a single flower in the umbel, but the additional floral segments makes for a fuller, much larger and rounder flower. This feature is not always stable and varies with the clone; some plants will produce a mix of six and eight tepals among the flowers of the same umbel. Eight tepal flowers appear to have emerged independently both in Japan and California.

DOUBLE FLOWERS. Other multipetalled types will have one or several extra petals inserted within the perianth ring. A true double might have several rows of tepals. This feature appears to be unstable, and an effort to stabilize doubleness is one goal of clivia breeders. Unfortunately, breeding stock is very rare. Most doubles appear to be in Japan and are simply not available for Western plant breeders. One frequent aberration is the fusion of two or more florets to make one large flower with many petals.

Close-up photographs of these tend to be misleading because clivia growers envisage an entire umbel made up of gigantic multipetalled blooms, which unfortunately is not the case. The giant double flower is normally the only one in the umbel and is usually accompanied by other ordinary flowers. Furthermore, this feature may not reoccur the next season. Many growers, however, find these aberrations intriguing novelties.

KEELED TEPALS. Running along the length of each tepal can be a ridge of tissue that may clasp the stamen filament. The ridge can be more than ½ inch (1.25 cm) in height. Keeled tepals occur in flowers of various shapes, but it is sometimes not a stable feature. In some clones only the petals may have keels. In others all the perianth parts carry keels. Not all the flowers in the umbel will produce keels.

Criteria for parent plants

There is little use in breeding flowers unless you have a specific goal in mind. Deciding on those goals is an individualistic endeavor. You may be forced to use two parents because those are the only plants available to you. If you have a choice in parents, then there are some nonfloral criteria that you might want to keep in mind. There are three aspects of the plant that one needs to think about. These are plant growth and vigor, characteristics of the inflorescence, and characteristics of the individual flower.

PLANT GROWTH AND VIGOR. People get so carried away by flowers that they often neglect to examine the plant itself. Disease resistance can be totally forgotten, although it is among the most important aspects. For the most part, clivias are so easy to grow and so undemanding that even sickly plants are able to limp along and flower. That does not mean one should neglect the plant's ability to resist disease. In clivias, there is a common fungus susceptibility that shows itself as rust markings on the leaves, and those leaves are then also susceptible to yellowing and discoloration. Other plants are totally resistant to this fungus.

Seedlings produced by this plant should be examined for signs of the disease and destroyed.

Other vegetative characteristics also need to be taken into account. For example, do you prefer narrow or broad leaves on the plant? Broad leaves are currently fashionable, but can they be too broad? Some plants clump rapidly after reaching mature size, but others can remain a single fan of leaves for most of their lives. Vigorous clumping plants may be ideal for the landscape but they are not so desirable as pot plants where space considerations are important. On the other hand, if you want to distribute your favorite cultivars, then clumping may be very important. If you are trying to perfect a seed strain, then clumping may be totally irrelevant. One aspect that is often neglected by flower breeders is the length of time the parent took to reach maturity. Some plants will flower in the second year, while others may take more than eight years. Choosing to use plants from the latter group in your breeding program may mean you have to wait a very long time before you see flowers, but if variegated leaves are your goal, the time to adulthood may not be important. All these choices will depend on your goals.

CHARACTERISTICS OF THE INFLORESCENCE. Clivia judges still argue about what makes a perfect inflorescence, but you might want to consider the following points. Does the plant have a flower stalk that holds the cluster well above the leaves so that the flowers are well displayed, or is it frequently buried in the crown on a short stem? There are plants that bear two flower heads simultaneously for each mature fan of leaves, and there are plants that flower several times a year on the same or different growths. Does the inflorescence have many flowers or just a few? How are the flowers arranged on the head? Are the peduncles and pedicels strong enough to carry the flowers? You may have no choice about what you use if you are pursuing a particular goal because you may be forced to use what is available, but it does not hurt to be aware of the shortcomings at the same time. Such awareness will put you on the lookout for ways to overcome the deficiencies when they present themselves.

CHARACTERISTICS OF INDIVIDUAL FLOWERS. The typical goals for flower breeding are unusual shapes, colors, and patterns, but there are some other factors as well. Sun resistance by orange- and red-colored flowers can be a problem in landscape plants, and even short exposures to direct sun can bleach many flowers. In other plants such as daffodils, orange colors in early hybrids used to burn in the sun. There has been some success in breeding for nonfade characteristics, and perhaps this is also possible for *Clivia*. On the other hand, you may want to deliberately breed yellow flowers that fade to white on exposure to sun.

You may also want to look at the stability of flower shape and the number of flower parts. There are plants that routinely make flowers with eight tepals called multipetals. Among their progeny may be plants that usually make flowers in the umbel with six tepals and just a few flowers with eight, while other plants will bear many more eight-tepal blooms. If you are breeding for multitepals, therefore, it would be better to use a clone that routinely makes flowers with eight tepals.

POLLINATION

The act of placing pollen on the stigmatic surface is called pollination. In the wild, some vector (probably sunbirds or butterflies) effects pollination. The pollen is so dry and light that simply jostling a plant can sometimes be enough to self-pollinate some of the flowers. Most clivias are at least partially self-fertile and will produce some viable seed following self-pollination. This can be annoying if you are trying to make a particular cross and find out five years later that the plants are not from the cross you were trying to make, but merely the results of self-pollination. You can control unintended self-pollination by removing the anthers before they dehisce, usually as the flower buds are opening. Gently pry the tepals apart and, using your fingers, pluck off the anthers. Take care not to damage the stigma; that way you can pollinate the stigma a few days after the flower is fully opened without the flower's own pollen getting in the way and being transferred to its own stigma. This operation can also be performed well before the buds open, but then there is a chance of bruising the flowers. If you do it later, there is still the chance of having undamaged flowers that you can appreciate.

If you carefully examine the development of the stigma during the days following anthesis or flower opening, you will see how the stigma expands and ripens. If the stigma is too fresh it is not receptive, and the pollen will not hold. Some hybridizers claim that a little saliva or sugar water applied to the stigma will help the pollen adhere without killing the stigma. Sometimes, when the stigmatic surface is too old or if it has been hot and the air dry, the surface cells on the stigma die and are no longer receptive to the pollen. In those instances, you can sever the style half way along its length with a sharp razor blade and place a droplet of sugar water on the cut surface. (The concentration of sugar used is six teaspoons of sugar to a cup of water, although there appears to be no need for accuracy in measuring the amount of sugar.) After waiting five minutes, dab pollen on the cut end. I have not tried this, but many clivia hybridizers swear by it.

If your breeding clivias are in pots, you might want to bring them into shelter (such as a shed or house) where you can pollinate them at your leisure without the additional "help" of birds, bees, or even wind. If your plants remain outside, isolate individual flowers after pollination with small paper or gauze bags. Do not use plastic as that causes the flowers to sweat and they may rot.

All of these methods of pollination presuppose that the pollen itself is viable and capable of growing on the stigma. Pollen is actually quite fragile and easily killed. Contact with rain or tap water appears to kill it immediately, whether it is water from dew, rain, sprinklers, or the watering can. After pollen has been wetted, it may dry and look good, but it is usually dead. Pollen also gets sunburned, which usually kills it too. Sunlight will bleach pollen, and its grains become

whitened. The lesson from this is that pollen is best used when harvested from freshly dehisced anthers. Always select pollen that looks
light and powdery. A crumbly appearance usually indicates that the
pollen was once wetted and has since dried, and it should be avoided.

POLLEN BANKS

It often happens that the two plants you want to cross do not flower
at the same time. Being able to store and retrieve pollen of the
desired parent at will is a very powerful technique. By using a pollen
bank, you could mate a fall-blooming species such as *Clivia gardenii*
with a late spring-flowering plant like *C. miniata*. At another
extreme, a visit to a friend in the Southern Hemisphere might elicit
a gift of some pollen that you could use six months later back at
home in the Northern Hemisphere.

Making a pollen bank is relatively simple and quite effective,
provided some simple rules are followed. The pollen needs to be
kept both cool and dry. I find it convenient to store the pollen in
empty gelatin capsules that are normally used to make powdered
medicines easy to swallow. They are usually available from pharma-
ceutical company, drug, or health food stores. I recommend you use
medium- to large-sized capsules. Select anthers that have filaments
with fresh, fluffy pollen from the flower under consideration.
Remove the filaments with a pair of fine tweezers or jeweler's for-
ceps and drop them into the open capsule. Replace the cap on the
capsule and tap the capsule to deposit the pollen over the capsule
wall. Anywhere from a single to all six filaments can be placed in a
single capsule. Use a permanent ink pen to write the name, number,
color, and so on of the pollen donor on the outside of the capsule.
The capsules can be stored in a jar in the refrigerator, which often
has a temperature of 5°C (40°F), for short periods of time such as a
few months. Most modern refrigerators circulate dry air through
them, which is ideal for pollen storage. If you use a jar with a lid,
make sure that the lid is *not* airtight.

For longer-term storage of one or two years, use the freezer compartment of the refrigerator. Pollen will stay viable for a long time under freezing conditions. You do need to season it by partially drying it before you place it in subzero temperatures or else ice crystals will form in the pollen grains, possibly damaging them. You can dry pollen by placing the capsules containing the pollen in the refrigerator for twenty-four to forty-eight hours before putting it into the freezer. Frozen pollen can only withstand a limited number of freezings and thawings before losing viability. You must be able to find and retrieve a sample without defrosting those capsules you do not want to use, so plan your frozen pollen bank carefully. One way to do this is to have a system of numbered, small, wide-mouthed vacuum jars in the freezer that you can open and from which you can select and withdraw a capsule without tipping the jar while it is still in the freezer. Another way is to put the capsules into a plastic bag that can be sealed and placed in the freezer. You can locate the desired capsule through the walls of the bag while holding it against the cold floor of the freezer. After you remove a capsule from the freezer, you can keep it in the refrigerator, where it is usually good for only about a week.

LABELS

A clivia inflorescence is an umbel bearing many flowers, so it stands to reason that you can make a number of different crosses using the same head of flowers. You will need some way of labeling the individual ovaries so you know the parentage of the cross when you harvest the seeds. There are several ways to do this, but usually labels are attached to the pedicel below each flower. The tags will have to last for at least one year (the time it takes clivia fruit to ripen) and be able to withstand a variety of different element conditions. If the plants are outside, string and paper labels usually do not last for the year to fifteen months that a set of fruits may take to mature. Paper tags on plants that are maintained in a greenhouse will typically end up covered in black mold. Pencil on a paper label is always better than even permanent ink, and if it lasts without disintegrating, you can often read it after soaking it for several minutes in bleach. I recommend using Scotch brand Magic tape over permanent ink writing for my own labels; they wrap easily around each pedicel, resist water damage, and seem to last for a very long time without disintegrating. Use wide-tipped pens for the writing as the script seems to weather better and is easier to read (you do not have to bend down). A friend of mine codes his crosses by tying several threads to each pedicel of different colors for each cross; he notes the crosses that they signify into his record book. If all of the flowers on an umbel are pollinated with the same pollen, then the cross could be written on a plastic label inserted into the pot near the base of the peduncle.

HARVESTING AND CARE OF SEEDS

The berries start to show their colors usually after about ten months and during the winter months. Some clivia breeders will remove the berries at this point. As the fruits can be quite decorative, you might want to leave them on the plant until the next season's buds start to show. Experiments suggest that one can remove the seeds from green berries after they are six months old and germinate them at that time. I have not tried that technique but it may be attractive to the impatient grower. The berries and their tagged pedicels can be broken off the umbel. Disposable paper cups are useful for keeping the berries from various crosses separate and organized until you can clean them and extract their seeds. They can be left in the cups for a month or two, but if you live in parts of the country that have freezing winter temperatures, take care to keep the fruits from freezing. There seems to be no clean way to extract the seeds; simply tear open the fruits and pluck out the individual seeds. Seeds can be kept organized by returning them to their paper cup containers, and if you have written— preferably in pencil—the parentage on a plastic label, you will save yourself work later and keep the results of your labors organized. You should also keep an electronic or written record, perhaps both.

HYBRIDIZING STRESS

In this section I address concerns about the costs of seed production to a plant. Many hybridizers notice that if they pollinate all the flowers in an inflorescence, and if these mature to make large fruit, they may get a poor inflorescence or no flowering the following season. Reproduction stresses the plant. If a plant has all its flowers pollinated, then it should be given a season or two to recover before being forced to make seed again. In the meantime, the plant's pollen remains available for breeding; the costs of making flowers appear to be negligible compared to the costs of seed production. A very large, multigrowth plant would not be as stressed as a single-growth plant and could be used every year, provided the flower quality does not seem to be going backward. To avoid reproductive stress, you could pollinate only a portion of the umbel, give the plant extra food, and alternate the seasons that the plant is forced to bear seed. Remember that every season you can get pollen to use.

SOME TERMINOLOGY

Whether you are a casual breeder making the occasional cross or an obsessed fanatic growing a whole plantation of clivia seedlings, the time will come when you want to communicate with other similarly inclined individuals. There are a few terms that you might want to know to converse in the jargon.

HYBRID. A plant that is the result of deliberate pollination. Hybrids are the results of a cross between two different parents, either within the same species or between different species.

F_1 HYBRIDS. The progeny in the first generation of a cross.

F_2 HYBRIDS. The progeny from crosses between F_1 hybrids. Usually F_2 plants will show more variation than F_1.

OUTCROSS. Usually refers to the progeny produced from two parents that are not closely related to each other.

BACKCROSS. Making a cross by pollinating an offspring back to one of its parents. It is sometimes used to retrieve parental characters.

ALLELE. The gene that occupies a certain position on the chromosome. Each plant normally has two genes (alleles) for a certain characteristic. The alleles are not necessarily the same; the genes for pointed leaf tips for example, are different from those for rounded leaf tips.

DOMINANT CHARACTERS. Features of a parent that invariably emerge in its direct offspring. Orange color is an example of a dominant character. Usually only one copy of the gene is needed in order for it to be expressed.

RECESSIVE CHARACTERS. Genes that are not expressed unless the plant possesses two identical copies of that gene are called recessive. The genes that block anthocyanin synthesis have this characteristic.

CODOMINANCE. Both genes of a pair of alleles are expressed in this situation, and if they are different, intermediate characters are produced.

LINE BREEDING. Mating parents with similar features together, and repeating this through several generations. Line breeding tends to produce more uniform offspring. It can also be oriented toward a goal, such as producing deeper red flowers by mating the two darkest reds together from each generation.

HETEROSIS. A term that refers to hybrid vigor. Often the resulting F_1 hybrid plants are larger and more vigorous growers than either parent.

PLOIDY. This term refers to the number of sets of chromosomes in the plant. Normally plants have two sets of each kind of chromosome and are called diploids. In many garden hybrids such as daylilies or daffodils, there are four sets of chromosomes, and those plants are referred to as tetraploids. Tetraploids are usually larger plants with bigger flowers and thicker tepals. There are no known tetraploids in *Clivia*, and all hybrids and species appear to be diploids. Triploids result from crossing diploids with tetraploids and they tend to be sterile. Clivia breeders are interested in making tetraploid clivias, but if any have been produced, they have not been well publicized.

POLYPLOIDS. Refers to more than two sets of chromosomes.

RECORD KEEPING

If you want merely to produce a lot of seeds or plants for landscaping, then there is no need to keep track of the crosses you make. However, if you have definite breeding goals, you will want to know the seedlings' parentage once they start flowering. Not all clivias are equivalent, and you will soon learn which are the better and more reliable parent plants. You may want to repeat a cross that produces an unusual or particularly desirable offspring, and by comparing parentage with offspring, you can learn a great deal about the breeding potential of individual clones.

There is an international code for the way parentages are recorded: the seed parent is written first, followed by the pollen parent. Thus, if you buy seed written as *Clivia miniata* 'Emmie Wittig's Pink' × *C. miniata* 'Chubb's Peach', for example, you know that 'Emmie Wittig's Pink' was the mother plant. It is important to know which is the mother plant because both plastids and mitochondria possess their own chromosomes, and both are inherited only through the mother plant, not from the pollen parent. Maternal inheritance is particularly important when breeding for variegated foliage. There may also be other, more subtle maternal influences that are not transmitted through the pollen, which is another reason why it is useful to keep track of pollen and pod parents.

Writing a seed's parentage on labels to go into pots can be tedious, especially if the parentages are very involved. It is easier to assign a code number to a cross. (Codes can contain information in addition to parentage.) One example would be a code such as K/2000/5, which translates into Koopowitz (the breeder), 2000 (the year of pollination), 5 (the fifth cross). The actual cross must be recorded in a register and cross-referenced to the code. As seedlings are selected they can be assigned additional numbers with short descriptions added to the register. Registers can be as simple as a notebook (make sure you use pencil or permanent ink) or as complex as an electronic spreadsheet (keep making updated hardcopies). Handwritten registers often get wet, especially if you go out in the rain or handle wet plants, and computers have a nasty habit of crashing when you least expect it.

An example of a cross's notation is given below. The first entry is the actual cross, and the other entries are the seedlings from the cross after they have flowered. Such notations will help you remember the plants' characteristics when they are not in bloom or after you have disposed of the plants.

K/2000/5 = *C. miniata* 'Yellow Fellow' × *C. nobilis* 'Slow Grower'.
K/2000/5-1: Leaves have unusually deep notches, flowers insignificant.
K/2000/5-2: Flowers peachy pink—exceptionally high flower count in the umbel.

In later years you may end up using seedling codes to denote parentage in your register as you depend more and more upon your own seedlings for breeding. Entries might appear as:

K/2007/4 = *C. miniata* 'Yellow Fellow' × K/2000/5-2.
K/2007/5 = K/2000/5-2 × K/2000/5-1

These record books become historical accounts of one's plant breeding endeavors, and they are often passed along from generation to generation of plant breeders. If they were produced by famous plants-people, then they are treasured as prize possessions. Even if you are not going to go down in history as the world's greatest clivia breeder, you will find that your own register is very helpful as a record of your own successes and failures.

Clivia seed waiting to be planted. Some roots are already starting to emerge from the seeds. A seedling with its two roots is placed over the seeds to provide a scale.

HANDLING SEEDS AND SEEDLINGS

There are many different ways of handling and germinating seeds. These differences, in themselves, illustrate how easy clivia seeds are to grow. I grow my seeds by arranging them on the surface of a light, sandy medium in a pot 4 inches (10 cm) square and 4 inches deep. A pot this size can accommodate up to twenty-five seeds, but as I keep the plants in the pot for two years, I usually put no more than sixteen seeds to a pot to decrease overcrowding. Often I will put in even fewer seeds, and I usually plant only seeds from the same cross in a single pot. Other people plant their seeds in shallow flats or trays, using dividers to keep the different crosses separate. Seed can also be started in some of the newer seedling cell trays by placing a single seed in each cell. The problem with the last method is that the seedlings may need to be moved much sooner than those in containers with more root room.

Seeds should not be buried but instead laid on the top of the medium and pressed down so that about half the seed is visible in the pot. Burying seed increases losses from rot. If the germination point is facing the medium, the seedling will have an easier time germinating. Positioning the seeds is impractical, however, when you deal with hundreds or thousands of them.

Any loose, friable, germinating medium will usually result in successful germination. Some growers use medium grade perlite as the sole medium, whereas others first germinate the seeds on damp paper or toweling in plastic boxes and only plant the seeds after germination. Gentle, bottom heat appears to hasten germination, and elaborate incubators for germinating clivia seed have been suggested by a number of hobbyists. Under my conditions in southern California I do not find that necessary. Seedlings will also germinate and succeed in any good soil mixture that is suitable for the adult clivia plants (see chapter 4).

Upon germination, a single thick root emerges from the seed. It appears quite ineffectual at penetrating the soil. The root of a buried seed that has escaped the rot and is growing will push the germinating seed out of the soil until the plantlet flops over. Once the root is long enough—about 2 inches (5 cm)—most growers will replant the individual seedlings by making a hole with a pencil and dropping the plantlet, root first, into the hole. The attached seed should remain at soil level. If you are germinating flats with hundreds of seeds, it is not feasible to replant each seed individually; simply cover the seedling roots with a layer of coarse sand. If the seeds are not replanted, the seedlings will flop onto the soil and will continue to grow as long as they are not subject to desiccation. Eventually the weight of the whole seedling surpasses the force at the growing root tip, and roots penetrate the soil. If there are a lot of seedlings, they soon become quite intertwined, and the next repotting stage can be a lot of work.

Remember that seedlings in the wild do not have anyone to replant them; most have roots that scramble onto the surface of the soil and are barely covered by mosses and loose leaf litter, yet they survive. However, if you want to optimize growth rates, you may need to give your seedlings a helping hand.

Seedlings appreciate buoyant air and need some air movement or there will be losses from damp-off microorganisms. Seedlings need to be kept moist but they should not be kept under soggy conditions. Although clivias are plants from forest floors and often grow among moss and ferns, they are subjected to occasional dry conditions and can withstand their pots being dried out for short periods without adverse effects. In some areas of South Africa there are substantial losses from damp-off fungi during germination, and growers routinely treat their seeds and seedlings with fungicides. It is my opinion that many of the problems are caused by poor air circulation, stagnant conditions, and overly high temperatures. In southern California, where I grow seedlings under continuous air movement, damp-off is no problem. Seedlings should not be exposed to direct sunlight; indirect or diffuse light is best. Under diffuse light conditions the leaves should be dark green.

There is a sufficient food reserve in the seed to build a strong root and about two leaves and to keep the seedling alive for several months. However, once the seedlings are growing they can be fed with a general, well-balanced fertilizer. The plants are vigorous feeders and appreciate consistent feeding regimes. Under ideal conditions the plants will constantly grow and reach maturity rapidly in three to four years.

The ideal temperatures appear to be between 60°F to 90°F (16°C to 32°C), but clivias tolerate temperatures that are just above freezing. They will certainly tolerate much higher temperatures, especially if there is a drop in evening temperatures. The fastest outdoor growth rates I have seen are when seedlings are grown under subtropical conditions, yet clivias succeed in so many temperate parts of the world that it is clear they can tolerate a very wide range of above freezing temperatures.

Seedlings that have been pushed out of the pot by their roots.

A variety of different kinds of seedlings may exist depending on the breeding history of the plants. Where plants are inbred, a certain percentage of the seedlings may emerge with variegated, pure white, or pure yellow leaves. The pure white- and yellow-leafed seedlings do not have functional chloroplasts and will die soon after they exhaust their food reserves in the seed's endosperm. Usually plants with varie gated leaves will survive, but they grow more slowly than plants with solid green leaves. The amount of green tissue varies in variegated seedlings, and the greater the extent of the green tissue, the faster the seedling growth. I will discuss seedling growth again in chapter 11, which deals with variegated clivias.

Seedlings typically have purple to red pigmentation at the base of their leaves. This pigmentation tends to disappear as the plant ma-

A series of clivia seedlings with different colored leaf bases. From left to right are a yellow *Clivia* Minicyrt, a variegated yellow *C. miniata*, a yellow *C. miniata*, an orange *C. miniata*, a variegated *C. miniata*, and a *C. caulescens.*

tures. The exception to this occurs in yellow-flowered clivias, where pigmentation is blocked and its plantlets possess leaf bases that are green. Such a distinction is very convenient as it allows you to select yellow flowered plants while they are still at the young seedling stage, long before they actually flower. There are some pastel-flowered seedlings, however, that can have what appear to be green bases.

As long as the seedlings are growing vigorously, they can be kept together in their community pots or trays. That arrangement presupposes that the seedlings in any one batch are uniform, and that depends on the genetic background of the parents. In some situations, such as breeding for a very small dwarf clivia plant, some of the smallest plants can get smothered by the more vigorous and, in this case, less desirable seedlings. Similarly, when variegated seedlings grow together, those with the greatest green area to their leaves will rapidly overtake the seedlings with more yellow or white areas. In both situations, you might want to separate and replant the seedlings so that those that deserve special attention are not over-grown and obscured by their siblings. Carefully tip the medium out of the pot and separate and sort the seedlings. Take care when unraveling intertwined roots so as not to break the tips or crack the roots along their length. Watering the pot well a day or two before attempting to sort them will help.

When the seedlings are large enough they can go into individual pots. Make sure the pots are not overly large or too deep. The size of the root system should match the size of the pot, although the pot also needs to be large enough to accommodate a plant that will increase in size severalfold during the following year as it approach-es mature size. During the second year the plant should achieve at least half of its adult size. Visualize how big that is going to be before selecting the pot. At the beginning of a plant's life there may be rel-atively few roots, but remember that if the ratio of root to pot vol-ume is too small, the plants may not be able to drain the pot effi-ciently. If stagnant, anaerobic conditions (sometimes gardeners refer to this as souring) arise, this will set the plants back. The best way to avoid souring is to have compost that is well draining. When you water your clivias, drench them so that the water flows out of the bottom of the pot. The volume of water will actually drag air after itself, bringing oxygen to the roots. It is better to let the pot dry between waterings because frequent sprinkles that keep the soil constantly moist and damp cause compaction of the soil, which in turn excludes oxygen. Most of the roots stay around the periphery of the pot and close to the wall; oxygen levels are probably higher here than in the center of the pot.

The number of pairs of leaves needed before a seedling will flower varies depending on the genetic background of the individual plant. Some strains are bred to mature and flower in their second or third year, and they usually need to have at least six pairs of leaves

View of Anna Meyer's stud house. Gauteng Province, South Africa.

before they can start to make flower buds. These plants are also responsive to seasonal changes in temperature.

ASSESSING YOUR EFFORTS

Every clivia grower has a heightened sense of anticipation when the first buds appear. This is the time when you can dream and fantasize about what will be flowering shortly. It is like holding a lottery ticket before the drawing of an exceptionally large prize. The actual flowering may be a rude disappointment—or it could be the culmination of your dreams. During the first few years of hybridizing one tends to be very forgiving of one's own efforts; after all, these are your own unique creations. They are your children that you have coddled for several years and finally brought to flowering. You should be proud, but at the same time you should try to measure these progeny against the goals that you had set for yourself.

Plants should not be dismissed on the first flowering. They can improve, especially in flower number and quality, as the plant continues to strengthen and mature. Of course, if you insist on putting seedpods on its first inflorescence, you may debilitate it and never see its full potential. If you do breed with the plant, use it as a pollen parent rather than making it set seeds. Even mature plants will not flower as well the season after bearing a heavy load of berries. One can destroy a very fine plant if one is overanxious to breed with it.

You should move the seedling you have selected for keeping out of the seedling blocks to an area where you can observe them over the next several seasons. Many growers maintain a stud house or area for their breeding plants that is separate from the seedlings. Once again, it helps to keep everything organized.

Chapter Seven

CLIVIA OBSESSION

T HE HORTICULTURAL HISTORY of any group of plants is really the story of a set of people who became interested in the plant and then proceeded to develop it. Why some plants are selected and worked with while others are neglected is not clear. Flower growing is a mixture of art and science, and the reason why some people prefer one flower over another is as much a mystery as why others prefer the impressionist style to abstract art. Clivias are impressive flowers, sometimes even overwhelming. The question is perhaps not why are some people smitten with the plants, but rather, why are others not?

There are several different ways that gardeners and plant enthusiasts react to the plants they like. At one end of the spectrum are those who like a plant but really could not be bothered to grow it. At the other extreme are the true collectors who need, desperately, to possess as many variants on the particular plant's theme that they can. It does not seem to matter what the plants actually are. They could be miniature coniferous evergreens, African violets, daffodils, orchids, or even clivias. In many cases the need for plants becomes a true obsession and the addict will often follow his or her particular fancy to extravagant lengths. When one encounters other gardeners with the same obsessions, the result is often instant empathy and communication that can develop into a lifelong friendship. It is among the great payoffs for this peculiar obsession.

Clivia 'Four Marys'. Dr. Earl Murphy traveled halfway around the world to get this plant.

In the course of researching this book I met a great many clivia enthusiasts. I looked for patterns in their personalities to see if it was possible to isolate some feature that had steered them toward clivias. Of course not every one fitted the same mold, and it was hard to pinpoint specific patterns. It goes without saying that they all seemed to like plants and were not monomaniacal about clivias; many appreciated and collected other types of plants and flowers as well. But a few people were so obsessive that they might be considered addicted to clivias. And there were also a fraction, albeit a small one, who regarded these plants merely as valuable objects for which other people were prepared to spend real money, and their interest was purely mercenary.

One similarity did occur among a high percentage of the enthusiasts: they had been initiated into growing clivias, sometimes unwittingly, by a parent or older relative. There were also clivia plants that had been passed through several generations in a single family and were regarded as heirlooms. Clivias, of course, lend themselves to this by their very nature; they are long-lived, tough plants that are hard to kill through neglect, and yet they reward a modicum of care with a spectacular display of flowers. I had not realized the common thread until I remembered that my mother had come home one day, very excited, with a "Port St. John's Lily", (that was the name then in the Eastern Cape for *Clivia miniata*). I was probably no more than ten years old at the time, and though the plant subsequently died before it flowered (it was exposed to a very hard frost), I remembered her excitement. When I was later exposed to a fine truss of orange flowers, I understood her excitement and realized clivias were worthwhile plants to grow. I was twenty when I visited the gardens of one of the earlier South African clivia hybridizers, Miss Blackbeard, (it was before she gave up her clivias), and her flowers more than confirmed my earlier assessment.

Clivias have several unusual features, besides their ease of growth and longevity, that make them a good hobbyist's plant. The plants are now of a manageable size—although there are some giant forms—but many modern clivias are small enough to be accommodated in reasonably sized containers. They can fit on a wide windowsill or grace the steps at the front door. They make big seeds that are easy to count and handle, and growing them is almost as easy as planting beans. In fact, making and growing clivia seeds is a great project for a small child. The earlier rarity and cost of yellow clivias gave them a reputation as something special horticulturally in that they were not only exotic but also highly desirable. Mass seed production has now made yellows accessible to all, and this has helped boost *Clivia*'s popularity. The formation of the Clivia Club in South Africa in 1992, and the two international shows and conventions held there in 1994 and 1998 helped promote this new hobby to an international level. The recent formation of an e-mail list of clivia enthusiasts helped strengthen the worldwide interest in this group of plants, and within a very few months, hundreds of enthusiasts were exchanging information and asking questions over the internet.

EUROPE

Clivias have long been an important pot plant for the European market, although interest has fluctuated. Pierre de Coster (1998) reviewed the history of the plant in Belgium. After the First World War, a new form of *Clivia* that was more suited to the pot trade was introduced by Bier and Ankersmit. It was a dwarf plant with much wider and shorter leaves than the type, and the leaves also had rounded tips. These appear to be the beginning of what would subsequently become known as the Belgian strain (also known sometimes as the Belgium strain). There were several nurseries, particularly in or near Ghent, that specialized in or grew considerable quantities of clivias.

After the Second World War the nursery industry turned to cheaper kinds of plants, and clivias lost their appeal. They took too long to mature, and hence were too expensive. It was in the early 1950s that Ernest de Coster started to select for rapid maturation and early bloom. He ended up with compact plants with leaves about half the width of the older Belgian strain. They started to flower in their second year from seed, and the majority could be sold the following season. These faster maturing plants have now supplanted the earlier strain but they are often still marketed under the same name. Belgium currently produces about 700,000 flowering plants a year.

There was considerable activity in breeding clivias in Germany during the later half of the nineteenth century. Little of that industry remains today, although people around the world still speak of "German Reds" when referring to one of the darker orange-red flowers. The German cultivars have probably contributed their genes to the California flowers through clivias originally bred by Zimmerman.

THE BODNANT ESTATE

The Bodnant estate in South Wales is renowned for its horticultural excellence. It is also well known for its clivias although, admittedly, few seem to have seen the collection. Clivias have been grown and bred under the leadership of three generations of Lords Aberconway, who were known particularly for their very fine yellow clivias. Another famous horticultural name—that of Westonbirt—lies behind the Bodnant clivias. At Westonbirt a series of *Clivia* Cyrtanthiflora Group hybrids were produced for Sir George Holford and were bred for several generations. In 1924, a few select plants from Westonbirt were transferred to Bodnant, and they formed the foundation of that collection. It was the addition of a fine yellow clivia plant in about 1930, however, that proved to be the touchstone for the second Lord Aberconway's head gardener, Mr. F. C. Puddle.

Many years ago I was able to get a division of what was then called *Clivia kewensis* var. 'Bodnant' from the New York Botanical Garden (NYBG), and I wrote to Gordon McNeil asking what he knew about the history of the plant. He wrote back that the name *kewensis* indicated that the plant had been bred at Kew. He then proceeded to relate the following little story. This fine yellow *Clivia* specimen happened to be in flower when Lord Aberconway was visiting the Royal Botanic Gardens, Kew. Like others of the clivia obsessed, Lord Aberconway had to have the plant. He was somehow able to apply enough pressure so that the plant was transferred to Bodnant. (It took Kew a long time to receive a division back again.) Meanwhile, this plant was being bred to the other fine clivias in his lordship's collection by Mr. F. C. Puddle. The gardener eventually achieved immortality of sorts for his plant breeding work, but not by breeding clivias; he is known today for his contributions to breeding white lady-slipper orchids. Nevertheless, a wide range of high quality yellows and several outstanding pastel clivias were produced at Bodnant.

ASIA

The Japanese fascination with *Clivia* trailed the European interests by only a few years with importations of both *C. nobilis* and *C. miniata* occurring in the mid-nineteenth century. The broad strap leaves, variegation, dwarf habits of some, and the overall plant form lent themselves to the particular Japanese appreciation and fascination with certain kinds of pot plants. It was almost as if the plants were attuned to the Japanese psyche and aesthetic. Clivias were soon regarded as special plants and were placed in the same category as traditional native plants like *Dendrobium moniliforme*, *Neofinetia falcata*, and others. Although clivias have long been considered traditional plants in Japan, it is only recently that small groups of enthusiasts have started to organize into clubs and hold clivia shows. It is part of the power of the internet that these people have come together to share their interest electronically as well. In contrast to Southern Africa, where clivia interest tends to be shown by middle-aged or retired people, it is the younger growers in Japan who take up the hobby.

During the Japanese expansion into Southeast Asia before the Second World War, particularly into Korea and Manchuria, the commanding Japanese officers took their clivias with them. The plants' special status was thereby introduced to those Asian communities, and when the Japanese had to abandon their plants after they lost the war, those plants formed the nucleus of what is now almost a plant industry, particularly in China. The fact that the Chinese name for *Clivia* is *lan*, meaning "orchid," and the Japanese name *kunshu ran* translates into "royal orchid" clearly indicates that these plants are regarded as exceptional, although of course they are not orchids. Japanese horticulture has even had an impact in Africa. Once the South African gardeners rediscovered clivias toward the end of the twentieth century, they started to look at what the rest of the world had developed from among their native flowers. They were surprised by the extent of Japanese interest and the unusual forms that

Clivia enthusiasts at a fair in China examining possible purchases.
Photograph courtesy of Yoshikazu Nakamura.

existed in Japan, such as plants with variegated leaves, miniature
plants, extra numbers of petals, and unusual color patterns. The

South Africans were anxious to incorporate Japanese clivia germplasm into their own breeding programs.

In recent years clivias have developed at a very fast rate in China, and it is said that the Japanese now visit China to buy the very best varieties. The prices that good clivias fetch in China are stupendous, and many of these plants find buyers in the domestic markets too. Even seed can command unusually high prices; the seed from the finest parents may fetch U.S. $500 dollars each. This situation resembles Holland's tulipomania period in 1636 and 1637. The clivias of China are bred for their leaves and the shapes of the plants, and there are many clivia nurseries in Dalton, Manchuria, and other provinces. In recent years, clivia shows have been held in China, where a judging system has been codified. The Chinese have developed clivias in different directions from the Japanese in that a good Chinese clivia would have rounded leaf tips and the leaves themselves should be broad, shiny, and held in a horizontal position. The veins in the leaf should be prominent, either raised above the leaf surface or sunken into it. The leaves themselves should offer a contrast between dark green veins and a bright yellow background.

Clivias are also grown in Korea (they seem to be more popular in the north than the south), but they have not developed to the same extent as in China and Japan. Other Oriental clivia enthusiasts do not consider the Korean plants as being highly developed yet.

JAPAN AND ITS CLIVIA AMBASSADOR

One person above all others has done much to bring the appreciation of Japanese clivias to South Africa and the United States. Yoshikazu Nakamura is an international ambassador for these plants, exposing and introducing Japanese clivias in their myriad forms, flower colors, and plant shapes to other growers around the world. He has also sold and shared seed—spreading both enthusiasm and goodwill for *Clivia* around the world.

Nakamura recalled that as a young boy he damaged one of his father's clivias with a knife. His grandfather rebuked him, and apparently in such a fashion that he never forgot about that mutilated clivia plant. He later acquired an interest in plants and started to grow alstroemerias and hippeastrums, and in the mid-1970s became infatuated with clivias. Nakamura was able to purchase a collection of clivias from a famous Japanese horticulturist named Dr. Hirao after Hirao's death, including a *Clivia miniata* 'Vico Yellow' plant he had obtained from Sir Peter Smithers. Nakamura brought that plant to the attention of the Miyoshi Company, where it was micropropagated. As one of the first mass-produced *Clivia* cultivars, it has taken its place among the most well known of the modern clivias. Over time Nakamura was able to get several additional clivia collections from other Japanese breeders. After collecting for about twelve years, he quit his regular job and turned his hobby into a commercial venture—although he claims that his interest in the plants is "80 percent as a hobbyist and 20 percent as a commercial grower." Nakamura's nursery is called the Clivia Plantation, and the excellence and variety of clivias grown there are recognized around the world. The nursery is quite large and contains well over fifty thousand plants. Nakamura produces and sows about ten thousand seeds each year, and it takes him about five years to bloom out a crop. Always on the lookout for unique novelties in both plants and flowers, Nakamura is considered to have the best collection of clivias in the world.

EARLY DAYS IN CALIFORNIA

Tracing back the origins of clivias in California is difficult. It is a common landscaping plant, and few seem to remember its origins. Many of the yellow forms appear to have been mutations that appeared "spontaneously." It is not clear if the genes for yellow had been mixed in Europe or if they were new mutations that appeared in California, where most of the plants were seed grown and not divisions. One person who had a great influence on the California flowers was E. P. Zimmerman. He had emigrated from Germany to the United States in 1907, and twenty years later when he was forty years old he settled in the Carlsbad area, a wonderful, frost-free, mild flower growing area in southern California. He must have brought his plants or seed—perhaps both—with him from Germany. William Drysdale (1990) reported that Zimmerman was "... proud to say that three generations of his family had worked for 75 years on *Clivia*." His grandfather must have been among the first Europeans to get involved with clivias. There is no information on where the clivias were during the twenty years between 1907 and 1927, when Zimmerman finally settled in California. Were they still in Germany, or had they accompanied the family as prized possessions during the family's sojourn in the New World?

Clivias grow very well in Carlsbad, and Zimmerman had five thousand pots growing under lath. He wanted to grow the plants for the cut flower market, but whether he succeeded in doing that is not known. Drysdale does record, however, that five hundred umbels were entered in the San Francisco World's Fair in 1939, and Zimmerman earned a gold medal for the display. He produced seed and plants for sale, and he listed thirty-eight types of flowers in six different colors. His plants were known as the Zimmerman strain, but of course they were not a strain in the strict sense of the word because of their variability. Current California breeders must all, at least in part, trace their clivia plants back to Zimmerman. In 1943, Jimmy Giridlian wrote in the Oakhurst Gardens catalog: "These [Zimmerman clivias] are the best hybrids in the world, showing great improvement in size and shape of the flowers, and the range of colors is truly marvelous, ranging from creamy yellow through all the shades of orange to deep red." He was still offering plants of that strain in 1968, twenty-five years later. It is likely that this "strain" also contributed to modern European clivias since Drysdale reports that at least ten thousand seeds were sent to Denmark and Germany. (It was not clear if that represents totals or merely one year's harvest.) Certainly by today's production levels in Europe that number seems small, but the market was very different then, and those seeds may have had a profound influence on the germ plasm that underlies today's market.

Horace Anderson was another important horticulturist. He was born in 1908 and initially not at all interested in plants. The story has it that he was a milkman and that the home of the Chancellor of the University of Southern California was part of his delivery route (Warren 1999). There, in the Chancellor's garden, he saw some philodendrons used in the landscaping and immediately became fascinated with them. This led to a general curiosity about plants. Anderson met his future wife, Mary, fell in love, and married. They set up a nursery and flower shop in or near Santa Monica, close to Los Angeles. Mary was well versed in horticulture and flowers, and Anderson took charge of plant propagation. At the beginning he could not tell a perennial from a tree, but soon he started to acquire a great deal of knowledge and experience. He became interested in subtropicals, including palms and clivias, and when he discovered how to hybridize and breed plants, it turned into a life-long obsession. In 1954 they bought a piece of land in Leucadia, where he had enough space to pursue his passion. Zimmerman lived nearby in Carlsbad, and Anderson must have known of that nursery with its thousands of clivia plants.

Another grower in Carlsbad at that time, Ed Hummel, was also growing and breeding clivias (he grew other plants for which he was to become more famous), and Hummel gave Anderson a division of what was then called *Clivia miniata* 'Aurea' that had a smallish yellow flower. As with all the early yellow clivias, it is impossible to decide if *C. miniata* 'Aurea' was a clone or merely an epithet applied to any yellow flower. Anderson crossed the yellow to an orange-flowered plant and bred with them for several generations, retrieving the yellow color, but with vastly improved forms. He was repeating the paradigm that had been used at Kew to improve the yellows. Anderson also achieved a wide range of other color varieties and forms, among

Joe Solomone in 1998 standing next to a block of yellow seedlings at his growing range in Watsonville, California.

them picotee flowers, doubles, flowers said to be close to white, and even one reputedly mauve flower. After Anderson died, Mary remarried one of his friends, Ron Chamberlain, who also breeds clivias. The nursery passed to Anderson's son and it still produces clivias for sale. Plants from the Anderson palette grace many gardens and collections in California, and they were probably the source of the yellow plants that formed the foundation of the current established clivia breeders, David Conway and Joe Solomone.

CURRENT CALIFORNIAN BREEDERS

Without a doubt Joe Solomone is the clivia king of North America. He has the best selection of yellow clivias of any I have seen around the world. Solomone is a nurseryman in central California who originally specialized in growing color perennials for the wholesale nursery market. He was able to keep his eyes open for unusual plants that had pos-

Views of the stud collection at Joe Solomone's growing range.
Watsonville, California.

sibilities for the nursery trade, and sometime in the early 1960s he found a seedling in a local nursery in southern California with a very pale yellow flower. The stem had not elongated and the flowers were hidden between the leaves. Realizing the potential of this plant, Solomone purchased it. He selfed the plant and crossed it onto a standard orange *Clivia* specimen. When the seedlings flowered, he backcrossed all of them to the yellow plant. He flowered a number of plants with yellow coloring in the next generation, and from then started to build up his numbers of yellow plants. It was not until the mid-1990s that he decided to emphasize the yellows. Maricela de la Torre has worked with Joe and the clivias for over twenty years, and she now does most of the selection and hybridizing. Plants are grown in 1-gallon (4½-liter) pots and then transferred to 2-gallon (9-liter) pots when large enough. Solomone uses a compost of 60 to 70 percent redwood saw-

dust mixed with a sandy loam, and the plants are either watered with
drip irrigation or by hand.

Solomone currently has about three acres (12,147 square meters)
of greenhouse growing space, of which 1½ acres (6073 square meters)
carries clivias, and he plans to expand the numbers of clivias to fill
the entire space. Over 90 percent of the clivias grown there are yellow, and the rest are oranges and variegated forms. The variegated
forms appeared spontaneously and have been selected out and
maintained. Solomone has brought in relatively little new genetic
material and he continues to utilize the genes derived from his original stock. He estimates that he now plants 100,000 seeds per year,
which allows him to explore the genetic potential of his founding
plants. An amazing amount of variation continues to be expressed,
and Solomone has found a wide range of shapes from spiders to
crinum-like bells. Size of individual blooms can approach 4 inches
(10 cm) in natural spread or less than 1½ inches (4 cm). A few dwarf
yellows have emerged, as have some giant plants with wide leaves.
Solomone has strongly variegated yellow clivias as well as variegates
with standard orange flowers, but it is his variegated leaf yellows
that are among the treasures of the plant world.

At first Solomone scheduled most of his yellow plants for the
Japanese market, but during the last few years he has found a steady
demand for his plants in the United States, especially in California.
Spring is the season with highest demand. Most plants are coming
into bud in spring, and they are easier to truck long distances before
the umbel elongates and expands. Plants that are in flower go to
local markets. Solomone's son-in-law markets the plants through
Monterey Bay Nurseries, and they are known throughout the
United States as Solomone Yellows.

David Conway is unique. His nursery sells divisions of named *Clivia*
cultivars, most of which he bred himself. There is probably no other
nursery in the world with as large an offering of named varieties.
Conway started collecting clivias in 1962 when he lived in central

California. At that time he was a landscape architect and bought some clivias for a job—broad leaf orange-reds, perhaps more red than orange. He visited a wholesale nursery in Carpinteria, just south of Santa Barbara, where he was impressed by the considerable variation between the flowers. Ted Kalil, another grower of clivias in that area, came across some clivias that had been bred by Mr. Webber of the Botanic Gardens (now called the Mildred E. Mathias Botanical Garden) of the University of California at Los Angeles and that had ended up in the landscape of a parking garage in the Santa Barbara area. Several of the plants had yellow flowers. He brought them to the attention of Conway, who was able to beg pieces of the plants, and he grew on the divisions. Eventually Conway named some of these 'Whipped Cream', 'Lemon Chiffon', and 'Supernova'. Sometime in either 1987 or 1988, Conway mixed up a batch of pollen from many different clivias, and taking a shotgun approach, he pollinated all the clivias in bloom in his garden. He harvested about one thousand seeds and grew up the seedlings, many of which flowered in 1993. From these he selected many of his named cultivars, and all his own clivias are named for women from his family. Clivias in his listing that do not have female names were obtained from other sources.

Other clivia enthusiasts also benefited from Webber's work. Both Dr. Glynne Couvillion and Roger Bodaert were able to get pieces of these plants from that same parking garage for their collections. Bodaert started a yellow strain of clivia that he named California Sunshine.

Among the younger generation of breeders is Randy Baldwin of San Marcos Growers, a large wholesale ornamental plant nursery in Santa Barbara. Randy obtained several yellow clivia plants from other growers in California and started to produce his own seed strain of yellow clivias. He obtained a plant of *Clivia* 'Lemon Chiffon' from Conway, another from Couvillion, and two Solomone Yellows. Some of his stock is also derived from Webber's. At first Baldwin found that some of the crosses yielded a percentage of orange-flowered types. In the second generation there were only 60 percent yellows, but by the next generation, 99.9 percent of the seeds yielded yellow flowers. It took only three generations of breeding and selection to produce a strain that is virtually true breeding, with only the very rare appearance of an orange-flowered plant.

Jim Comstock, the photographer for this book, is a landscape contractor by profession and a contemporary of Randy Baldwin. Comstock, a modest man who has created an exceptional array of the highest quality plants, remembers being moved by the sight of a blooming clivia plant when he was ten years old. He was always interested in plants and grew anything he could lay his hands on. His grandmother, a great gardener herself, encouraged this interest. Comstock has grown clivias of some sort since he was a child, and in 1986 he made his first hybrids. At that time he did not know any other clivia people and was unaware that there might be breeders working in this field. He found some unusual clivias and realized that producing new kinds of flowers was an exciting avenue to follow, particularly since it was relatively easy to manipulate the plants and grow seedlings.

Comstock's first seedlings flowered in 1992, and he was surprised at their variation and quality. A few of these plants later proved to be very good parents themselves. Before the first seedlings had flowered, however, he had already accumulated better and superior parents and was making seedlings with greater potential. As much as Comstock thought he could predict the results of a cross, he was surprised by the variety he got from any particular mating. This both delighted and exasperated him, but he was sufficiently encouraged to do crosses between very disparate parents to increase the chances of getting unusual genetic combinations. He worked out on his own how to breed yellows and select potential yellow seedlings from their green leaf bases. Only when he had to annex the backyards of several of his friends did Comstock realize that his obsession was out of control. (He admits being in denial for several years before that.) Today Comstock grows about one thousand flowering-sized clivias and about four thousand seedlings. He makes about 380 crosses a year, and while not all are successful, he harvests approximately fifteen hundred seeds a year. Where they are all to grow up and flower has become a slight problem, but one that is not unusual for someone who is truly obsessed.

I have seen the results of many hybridizing programs around the world and have had the good fortune to examine Comstock's plants for several seasons. He has created and produced some of the most stunning hybrids that I have seen, and I would rank him near the top of the world's hybridizers. He maintains an extensive frozen pollen bank that gives him special freedom in choosing parents. Comstock keeps good records that he can study to learn about the specific qualities of the various parents when their offspring flower. Unlike many other growers, he sets out specific hybridizing goals for himself. At the same time he exhorts hyrbridizers not to be hampered by rigid goals but to keep an open mind and recognize the potential of unusual plants. The commercial producers did have specific goals, and the Belgian hybrids have been selected for those specific characteristics. Backyard enthusiasts, by contrast, often slap two parents together to see what might happen. Extending the spectrum of colors and patterns seems an obvious goal, but being able to pick out what might be muddy color to some and breed with it to enhance that characteristic to make brick- or terracotta-colored flowers takes both talent and courage. Be warned, however, that when you see hints of purple in a plant and tell others that you want to create a purple *Clivia* specimen, you will encounter knowing nods and some may exchange grins behind your back—until your goal is achieved. Of course you will then be acclaimed a genius instead of a fool.

FROM AMERICA TO SOUTH AFRICA: CHASING THE *CLIVIA MINIATA* 'FOUR MARYS'

The year was 1984, the man was Dr. Earl Murphy (an American psychiatrist who just happened to be black), and the country was South

Africa. Apartheid, that country's notorious policy of legal racial segregation, was firmly entrenched. For a foreign black person to visit
South Africa at that time was almost, but not quite, tantamount to
a Jew visiting Nazi Germany. So what was our Dr. Murphy doing in
South Africa? He was chasing a clivia plant!

Tropical plants fascinated Murphy, and he cultivated a wide
range of exotic species in his garden near Oakland across the bay
from San Francisco. He assembled collections ranging from small,
cool growing masdevallia orchids to gingers and heliconias to unusual exotic shrubs and trees. Among these plants were several special
clivias. He was always on the lookout for exceptional clones of
Clivia. Murphy and I had met when he bought a division of the so-
called *Clivia kewensis* var. 'Bodnant' from the Arboretum at UCI
(University of California at Irvine), where at that time I was
involved in building up a collection of rare African bulbous plants.
On his infrequent trips to southern California, Murphy would stop
by to chat about various obscure and desirable plants. He was particularly curious about a clivia plant hybridized by Gordon McNeil,
who lived in South Africa, and which I had photographed on a previous visit to that country. McNeil was inordinately proud of this
plant and called it *Clivia miniata* 'Four Marys'. While he allowed me
almost free choice from among his collection of plants to take back
to UCI, it was understood that *C. miniata* 'Four Marys' would be
excluded because it was slow in making offsets and not a large
enough plant to be divided. Only other clivia enthusiasts can understand that Murphy *needed* a piece of *C. miniata* 'Four Marys'.

Never one to let the grass grow under his feet, Murphy contact-
ed McNeil, who invited him out to South Africa to collect a piece of
the plant. Murphy accepted. He flew in to the international airport
outside of Johannesburg and spent the night at a nearby Holiday
Inn, one of the few hotels in the country at that time that accepted
black guests. By allowing different races to occupy the same hotel,
this hotel was both innovative and daring. I asked Murphy how he
felt during his visit, and he commented that as a boy he had grown

up in the segregated southern states and was used to the situation; South Africa did not seem so radically different to him.

The next day McNeil and his wife, Margaret-Rose, collected Murphy and drove him to their home. McNeil was a fruit farmer and a mango hybridizer who lived on a farm called Dindinnie outside the village Ofcolaco in what is now the Northern Transvaal province. He also owned a second piece of property on a forested hillside, much of which he terraced so he could grow his clivias in the shade of the natural forest trees. It was here where I had earlier seen *Clivia miniata* 'Four Marys' in flower. McNeil had built a unique home tunneled into the hillside on that forested property. He called it "the shack," though it was anything but a shack. It was a substantial home. Some of the walls were naked rock where the giant boulders were too big to remove without blasting. In some places the floors and passageways were uneven where the rock bulged up into the floor, and yet it also had all the conveniences of a modern house. The road to the shack wound up a narrow twisted road through a steep canyon. Growing wild on the cliff faces were *Clivia caulescens* and the bright, brick-red, spidery daisy known as *Gerbera jamesonii*, which was bred into the stunning florist flowers we know today.

Murphy spent a few days both at the farm and at the shack enjoying the clivias, but he recounts two unsettling experiences. One morning he went into town with Margaret-Rose to mail a parcel. He helped carry the package for his host and followed behind her into the post office. He received glares from the other customers; apparently he had entered through the "whites only" door, but as he was obviously carrying the parcel for his white "madam," no one created a real fuss.

The second event was somewhat scarier. The McNeil farm was an easy drive from the famous Kruger National Park, one of the world's foremost big-game preserves. At the entrance McNeil, somewhat apprehensively, asked for special permission to take his black American guest inside to see the animals. He received the go-ahead from the park's officials. They had an interesting day, but on the drive home in the early evening Murphy noticed that his hosts were muttering together and that Margaret-Rose kept glancing apprehensively over her shoulder. Behind them was another car that kept a constant distance behind them but appeared to be following; it made the same turns and road changes that they were making. Were they under surveillance? This would not have been unusual in those days because Margaret-Rose was a volunteer worker in a nearby forced settlement area where South African blacks were herded and kept against their will under impoverished conditions. Her friendship with a black visitor would have been noted by the paranoid authorities of that time. The road back to the farm had many twists and turns, yet the pair of headlights maintained its presence. McNeil and his wife tried not to alarm Murphy, but their anxiety was clearly evident to him, as was their relief as they turned into their farm and the second car sped past.

Murphy came back to the United States with *Clivia miniata* 'Four Marys'. He still grows the plant but it is as recalcitrant today at producing offsets as it was during McNeil's time.

THE SOUTH AFRICAN CONNECTION

Clivias are indigenous to Southern Africa but are only one of the many botanical wonders of that region. There had been a tendency over the centuries for South African horticulturists to focus on petunias and hippeastrums and ignore their own native flora. It was the Europeans who developed geraniums (pelargoniums), and the Americans who bred gladiolus, and watsonias. The British did nemesias and lobelias, the Irish played with diermas. The Dutch developed a whole array of other Cape bulbous plants. The South Africans were, for the most part, content to grow roses and pansies. It was not until 1992 that the Clivia Club emerged in South Africa and focused attention on this genus. It has since become a popular hobby.

Among the first of the great South African clivia hybridizers was Gladys Blackbeard. She was an elderly spinster when I met her in the early 1960s. She and her sister lived in an old house at the edge of Grahamstown, South Africa. At that time, their home was in a black township, and the South African government was forcing them to sell the property and relocate to a "white area." Miss Blackbeard, then in her eighties, had to sell her collection, and I was asked by Gordon McNeil to visit and assess it. Miss Blackbeard lived on a smallholding named Scott's Farm. She had a penchant for rescuing wounded birds and other small animals, and I remember a rather noisy shrike and a large Blue (Stanley) crane that hovered protectively around her. She showed me around the garden and showed off her excellent clivias.

There are a few articles in *Herbertia* about Gladys Blackbeard and her program, but unfortunately they give little information about either the many crosses she made or her approach to hybridizing. Most of her hybrids could be traced back to a single plant of *Clivia miniata* her mother had planted on the farm (Forssman 1948). She incorporated the local species, *C. nobilis*, early into her program, describing the initial results of a cross between a yellow form of *C. miniata* and *C. nobilis* in 1939. By the time I saw these crosses in 1964, twenty-five years had passed and there were several generations of *C.* Cyrtanthiflora siblings and backcrosses to *C. miniata* types. Nearly all of the plants were container grown, and many were quite tall with numerous umbels bearing large pendent or semipendent flowers. They were carried in large, well-filled umbels. I was particularly impressed by the array of soft pastel colors she had produced ranging from apricot and peach to definite pinkish tones. There were many plants with standard flowers as well, also in a range of pastel colors. They seemed quite unique to my limited knowledge at the time, and I urged McNeil to purchase the collection, which he did. It took at least one boxcar load to move them to his farm. Much of the Blackbeard collection was then sold off, and when I settled in California in the mid-sixties, I was surprised to see a local nursery offering clivias of the Blackbeard strain.

McNeil terraced a hillside under native trees for the Blackbeard clivias. He sold off some of them, but he also added his own plants and bred them with the Blackbeard clivias. He produced a range of unusual flowers and gave several of them names such as *Clivia miniata* 'Green Girl' and *C. miniata* 'Four Marys'. How much his novel clivias actually gained from the influx of Blackbeard genes is hard to determine. Unfortunately, McNeil detracted from his good *Clivia* hybrids by promoting a series of *faux* intergeneric *Clivia* hybrids that created great confusion. He was convinced he had remade the intergeneric cross between *Eucharis grandiflora* and *C. miniata*, which had been reported in the gardening literature of the late nineteenth century. The plant, however, looked exactly like a specimen of *C. miniata*, although it had a green throat and a fragrance he thought resembled that of the Eucharis lily. McNeil decided that *C. miniata* genes were dominant for shape and that most of the Eucharis genes were recessive. Of course green throats and fragrance are not uncommon in *C. miniata* hybrids anyway.

Another hybrid McNeil touted involved putting *Clivia miniata* pollen onto a red hippeastrum. The offspring were all red hippeastrums, but McNeil seemed convinced that they had clivia blood in them. He also showed me liners of seedlings of a putative cross between a very dark agapanthus and a clivia plant, pointing out that the dark purple leaf bases of the seedlings resembled the color of the leaf bases of the *Agapanthus* parent. He ignored the other liners of seedlings nearby that were made with two clivia parents that also had similarly colored leaf bases. Nevertheless, McNeil was an important clivia personage who made important contributions to the development of the flower. His work is being continued by Mary Lynne Lubke, his niece, who is especially interested in green-throated clivias and who has been able extend the green flush from the throat all the way to the tepal tips.

Wessel Lötter started breeding clivias in approximately 1975. He was trying to find a natural way of dealing with the lily borer caterpillar that plagues so many South African growers. He had noticed that both *Clivia gardenii* and *C. nobilis* were less favored by the caterpillar and thought those species might have some natural resistance. He crossed each of the two species with *C. miniata* types. The resultant hybrids have been called Cyrtanthiflora-types and tend to have pendent and curved florets. As Wessel himself said, "The first generation of hybrids were ugly." The F_2 generation, however, started to show some interesting characteristics, and some uniquely attractive selections emerged from among the variety of new genetic recombinations. Wessel put much energy and thought into trying to understand and sort out the various breeding patterns of yellow clivias, some of which breed true while others produce normal orange flowers. Wessel's son, Rudo, has taken over his father's interest in clivias. Rudo is himself now emerging as an important clivia leader, and he has organized the current clivia e-mail list, a very active group of clivia devotees who discuss and disseminate information on all aspects of clivias.

Among the most influential of the modern clivia growers is Nicholas William Primich. Born in Johannesburg in 1933, he is the father of the Clivia Club, the international organization of clivia enthusiasts that has grown faster than anyone ever expected. Much of Primich's early memories involve studying nature in the surrounding veldt. Although too busy in his varied career to garden seriously, he nevertheless remembers when he saw a *Clivia miniata* in bloom at a local nursery in the 1970s and was smitten. It was rather expensive, and by the time he had made up his mind to purchase the plant, it had already been sold.

When Primich retired to run a boarding house in 1984, he was at last free to garden. He started with succulents, then graduated to bulbs and orchids. Since he was more attracted to bulbs, his first clivia plant was *Clivia nobilis*. He became interested in the group but found it impossible to get a yellow *C. miniata* from the few yellow clivia producers in South Africa. Undeterred by the unwillingness of local nurseries to supply him with seeds of yellow clivias, he started to correspond with three enthusiasts in Australia and was able to exchange indigenous bulbs for seeds of yellow varieties. He started to correspond with other growers and soon had formed a coterie of about fifty bulb enthusiasts. It was then that Primich conceived of starting a newsletter that focused primarily on clivias. He persuaded some of his friends to write a few articles and sent free copies of the first three newsletters to his correspondents. An advertisement in the RHS journal brought in additional subscribers, and the Clivia Club was born. The first issue of the quarterly *Clivia Club Newsletter* was published in July 1992. By September 1994, about 110 people were members of the Clivia Club. At that time, a show and seminar were held in Pretoria, and it attracted participants from several different countries. By the time a second international Clivia Conference was held in Cape Town four years later, there were over four hundred members and over two hundred attendees including a number of participants from around the world. Membership continues to grow and in addition to the newsletter, the Clivia Club also publishes an annual with articles on various aspects of clivias.

When Primich started the newsletter it blossomed in ways he never anticipated; it is now a quarterly magazine with colored pictures. The Clivia Club and its branches sponsor clivia shows, and the standards by which to judge the flowers are being formalized. The Club is now the International Register for *Clivia* cultivars. Contacts for the Clivia Club now exist in several other countries, and more and more members are joining. Symposia devoted to clivias are becoming more common. Yet one senses that this is still only the beginning, that interest in clivia growing, and that collecting is still in its infancy.

Anna Meyer lives in Gauteng Province, the modern name for the area that incorporates Johannesburg and Pretoria. Her parents had moved from Germany and settled in South Africa. Meyer remembers examining one of her mother's clivias and thinking it a "nice thing." Her mother gave her a piece of the plant and she eventually had an entire bed of divisions from it near her front door. It is an interesting clivia plant that opens a medium orange with a touch of green in the throat that then fades to yellow. The orange sections have a hint of pink that becomes more obvious as the flower ages. Meyer crossed her mother's plant to a darker orange-red clivia and thus began her involvement with breeding these flowers.

Meyer lives on a fairly large estate with beds of clivias—among them some truly unusual varieties—displayed under both trees and in a large shade structure, where her best clivias are grown in pots. Also on her estate are a number of pet birds, including peacocks and swans, that provide Meyer with a unique method for pollinating her clivias. During the clivia pollinating season, some of the peacocks surrender their tail feathers for a good cause; Meyer twirls a feather in the flowers, gathering pollen from one flower and transferring it to the next as the feather brushes against the anthers and stigma. The feathers are long enough so that she does not have to stoop, and it is really quite an efficient way for transferring mixed pollen for mass seed production. The three large swans on the estate are aggressive watchdogs that dote on Meyer. She showed me how they courted and pranced before her when she sang to them. The scene stuck in my mind as "Anna and the dancing swans." She collects and sows about 87½ pints (50 liters) of cleaned seed a year, and she has a large retail plant nursery that sells about five thousand clivias per annum—all produced from her own hybridizing efforts with the help, of course, of her birds.

Val Thurston is a real clivia enthusiast. She studies the plants in her garden as well as those that grow wild in KwaZulu-Natal, where she lives, and she has self-published an information-packed book on clivias. She was involved with the rediscovery of a wild yellow clone of *Clivia miniata* that has since become known as 'Ndwedwe Alpha Thurston'. Val had permission from the local tribal chief to remove that plant. Any yellows found since the late nineteenth century have not been talked about, so her find was very exciting.

Val's find also illustrates the lengths a true clivia addict will go in pursuit of her avocation. Soon after she was involved in a head-on collision in 1995 with a tractor on a farm road, her husband, Roy, said he was going to the Ndwedwe area to check up on some sugarcane farms. Val, still feeling stiff and miserable, jokingly asked him to bring her back some clivia seeds and a yellow clivia. Three hours later Roy returned with a grin and about fifteen clivia seeds. When Val asked if that was all he managed to get, he replied, "Yes, but I also found a yellow clivia." She did not at first believe him, but he agreed to take her to the forest to see for herself. She was still in a great deal of pain and discomfort, and needed his help getting to the site. They first crossed a shallow river filled with large slippery boulders, and Val not only had to maintain her balance as she climbed over them, but she also had to keep her camera dry. Once on the other side they negotiated a steep rocky slope while keeping an eye open for black mambas, particularly vicious and poisonous snakes that inhabit the area. The scratchy brambles and biting insects were merely minor irritations for Val as her husband pushed and pulled her up the slope. She was just about to give up—it was taking forever to reach the spot where Roy had seen the clivia, and the heat and humidity were intense—when she looked up over a huge boulder and saw "this amazing, large yellow clivia umbel—a really wonderful sight." Their toils were not yet over, however, because they then had to photograph the plant in situ, dig it out, and gingerly carry it down the slope, across the river, and home without damaging any of the flowers so they could rephotograph it. Although Val was hot, sore, and exhausted by the end of the day, she was also replete with the kind of satisfaction only achieved when one who is clivia obsessed comes upon a prized specimen.

Sean Chubb is a young farmer who lives near Pietermaritzburg in KwaZulu-Natal. He remembers clivias growing wild while he was still a schoolboy and has been interested in these plants for most of his life. Although he grows and hybridizes a wide variety of clivias, Chubb is famous for one clone called *Clivia miniata* 'Chubb's Peach'. Besides flowers, he breeds *Nguni*, a disease resistant strain of African cattle. These were the indigenous cattle of the Zulu people that were long ignored and pooh-poohed by the white settlers in favor of European strains. But the *Nguni* prosper where other cattle fail, and they produce a milk rich in butterfat and protein. Much attention is now given to them.

Chubb's interest in and obsession with clivias can be gauged by the following story he related to us. On an outing along the Intumeni River one day in 1989, he came to a place where it dropped some 40 feet (12 m) as a waterfall. On the lip of the waterfall across the other side of the river grew clumps of *Clivia gardenii*. They were in flower, and Chubb was astute enough to realize that one flowering clump was considerably shorter than the others; it was a dwarf form of the species. Like any other true clivia addict, Chubb needed that plant! He waded across the river, ignoring the current that threatened to sweep him over the falls, and reached the other side. Even a dwarf clump of *C. gardenii* is sizable, so Chubb, now burdened with a large chunk of the plant, had to wade back the way he had come. Only a true fanatic would have performed the task, but it was worth the risk because the plant now grows happily in his collection. He has distributed its seed, making it possible for others to share this unique form.

Only a few people have been singled out in this chapter for attention—there are many others scattered around the world who are equally worthy of regard. One could probably write an entire book on all the personages involved with clivias, but I can give brief mention to just several others. Les Hannibal and Herbert Kelly in California, both students of the Amaryllidaceae and other bulbous plants, amassed good collections of the plants. Kees Sahin in the Netherlands is well known for his interest in clivias, and he grows a fine collection under glass. In Australia, Bill Morris and Ken Smith have propagated their enthusiasm as well as their plants, and Les Larsen has been a good ambassador there for clivias. Pen Henry runs what is probably the first—if not the only—Australian nursery that deals exclusively with clivias. New Zealand has given the clivia world Keith Hammet, a man of boundless enthusiasm for clivias, as well as Mike Styles, who seems to be equally besotted with these plants. No doubt there are many others whose lives have become enmeshed with this group of plants, and we expect that as more people get to know clivias, they too will become ensnared.

Chapter Eight

Standard *Clivia miniata* Hybrids: Orange and Red

S TANDARD CLIVIAS are bred from *Clivia miniata* and are large plants with either wide or narrow leaves. Until very recently there had been relatively little work on deliberate breeding for specific flower shapes. Many of the various forms that we now possess were created purely by chance. Most clivia propagation is by seed, and with relatively little selection of parents, there is now enormous variation among individuals from within seedling batches. Chance combinations of genes have provided many of the novelties, and some hobbyists now comb the nurseries for variants that they think are worthy of collection.

It is only in the last decade that intense breeding activity for specific orange types has started. At the beginning of the twentieth century and again in the 1970s and 1980s there was much enthusiasm for yellow clivias, and special efforts were directed toward breeding for that color phase. Standard yellow clivias will be dealt with in chapter 9. There is so much breeding activity with all forms of clivias now that in the future many new and unusual types are bound to surface. Some will be found by chance, but others will be created through deliberate breeding programs. Clivia growers are aware of the increasing popularity of hybridizing all types of clivias and they await future developments with eager anticipation.

FLOWER COLORS

There is a surprising range of shades and patterns within the group of orange flowers. There is a continuum that ranges from the softest pastel oranges through wonderfully bright, strong orange shades to deep orange-reds to almost reddish black colors. Between the extremes there are a myriad of tones and patterns. When green underlies the orange colors, rich shades of terracotta or even brown can appear. The intensity of color changes depending on the available sunlight and the age of the floret, and some flowers deepen in color and others fade depending on the clone. Flowers that develop indoors tend to be paler than those that open up and mature outside.

The basal portion inside the flower is called the throat, and this is normally of contrasting color to the rest of the tepals. The portion of the tepal that makes the throat usually has a central yellow region that is flanked with white patches, but throats may also be entirely yellow or white. As the flower ages the throat may be reduced and can even disappear. At the other extreme, the throat could be so large that it leaves merely a picotee rim of orange or red. Both of these extremes in the throat are very rare and much sought after.

The addition of green chloroplasts to the flowers can produce vivid green lines in the throat that extend to the rest of the tepal. If green chloroplasts occur together with the orange or red flavones, the flowers can be terracotta, brick, or even brown in color. Green stripes in the throat are not rare but give a distinctive flare to the flower, whereas brick or brown flowers are quite unusual and considered choice.

Color is often more important than form, and people will often grow and treasure flowers with exceptionally poor form as long as the flowers have unusual colors or patterns.

WHAT MAKES A SUPERIOR CLIVIA PLANT?

As with many esthetic questions, there are many different answers depending on the person queried. Some people think only in terms of

Clivia miniata Flame™ is considered to be among the best of the red clivias.

the flowers, others in terms of the whole plant. Clivias are more frequently used as pot plants, and because the entire plant is displayed, one needs to take both plant and flower habit into account. In

Western flower-judging systems for other plants such as dahlias, daffodils, or orchids, there is a common slate of characteristics that people breed for. Only a few breeding systems—for example, daylilies—have been able to throw off the shackles imposed by the judges, and even then they have not been able to do it entirely. Many of these common flower criteria apply to clivia flowers as well, although the vegetative characters must obviously be unique to clivias.

Flowers

SIZE. For most flower groups, bigger is always better. Even if size is only allocated 10 percent of the points on a scorecard, it is often the first ten to which the judges pay attention. To my mind there is a range of permissible flower size from quite small to quite large, but it should be in proportion to the stature of the plant itself.

SHAPE. Hybridizers and flower judges tend to focus on flowers that have rounded and overlapping parts; the wider each petal segment, the better. Also important is that the flower parts be symmetrically arranged. Preferably, the basal third or half of the tepals should overlap, and there should be no fenestration (gaps) between the bases of petals and sepals. The exceptions to this are the spider forms where long thin segments are desirable. The tepals in those spider forms will give a better display if the flower is fairly flat.

COLOR. Color is probably more important than shape as that is what first catches the eye. There appears to be a trend in the history of breeding any flower in which breeders first attempt to produce pure and intense colors with definite demarcations of patterns, and then, after achieving that, they return to creating subtle blends and pastels. (Are the judges becoming more sophisticated or merely blasé?) Currently intense red in clivia flowers is much desired. Strongly contrasting white, yellow, or green throats would look good with the more mid-orange shades.

INFLORESCENCE. The number of florets in the umbel is important. However, the flowers should not be too crowded but spaced in a way that individual flowers can be seen and appreciated. The number of flowers should be evenly arranged and not bunched, and there should be no obvious gaps where flowers look as if they are missing. Enough flowers should open at once to make a pleasing head. Too often there are dying flowers before most of the buds have developed. In the ideal case the inflorescence should have a stage where all flowers are open and looking fresh. Obviously the peduncle must be tall and strong enough to hold the flowers away from the leaves. Weak peduncles that droop under the weight of the flowers, or peduncles that split or curve, are also obvious faults, and some clones are more prone to these faults than others. There is some argument about whether the umbel should form a sphere of flowers or a half sphere. Some strains, in particular those with tulip-shaped flowers, have all the florets arranged in an upward facing bunch, almost like a paintbrush.

If you want to produce a perfect inflorescence, you will need to ensure that the flowers open and mature under protection. Some people bring the pots onto covered porches, verandas, or even into their homes. Flowers will develop quite happily indoors, but the color intensity will not be as dense as when they have been developed outside.

The plant

What makes an ideal plant is harder to define. The leaves of a show plant should have no mechanical damage, either from handling, disease, or insects. The leaves should be entire and without sun or chemical damage. Some varieties of *Clivia* seem particularly susceptible to various fungal infections, and those will disfigure the leaves. There are also clones that seem to have weak constitutions and produce brown necrotic blotches. Fortunately, the fungal infections do not seem to be particularly infectious.

People tend to prefer plants that have broad leaves, the wider the better. I have seen plants with leaves as wide as 6 inches (15 cm), but those are exceptional. The leaves should be arranged in two ranks with each leaf neatly stacked above the over. The leaves can be more or less erect, gently arching, held in horizontal stacks, or even have an exaggerated downward arch encompassing the pot. Very long leaves cannot support themselves well, and clones with long leaves tend to be untidy. The longest leaves I have seen on were on wild *Clivia miniata* and measured over 6 feet (1.8 m).

The depth of green color in the leaves usually depends on the amount of light to which they are exposed. A dark bottle green results from very low light exposure, and leaves that color make a wonderful contrast to the flowers. Pale green to yellow-green coloration indicates too much light. The Chinese, however, have bred for yellow leaves with green veins, and the veins may be prominently raised or sunken depending on the variety. Chinese clivias often have short and stubby leaves with nicely rounded tips that are preferred over leaves with acute ends.

The sheaths at the bases of the leaves can make a nice, regular, symmetrical, and imbricate pattern. Sheaths can also be thickened and can produce a basal bulge that makes the plant appear to have an incipient bulb. One does not want too many growths on a plant used in indoor display, but large clumps out of doors and in the landscape can look magnificent. Large clumps in very big containers are also difficult to move, although they admittedly make a spectacular display if one has either the space or manpower to deal with them.

Beginners are usually more tolerant of divergences from the norm in both flowers and leaves, but as they gain experience they tend to become more picky. What were once treasures get discarded in favor of newer and more refined plants and flowers. There is some truth to the saying that while experience in plants may make one more discerning, it also diminishes ones appreciation of beauty because the criteria for beauty becomes more restricted. Perhaps as long as one is comfortable and appreciative of the innate beauty of the flower, one is wise not to take judging criteria too seriously. On the other hand there is the gardening adage that says because it takes as much—if not more—effort to grow a poor plant as a good one, the gardener might as well grow the best that are available. But it is deciding which are the best that is the problem.

SIZE

Clivias come in all sizes ranging from tall plants standing over 3 feet (90 cm) tall to very tiny plants less than 6 inches (15 cm) high. The continuum in sizes from the largest to the smallest makes it difficult to demarcate one size from another. Growers tend to lump plants into either standard varieties or dwarf types, but this is not very satisfactory as the medium-sized plants are too small to be standards and too large to be dwarfs, and the tiniest plants are far too small to be lumped together with the dwarfs. Perhaps the answer will come from following the procedure used for *Cyclamen persicum* hybrids, which C. Grey-Wilson (1997) classifies according to their size as follows:

MAGNUM PLANTS, which are much larger than normal plants.
MAXI PLANTS, which are plants of standard size.
MIDI PLANTS, which are medium-sized plants.
MINI PLANTS, which are the miniatures.
MICRO PLANTS, which are the smallest.

With a little experience one can generally look at a plant and put it into a size category without resorting to measurements. Some people would like exact numerical measurements as category boundaries, but there really is no need. Mini and micro plants are often assigned to the dwarf category, but the very smallest plants are so much smaller than other dwarfs that it would be useful to have a separate descriptor for them. Of course there are always borderline plants that are difficult to assign to specific classes, but it is nevertheless useful to have some plant size categories. Modern seed-grown types, such as Belgian and French strains, often fall on the border between standard and dwarf types. Plants designed for windowsills must not be too large, and there has been a tendency to breed for smaller plants even among the standard types. It is a trend that is likely to continue.

ORANGE STRAINS OF *CLIVIA MINIATA*

German Reds (Friesdorfer-type)
It is thought that this strain introduced the darker orange-red colors. Prior to this strain, mid-orange colors were the common type. The very dark orange-reds do not seem to have been found in wild populations. A Mr. Lobner in Bonn-Friesdorf is said to have developed a very deep orange flower in 1917, and it gave rise to what was called the Friesdorfer-type. Some of these may have found their way to California and possibly contributed toward the Zimmerman strain.

Belgian strain
Two different types of plants are now known by this name. The older form was a compact plant with wide and thick leaves. In recent years these have been replaced by a fast maturing strain with narrower leaves. Sometimes flowering in the second year from seed, they make ideal pot plants. They can be considered either small standards or large dwarfs. Flowers are often tulip shaped and borne in upward facing clusters, although a few have the more traditional semispherical umbels. Seven hundred thousand plants of this strain are produced and sold each year in Europe (van Huylenbroeck 1998). Flowers tend to be medium sized and a mid-orange color.

A number of other strains masquerade as Belgian hybrids. While some are dwarf, they usually do not have the same flower configuration. In California any clivia plant of European origin is sometimes called a Belgian hybrid. Many of these can be quite small plants, but with variable forms and colors.

French strain
One of the biggest wholesale producers on the west coast of North America has marketed a seed strain called French Hybrids for

many years. These are standard orange clivias. There is nothing particularly distinctive that sets them apart, although one can find the occasional outstanding clone. The plant is taller than the Belgian strain.

Solomone's Charm series

Not yet introduced, Joe Solomone has selected out a series of plants from his breeding program that have distinctively different flowers, both in size and shape. These are diminutive flowers that can occur in medium-sized umbels. The flowers are narrow trumpets with pointed tepals that open somewhat for their distal third. Natural spread is less than 2 inches (5 cm). The tepals overlap for about two-thirds of their length and end in pointed and narrow tips. Sepals are less than $1/2$ inch (1.25 cm) wide and petals less than $3/4$ inch (2 cm). Colors are soft oranges and a few salmon-pinks. Most of the over-lapped portion has an ivory throat. Plants are medium to small in size. This group is still being developed and strictly speaking should not be called a strain.

Older diploid strain

In southern California there appear to be two different types of orange clivias. Some landscapers differentiate them into an older diploid type and the modern tetraploid types. None of the modern types in California has been counted, and it is doubtful that any might actually be tetraploids. At the 1998 Second International Clivia Conference, Keith Hammet suggested that most, if not all, of the big modern hybrids are diploids. One clone in Japan called 'Taikohden' is published as being a tetraploid (Mori 1990), but Hammet, who has counted many different varieties, doubts that any of the big, modern, wide-leafed forms are tetraploids. The Japanese Daruma-type clivias, which have wide thick and often corrugated leaves, are probably also diploids.

I have seen this old diploid-type plant in some of the older gardens in South Africa and Australia. They have relatively narrow and more erect leaves, and the flowers are relatively pale orange with narrow floral segments that are quite open—unattractive flowers compared to the large showy modern varieties. Plants clump readily but do not get overly tall. This is a tough garden plant capable of taking considerable neglect and drought, provided it gets enough shade. The leaves do not seem to burn in the sun as readily as the modern varieties.

"Green Girl"
Gordon McNeil in South Africa found clivias that had distinctive green markings in their throats. He used the name *Green Girl* for this type. It was never clear to me, even during my several visits to McNeil when he was alive, if he used the name to refer to a strain of his or a specific clone. Sometimes he even seemed to refer to his putative *Hippeastrum* × *Clivia* as "Green Girl." Many different clones now appear to carry this name, but it is likely that these do not represent a single strain because green throats appear quite regularly and spontaneously in nursery offerings all over the world. Some people still refer to any clivia plant with a green throat as a Green Girl and even talk of hybridizing to produce a yellow Green Girl. One clone has already been called 'Yellow Green Girl'.

Zimmerman strain
This was an early strain of quite variable clivias that was produced by E. P. Zimmerman in southern California. He claimed that they represented seventy-five years of breeding going back to their original German stock. Their genes probably feature in the breeding programs of other Californians such as Horace Anderson and Ted Kalil.

THE FIRST TIME AROUND

The current intense focus on breeding clivias is not a new phenomenon. From 1880 to 1900 there was significant interest in their breeding, and there are reports in the old *Gardeners' Chronicle* (1888) of flower shows where named standard clivias were described.

Among them are names like *Clivia* 'Meteor', *C.* 'Cruentum', *C.* 'Martha Ricmers', *C.* 'Baroness Schroeder', *C.* 'Van Houtte', and *C.* 'Ambroise Verschaffelt'. They were described as ranging from orange-scarlet to orange vermilion and as having yellow throats. Similar interest occurred in Belgium, where Jean Linden published lithographs of some of the selected clones in *L'Illustration Horticole.* In the years 1875—1913 the *Revue de l'Horticulture Belge et Etrangère* also described many varieties. Most of the plants were named to honor specific people, and the quality of the flowers was stunning, equal to some of the most modern standard hybrids. Why interest in the plants waned for so many years is not clear, but the fault can probably be laid upon the First World War, where so many young men were killed (including a generation of gardeners) and the result was social upheaval and a change in lifestyle.

'Lindeni'

Among the most famous of these early clones is *Clivia miniata* 'Lindeni'. It was the major impetus for breeding good clivias. The flowers were very large, approximately 4 inches (10 cm) in natural spread. The floral segments were slightly narrow by modern standards, but their size and arrangement on the umbel made for a spectacular display. The umbel itself was nearly 12 inches (31 cm) in diameter and reputedly carried up to thirty-nine flowers. This was among the first clivias with wide leaves. The plant is said to have been bred by Theodore Reimers, the chief gardener for a Mrs. Donner who lived in Ottenhausen near Hamburg in Germany (de Coster 1998). Whether or not the plant still exists is not known, but its genes are probably widespread in the background of most modern orange clivias of European descent. It created a sensation at the time it was displayed. From the painting of it that exists, it would still rank as a great flower.

'Mlle. Alice Rodigas'

This is among the most stunning among the earlier illustrated clones that was published. The individual flowers are a strong orange-red

Clivia miniata 'Lindeni'.

with almost no contrast in the throat. Petals are very rounded and have much overlap with close to thirty flowers in the inflorescence. Sepals and petals were wide spreading, and there is some reflexing of the petals to make for a flat flower. The flowers are perfectly arranged in a large semispherical head.

'Mme. Paul Buquet'

This was a flower that looked like an improved *Clivia miniata* 'Lindeni' with wider orange petals and a striking throat of yellow. Flowers were arranged in a nice umbel, but with fewer flowers than *C. miniata* 'Lindeni'—probably no more than twelve flowers in the umbel.

Clivias are long-lived plants, but how many of these plants still exist is not known. Some may still be held in private hands, but few, if any, were propagated and dispersed under their cultivar names.

Clivia miniata 'Mlle. Alice Rodigas'.

A SELECTION OF MODERN ORANGE CULTIVARS

Most of the modern standard clivias are seed grown and quite variable. They are usually not given names, but that trend is returning now that there is a need to keep track of parent plants. Relatively few named clones are actually available on the market, but specialty clivia nurseries and some businesses specializing in subtropical plants do list divisions from time to time. One very well known nursery that is run by David Conway in Santa Barbara, California, specializes in clivias. Conway has assembled one of the best collections of clivias in the United States and the majority of the plants he offers are divisions of selected plants from his own breeding program.

Below is a sampling of some plants from various sources that have cultivar names. This is a biased selection because it is easier for me to focus on Californian plants, but there are many good clones in

Clivia miniata 'Adam'.

South Africa, Australia, and Japan to which I did not have ready access. Standard clivias are common landscape plants in southern California, and during the season one often finds plantings that contain unnamed clivias with flowers that often surpass those I describe below. The measurements of flower parts and plant dimensions are given only as a guide. One should remember that any plant's dimensions can vary depending on the season, health, and potting regime.

'Adam'
Without a doubt, this is among the finest modern orange clivias. It produces a spherical umbel with evenly arranged flowers, usually two a season. The sphere of flowers is about 9 inches (23 cm) in diameter. Each head contains more than thirty flowers of a strong mid-orange

Clivia miniata 'Antz'.

color with a small, well-defined throat. The sepals are pointed with a contrasting white mucro. (A mucro is a small triangular appendage at the tip of a tepal.) Petals are more rounded than the sepals and reflex nicely. The flowers have long protruding styles and are fragrant, and both these characteristics are from Comstock's peach-colored *Clivia miniata* 'Morning Light', one of its parents. The other parent was an unnamed orange clivia plant from yellow breeding, and as a result when 'Adam' is crossed to a yellow, it will produce some yellow seedlings. Likewise, if crossed to a peach it will produce wonderful pastel shades. Many of its 'Adam's' seedlings inherit its parent's good qualities such as fragrance, high flower count, and full umbels, all of which result from Comstock's breeding. In some respects the flower shape and arrangement are reminiscent of the old *C. miniata* 'Lindeni'.

Clivia miniata 'Anna Meyer's Tulip'.

'Antz'
One of Comstock's spiders, this has very narrow tepals that open out.
The creamy white throat area occupies the basal third of the tepals.
With about ten flowers to the umbel, this cultivar is a little low on the
flower count but it has excellent potential for breeding spiders.

'Anna Meyer's Tulip'
This is a classic tulip-shaped clivia plant with a deep red flower. The
dense umbels stand out even in a crowd of other clivias.

'Bessie'
The flower count is somewhat on the low side—about fifteen florets
to the umbel—but individual flower quality is very good. The flower
is a soft orange color with an extended cream and yellow throat.
Flower shape is full, and the tepals are overlapping with rounded

tips. This Conway selection grows leaves that are 24 inches (62 cm) long and 3 inches (7.5 cm) wide.

'Brown-Eyed Girl'
Bred by Doug McGavin of California, this resembles 'Jean Delphine' and is among the brown or terracotta clivias. The small florets are slightly more flaring than 'Jean Delphine', but the color is not quite as intense. Nevertheless the mixture of green and orange makes for rich brown tepals that contrast with a small but bright lime-green throat. The florets barely measure 2 inches (5 cm) in diameter and are made up from rounded petals that are just over 1 inch (2.5 cm) in width and pointed sepals that measure 3/4 inch (2 cm) wide. The nine to eleven flowers are held in a flattish head on a short peduncle some 10 to 12 inches (25 to 31 cm) tall that in turn is among erect leaves 12 inches (31 cm) tall and 2 inches (5 cm) broad. The small flower count and poorly held inflorescence can be forgiven in light of the unusual flower color.

'Deuce'
This is one of Comstock's darkest clivias. It is considerably deeper red in color than Flame™. This plant was bred from a variegated *Clivia* specimen and it shows faint variegation in its leaves. It carries twenty flowers in the umbel on a 12-inch (31-cm) peduncle. The flowers open a dark orange with a yellow throat that soon flushes a dark red color, obliterating the yellow. The florets are narrow with a natural spread of only 2½ inches (5.6 cm) and are trumpet-shaped with good overlap between the parts. Petals are 1¼ inches (3.1 cm) long, while sepals are slightly less than 1 inch (2.5 cm) across the widest parts. Leaves are a modest 3 inches (7.5 cm) wide and only 15 inches (37.5 cm) long.

'Doris'
This is a nice, dark, orange-red from Conway. 'Doris' is another clone that darkens as the flower matures. At its peak, the narrow

Clivia miniata 'Doris'.

trumpet flower is a solid orange-red color that extends all of the way down to the bottom of the throat. Petals are rounded and the sepals pointed, and there is good overlap between the two. The umbel is made up of a nice, tight cluster of about twenty flowers. It is among the better reds available and is recommended for those who are serious about breeding for dark colors. Vegetatively, it is a good грower, and it produces leaves just under 24 inches (62 cm) long and about 2½ inches (6.25 cm) broad.

'Emperor'
One of Comstock's selections, this plant approaches his 'Galaxy Quest' in size and impact. 'Emperor' is a magnificent plant with enormous rounded, fairly flat flowers of a clear pastel but true orange. The very edge of the petals has a thin rim of soft pink. Flowers have a soft, cream-colored throat. Individual flowers can

Clivia miniata 'Emperor'.

easily reach 4 inches (10 cm) or more in natural spread. The rounded petals are over 1½ inches (3.75 cm) wide and the sepals are 1¼ inches (3.1 cm) across their widest part. The impression is of a widely flared and almost flat flower, but close inspection of this widely flaring flower reveals that the petal edges roll back while the sepal edges are incurved. The umbel carries only ten to thirteen flowers, but their size and stance make for a very full head that is carried on a 15-inch (37.5-cm) peduncle that is somewhat brittle. The plant itself, however, is very strong and robust, producing very wide leaves averaging 4 inches (10 cm) in breadth and 22 inches (57 cm) in length.

Flame™
This is among the few clivias that have been both trademarked and patented for commercial protection. The plant's patent registration

designation is 'Moyna' (P.P. no. 6205). This is a large plant that is quite vigorous, and as the name suggests, it is among the redder flowers available. It has flowers that open a strong orange with a relatively small yellow throat. As the flowers mature, the orange takes on deep red tones, and the yellow throat recedes as the orange coloring moves down to the base of the flower. Intensity of color varies somewhat with light exposure and from season to season, but it is still among the darkest clones available at a reasonable price. When flowers develop outdoors and in colder areas like the San Francisco bay area or during a cold winter in southern California, the rich red color can be quite stunning. If flowered under glass or during a warmer season, they may be paler. This is a ready bloomer that flowers relatively early in the season, typically in the first days of February in southern California. It is a rebloomer, and a large clump often throws additional umbels during the summer and fall. The umbel carries about twenty-five flowers in a 9-inch (23-cm) diameter umbel. Each flower has a natural spread of 3 inches (7.5 cm). Petals are rounded and somewhat over an inch in diameter (2.5 cm); sepals are narrower, considerably less about $3/4$ inch (2 cm) in width and with acute tips. Leaves are about $2^{3}/4$ inches (6 to 7 cm) wide and about 22 inches (55 to 60 cm) long. This plant is much in demand as a breeding plant but is partially self-sterile.

Flame™ is also known informally as 'Mirken's Flame', a name that is recognized all over the world although relatively few growers outside the West Coast of the United States have actually seen it. Hodge Amemiya found the plant originally, and he recognized the flower as being distinctive when he saw it in the private garden of a Dr. Mirken in the spring of 1953. For a time the plant was actively propagated at Mariposa Nurseries. It took nearly forty years to build up sufficient stock before it could be introduced into the trade, and it was first listed by Monrovia Nurseries in 1990. There was some confusion between the two names among clivia growers, but Amemiya confirmed that both of the names, Flame™ and 'Mirkin's Flame' refer to the same plant.

Clivia miniata 'Brown-Eyed Girl'.

'Fleur-de-lis'

One of the two iris-shaped flowers I have seen, 'Fleur-de-lis' has sepals that recurve back while the rounded petals extend forward for much of their life. This is a deep red flower that has a small white star

Clivia miniata 'Green Mile'.

deep at the base of the throat. Petals are 1½ inches (3.75 cm) wide while the sepals measure only ¾ inch (2 cm) at their widest. Stamen filaments are deep red. More than twenty flowers are clustered in an upward facing umbel held above the foliage. Leaves are 2 inches (5 cm) wide and 18 inches (45 cm) long. The plant is vigorous and suckers freely.

'Grandmère'
This superb mid-orange flower has a creamy yellow throat. It has proved to be a great breeding plant, transmitting its full shape and high flower count to its progeny. A Comstock selection.

'Green Girl'
There are several clones using this name. The name appears to have started with McNeil, but it is not clear if he was referring to a single

clone or merely used the name to specifically designate those with a lot of green color in their throats. One of his so-called intergenerics with *Hippeastrum* was at one time called 'Green Girl', but he also once showed me a normal clivia plant with a green throat and referred to that as 'Green Girl'.

'Green Mile'

A stunning, dark, orange-red flower with very full tepals, 'Green Mile' is unusual with its white throat and deep emerald-green central stripes that extend into the orange portion of each tepal. The green color is relatively color-fast in the sun, and unlike some cultivars, it lasts for the life of the blossom. The petals are slightly notched, and the sepals have a small white micro. A fault with this cultivar is the small number of flowers to the umbel. It is another of Comstock's selections.

'Green Stripe'

Green throats are not that uncommon among standard clivias—they occur spontaneously in many strains of *Clivia*—although when you want one they seem hard to find. The 'Green Stripe' clone is unusual in that it is a multipetalled flower with some flowers possessing more than six tepals. The almost flat flowers have a white base and a yellow-green contrasting central stripe. This is one of Comstock's plants.

'Jean Delphine'

This is among the most distinctive of the Conway clivias with unusually rich, dark, brownish orange-red flowers. The florets are quite narrow with a natural spread of less than 2 inches (5 cm). The petals are 3/4 inch (2 cm) wide. Rather curiously, the sepals are very much shorter than the petals, but unfortunately I did not measure them. It is among the deepest brown flowers available in clivias. Florets also have a considerable amount of emerald green in the throat, and the brown color presumably reflects a background of chlorophyll under the orange-red of the tepals. Umbels tend to be a

Clivia miniata 'Green Stripe'.

little irregular in presentation, but one is willing to forgive this considering the very rare color. The plant carries leaves that measure 21
inches (52.5 cm) in length and 2 inches (5 cm) in width. 'Sabrine
Delphine', another of the Conway selections, is similar.

'Judy'
A modern and strongly colored orange clivia plant from Conway, this
cultivar has very shapely flowers. The flowers have the bugle shape
with flared and spreading tepals. The perianth is broad and overlapping. It could be improved by an increased flower count to the umbel.

'Laura'
Conway has produced this clone, and it appears to be darker than
many of the reds described above. It has narrow, trumpet-shaped

Clivia miniata 'Judy'.

flowers that open orange-red with a very small yellow throat. The entire flower then, even when young, rapidly changes to a very dark red that colors down to the base of the tepals. The stamen filaments, too, become red as the flower matures. The flowers have a natural spread of 2 inches (5 cm) and petals are just under 1 inch (2.5 cm) in width. Each trumpet is 2¾ inches (7 cm) long and there are approximately sixteen florets to each umbel. Parentage is said to be 'Doris' × 'Abigail'. Conway is now using this clone to breed deeper red colors. Foliage is moderate with leaves 22 inches (57 cm) long and 2½ inches (6.25 cm) wide.

'Leta Belle'
Another shapely, mid-orange flower from Conway, this cultivar also has a lot of green coloring at the base of the throat. The green color

fades as the flower matures. Flower count is low, but the coloring makes it a distinctive plant. It is a dwarf plant with 18-inch (45-cm) leaves that curve down and makes the plant appear shorter. The leaves measure $2\frac{1}{4}$ inches (5.6 cm) in width.

'Leta Clare'
This clone also portrays brown tones but is not as distinctive as 'Jean Delphine'. The additional brown tones make both the orange and green colors in the throat appear darker when compared to that of 'Leta Belle'. With only fifteen to sixteen florets in the umbel, flower count is also lower than one would like, but flower quality and the rounded tepals compensate for the low flower number. The leaves are only 15 inches (37.5 cm) long and 2 inches (5 cm) wide, making for a petite plant.

'Lollipop'
One of my own plants, this has an almost entire sphere of very shapely flowers and rounded tepal tips. 'Lollipop' has some of the widest and roundest overlapping perianth parts of any of the standard clivias I have seen. The flower color is a rich, smooth mid-orange with a contrasting wide throat. I happened across it by chance growing in a pot while I was in an artist's studio, and after much haggling with the artist's wife, managed to buy it. To my mind, the umbel has an almost perfect placement of flowers. The plant's stature is a little too large for it to be considered a dwarf. The gracefully arching leaves are just over 3 inches (7.5 cm) wide and 18 inches (45 cm) long. Two inflorescences are usually borne simultaneously and held just above the foliage.

'Lush Life'
Large, wide, and soft orange flowers frame a creamy throat. The paler *Clivia* varieties can be very handsome. The broad tepals are spreading and slightly reflexed. High flower count and good placement on the umbel are some of its good qualities. Comstock named this plant.

Clivia miniata 'Lollipop'.

'Midnight'

This is a very dark red flower that seems to have a dark brown flush, making for a deeply colored flower. It is produced when there is a flush of green underlying the surface anthocyanin. As you might expect, you will often find that these plants have strong green coloring in their throats. Comstock bred this one using another dark red clivia plant he called 'Ruby' that he crossed with an unnamed red with a green throat. 'Midnight' opens as an orange flower with a dark, emerald-green throat. The base of the sepals is solid green, but the petals have a fine white border to the green in the throat. Examining the outside of the perianth reveals that there is a flush of green that extends all the way to the petal tips. As the flower ages, the entire bloom flushes with a deep red. Among this cultivar's good points is the way the umbel, with its sixteen florets, is

Clivia miniata 'Painted Lady'.

presented on an 18-inch (45-cm) peduncle that is held well above the foliage. The basal edges of the petals furl inwards, a character-istic that it inherits from its mother 'Ruby', a small flower with a pronounced pinch that makes its petals spoon-shaped. This plant has 3-inch (7.5-cm) wide arching leaves that achieve a length of about 24 inches (62 cm).

'Orange Spider'
This Conway selection is among the better spiders, although there is considerable room for improvement in this type. The flower is fairly open with narrow segments that are splayed out. Tepals are flat and disciplined, especially at their margins. Color is a mid-orange and the basal third of each segment is creamy yellow. Flower count is lower than one would like. This is a standard-sized plant with

Clivia miniata 'Ramona'.

fairly long, narrow leaves reaching up to 42 inches (105 cm) in length but only 1½ inches (3.75 cm) wide.

'Painted Lady'
This is another older and well-known picotee *Clivia* specimen that was bred by Anderson of California. The color is not as intense as that of 'Ramona', but other than that, the flowers are quite similar. They measure 2½ inches (6.25 cm) in natural spread, the petals are also notched, and the sepals are mucronate. The paler orange border to the tepals averages ½ inch (1.25 cm) wide and it is feathered toward the large throat of pale white-cream. The umbel contains thirty flowers making for a very full and packed head. A nice feature of this cultivar is the diamond dusting in the throat and gold dusting on the picotee border. Petals measure 1½ inches (3.75 cm),

and sepals are just slightly more than 1 inch (2.5 cm) in width. The umbel is carried on an 18-inch (45-cm) peduncle. Leaves are longer and not as wide as those of 'Ramona'. Both 'Ramona' and 'Painted Lady' breed, and they should be important stud plants for this very desirable pattern, especially since many of the other picotee patterns are carried on flowers with poor quality.

'Ramona'
This is a Conway plant that deserves whatever superlatives can be thrown at it. It is among the best picotee flowers available and makes a stunning display. The umbel carries large, widely flaring, flattish flowers with overlapping tepals and enormous, central creamy yellow throats that extend toward the tepal tips. The tepal tips are edged with a vivid border of dark orange, which makes a strong contrast with the colors in the throat. The cream-yellow of the throat contains more bright yellow than normally seen in the yellow clivias. This is essentially a creamy yellow flower with about a 3/8- to 1/2-inch (1- to 1.25-cm) rim of orange. The petals are obcordate (notched) and the somewhat pointed sepals have obvious mucrones (small thornlike appendages) at their tips. The petals are slightly more than 1 inch (2.5 cm) at their widest, and the sepals are 1 inch (2.5 cm) wide, making a flower that is 3 inches (7.5 cm) in diameter. I counted sixteen florets to the umbel, which is formed on a rounded head and borne on an 18-inch (45-cm) peduncle. The somewhat short leaves are 20 inches (50 cm) long and 3½ inches (9 cm) wide. The leaves recurve, exposing the inflorescence above the foliage and making a very handsome picture. Without a doubt this is among the finest clivias available today.

'Redgrove'
I have not seen this cultivar, which is said to have been tissue cultured in New Zealand. Descriptions I have read refer to the flowers as being the same salmon-pink with orange throats as the species (I do not know what species is being referred to; I

Clivia miniata 'Saber Dance'.

certainly have not seen that combination in *Clivia miniata*) but with superb, much larger and fuller rounded heads. Apparently the accompanying photograph in the *Parva Plants Catalog* showed a more usual orange flower with a yellow throat. Nick Primich thought the plant looked like 'Relly Williams', a well-known Australian cultivar.

'Red Spider'
Here is another Conway selection of much deeper red coloration than 'Orange Spider', but not nearly as refined. The florets do not open as widely, and the perianth is not nearly as open or flat. While distinctly different, the form of the flowers—their poor spacing and low flower count—presents a rather messy appearance. Nevertheless, there are so few spiders available that it might still be worth having in a breeding program.

'Saber Dance'

Comstock has selected this spider for its well-disciplined shape. The narrow petals are only $^3/_4$ inch (2 cm) broad, but they are 3 inches (7.5 cm) long. The sepals are $^1/_2$ inch (1.25 cm) wide. There is a clear separation between tepals down to the base of the flower. Tepals are held rigidly in place without the rolling and twisting often seen in this type. Each floret is a rich orange-red with a small cream-colored throat. The umbel contains fifteen flowers in a globular cluster, and flowers are evenly spaced to display their distinctive shape. The peduncle is 22 inches (57 cm) tall, and the ball of flowers is held just above the foliage. Leaves arch slightly and are 30 inches (75 cm) long and quite narrow, measuring less than $1^3/_4$ inches (4.5 cm) in width. This is another robust plant that clumps readily.

'Sabrine Delphine'

Looking like an improved 'Jean Delphine', this Conway selection has the darkest of all clivia flowers to date. Flowers are similar in size and shape to 'Jean Delphine' but with sepals and petals of almost equal length. The flower opens brick with a strong green throat, and as the flower matures the red color deepens and creeps down to the bottom of the throat. The end effect is a flower that is a deep maroon color. This is a truly unique flower, and although it has been used for breeding, we have yet to see some of its seedlings in flower.

'Shimoda-Daruma'

This is a Japanese cultivar that has shapely, scarlet-red flowers with rounded petals. Leaves are up to 4 inches (10 cm) wide and 15 inches (37.5 cm) long. *Daruma* is used for many dwarf clivias. (The term *daruma* comes from the name of a wooden doll that is painted red around its face and has a swollen base, rather like a fat skittle. When tipped, the doll always rights itself.) This particular clone has the leaves arched into a wide base. It is another borderline plant for stature and is an important breeder for dwarf plants.

Clivia miniata 'Sabrine Delphine'.

'Soft Bricks'
Comstock is partial to the brown shades in clivias. A solid jade green fills the throat and lights up the soft terracotta colors of the rest of the flower. This flower is unique in terms of its color, and the selected name is very apt. Add to the color the rounded tepals overlapping in the throat, and one has a winning flower.

'Taikohden'
Another Japanese cultivar, this plant is reputed to be a tetraploid. It is one of those plants that can be considered either a large dwarf or a small standard. Photographs I have seen of this clone suggest that it is a pastel orange, although written descriptions suggest that it is dark orange. There is a contrasting green central stripe radiating out from the base of each tepal. This is said to be a famous clone in Japan.

Clivia miniata 'Thumbellina'.

'Taiyou'
This is a Japanese cultivar with large, dark scarlet flowers with rounded petals. The umbel contains many flowers. Its leaves can reach 4 inches (10 cm) in diameter and 28 inches (70 cm) in length.

'Thumbellina'
A small, tulip-shaped flower makes this Conway a special flower. Like many other tulip-shaped clivias, the umbel is primarily made from upward facing flowers with incurved tepals. There are about eighteen to twenty flowers to the umbel. Flowers are a rich orange color with a hint of green in freshly opened flowers.

'Wide-Body #2'
Comstock has bred a series of spectacular orange flowers that he refers to as his 'Wide-body' series. Only cultivar '#2' is described

here, but all the siblings are equally impressive. These are exceptional flowers that open wide and are quite flat, displaying their enormous rounded tepals. This series is among the best clivias in the world today. This clone has flowers that approach 4 inches (10 cm) in natural spread, having petals over 1¾ inches (4.5 cm) wide, and sepals measuring over 1¼ inches (3.1 cm) wide. The perianth parts are nicely rounded and look nearly circular. Flowers open a deep orange with a vivid contrasting throat of creamy white containing a central yellow stripe. As the blooms mature, the central yellow stripe is replaced with orange, leaving narrow cream edges. More than twenty flowers are usually carried in each umbel on top of a short 12-inch (31-cm) peduncle. The 3-inch (7.5-cm) wide leaves are only 18 inches (45 cm) long, and because they arch over they do not obstruct the flowers. The group was the result of crossing a pastel flower that Comstock calls *Clivia miniata* 'Morning Light' with a very full and rounded orange flower of his he calls 'Grandmère'. The latter has a spectacular contrasting throat. Compared to the Wide Body group, *C.* 'Morning Light' has relatively narrow petals, but this seems to be a recessive characteristic.

Very few of these modern orange cultivars are ever offered for sale. When they are available they often command prices that would put an orchid to shame. I have provided descriptions to give the reader a sense of the variation in plant size and flower form among the standard *Clivia miniata* hybrids. Among the best ways of getting good clones is to buy seeds from a reputable dealer. Alternatively, if you live in an area where clivias are used in the landscape, keep your eyes open for good forms and then talk the owner out of pollen or even a division. Join the Clivia Club and correspond with the major breeders.

Chapter Nine

STANDARD *CLIVIA MINIATA* HYBRIDS: YELLOW

YELLOW CLIVIAS are mutations of the normal orange-red standard forms that have appeared spontaneously in both wild and garden populations. Being both rare and desirable, yellow clivias have acquired a distinction that ranks them among the very special plants of the world. Over the last few decades special effort has been spent breeding and propagating yellow forms, and this effort has succeeded to a large extent. Throughout the primary clivia-growing areas of the world—excluding Europe—there are now nurseries that specialize in the production of yellows. Consequently, the price of yellow clivias has dropped from being exorbitant to merely expensive. With another decade or so, there should be little difference in price between the two major color phases, yellow and orange. Nevertheless, good yellow clivias can still fetch extravagant prices; at the Longwood Gardens Rare Plant Auction in 2000, a yellow clivia plant fetched the highest price. It was reported to have sold for U.S. $2200.

The yellows are distinguished in the literature under a number of botanical names, none of which is either correct or used correctly. When the first yellow *Clivia* specimen was discovered, it was described as *Clivia miniata* var. *citrina*. This name has precedence and appears frequently in modern literature. In modern usage,

An unnamed yellow clivia plant from Joe Solomone's breeding program. Owing to light conditions and film development, the color of the flower in this photograph is more intensely yellow than in real life. Breeders are still striving to achieve this depth of color.

however, the word variety indicates plants derived from a population that differs from the originally described form of the species. The first yellow clivia plant was merely a single clonal variant and not representative of a yellow natural population. The term *variety* in its modern taxonomic sense is not appropriate. When it was originally used for *C. miniata* var. *citrina*, *variety* was equivalent to the modern term of *cultivar* or *forma*. No yellow forms found since then should be called *citrina* or any of the other earlier names unless the names refer directly to the appropriate original clones.

Although there are still rumors of populations of *Clivia miniata* that have only yellow flowers, there is no strong evidence that such taxa actually exist. Many of the wild yellow clones were found in widely separate geographic areas and thus cannot really be considered part of the same population. They therefore do not deserve to share a common varietal name. A more appropriate designation of this plant as a horticultural selection would be *Clivia miniata* 'Citrina'. Although modern yellows need new names, one will still find yellows designated as *C. miniata* var. *citrina*, *C. miniata* var. *aurea*, and *C. kewensis* var. 'Bodnant'. This last name is especially confusing because it looks like a species name, but it was merely a certain yellow form of *C. miniata* that originated at the Royal Botanic Gardens, Kew. It is not even a grex name because it is pure *C. miniata* and not an interspecific hybrid. The latter plant should be referred to as *C. miniata* 'Kewensis' or *C. miniata* 'Bodnant Variety'.

THE FIRST YELLOW CLIVIAS

When the first yellow mutant clivia plant reached Europe it created a sensation. The flower was described by Watson in 1899 as *Clivia miniata* var. *citrina*, but it had been discovered in 1892 in Eshowe in KwaZulu-Natal (Thurston 1998). The resident commissioner at the time was Sir Melmoth Osborne, and his Zulu cook, who was out collecting firewood, came across the yellow-flowered plant. The cook was perspicacious enough to realize the significance of his find, and he dug up the plant, which must have been a large clump, and brought it back to the residence. Sir Melmoth's assistant Sir Charles Saunders managed to beg two pieces of the original plant. One piece was sent to his mother, Katharine Saunders, who lived in Tongaat about 62½ miles (100 km) to the south. The portion sent to Mrs. Saunders was in flower when it was dispatched, but it made the trip by slow ox wagon, and by the time she received it the flowers were aged and much the worse for wear. Nevertheless, she made a watercolor painting of the new find, which still exists today. A piece of the plant was sent to the Royal Botanic Gardens, Kew, where it flowered and was described in an issue of *The Garden*.

An alternative history to the discovery of yellow clivias was published in *The Gardeners' Chronicle* in 1899. There it was suggested that *Clivia miniata* var. *citrina* had been collected in the wild in Zululand by Captain Mansell and first flowered by Mrs. Powys Rogers of Perrenwell in Cornwall, England, in April 1897. These flowers, together with a small offset of the plant, were sent to Kew, and they were probably what Watson described. Kew already had a plant that had been donated by Rev. W. H. Bowden from North Devon, and that plant flowered at Kew in 1899. The plant was described as having a clear, pale cream flower with a faint tinge of orange at the base of the floral segments. Katharine Saunder's painting does not show this orange tinge, so it is possible that at least two different yellow clones had reached England at about the same time.

Although yellow mutants are rare in the wild, several distinct clones have been discovered, and a few are still being found at the present time (Thurston 1998). Yellow forms are also reputed to occur and be in cultivation for *Clivia nobilis* and *C. gardenii*.

Yellow *Clivia miniata* in the wild result from mutations that occur in the pathways used to make anthocyanins. Many genes underlie the synthesis of anthocyanin, and one of any number of different mutations could eventually result in the yellow coloring. (See chapter 6 for a detailed discussion on the basis and inheritance of yellow coloring in clivias.) Without the orange-red pigments, one merely sees the carotenoids, which are yellow. Mutations like this are usually recessive and can occur at several positions along the pathway, meaning they could involve different genes. They may be carried in wild populations but are not expressed except in those rare instances when a plant becomes homozygous for the same mutation. Breeding two yellow plants together can result in orange flowers unless both parents possess mutations for the same alleles. Yellow coloring tends to be pale, usually a creamy butter color with some flowers having a deeper yellow throat. Just as there are many different forms of flavonoids, there can also be different types of carotenoids. In daffodils, all the colors except white are different sorts of carotenoids. There are yellow, orange, pink, and red carotenoids in those flowers.

There are many different shades and tones of yellow, and within this one color breeders are finding an expanding range of shades. One goal of modern clivia breeding was to produce flowers of an intense, vibrant gold color, but for a long time that goal seemed to be unobtainable. It was only in 1999 and 2000 that golden-yellow clivias appeared in a few nurseries. Honey-toned or amber-yellow clivias, which could result from differences in the carotenoids, also occur. At the other end of the spectrum are the palest yellows, which breeders are selecting for in an effort to achieve a white clivia plant. That goal is as elusive as achieving golden-yellow clivias was once. Yellowish green clivias are quite rare but do seem to be turning up in various collections. The hope is that the greenish flowers will eventually lead to better deep green blooms.

YELLOW CLIVIA HISTORIES

There is much confusion about the lineages of yellow clivias, though a few breeding lines are relatively well known. However, there has been little attempt to keep pedigrees of many yellow clivias straight, and the ancestry of most yellow plants is simply not known or else is someone's best guess. Myths are passed down from grower to grower, and the same plant names are often used interchangeably, sometimes for specific cultivars, sometimes for variable seed strains. There is little recognition that two quite different clones may have the same name. This would not be too bad if all yellows resulted from the same mutations at the same locus or position on the chromosome, but there are many loci where mutations can result in yellow flowers. When two yellows carrying mutations at different loci are mated, they compensate for each other. The result is a series of often mediocre, orange wild-type flowers. Nevertheless, there is more information on the history of specific yellow lines of breeding than there is on standard orange clivias.

MODERN YELLOW STRAINS

The yellow clivias are so much in demand that until recently there were simply not enough plants to go around. There was little breeding of yellows, division of mature plants was not fast enough, and tissue culture techniques were either not advanced enough or were closely held secrets. Several enterprising nurserymen in different parts of the world realized the potential of mass producing yellow clivias and were able to produce seed strains that guaranteed yellow flowers. Consequently, the price of yellow clivias, while still high, has dropped markedly in some areas. If the trends continue we expect that within the next decade or so there will be little difference in price between orange and yellow clivias.

Solomone Yellows

Despite the very narrow genetic base caused by starting with a very small breeding population, Solomone has been able to produce amazing diversity in his yellow clivias. Some of these are described in chapter 13 dealing with novelty clivias. Nearly all yellow clivias are soft, creamy yellow colors that fade toward the tepal edges, and most of those Solomone has produced are also of that type. However, among the thousands of plants that he flowers every year are some unusual treasures — flowers of a deeper yellow with unusual warm amber or honey-colored undertones. In most of these cases, the color is married to flowers of good shape that are produced in large heads. Most of the yellow clivias that are sold in retail nurseries in the United States as Solomone Yellows are first bloom seedlings that are shipped in bud. There is the potential for finding some superb plants in the seedlings offered for sale from the Solomone range, some of which will surpass the named varieties described below. Among Solomone's great yellows are some particularly fine variegated plants. Unfortunately, he does not name the plants, although in some cases he may assign them a number.

Jim Holmes's New Dawn strain

Halfway around the globe in South Africa, Jim Holmes also realized that seed production of yellow clivias was a good idea. He grows his clivias outside the small university town of Stellenbosch in a nursery situated in a picturesque valley surrounded by towering mountains. During my visit in September 1999, the mountains were blanketed in snow, not the usual image of the African countryside. Holmes's background is in horticulture, and over the years he has hybridized plants of many types. He has an excellent eye for flowers and an uncanny ability to see how to make a breakthrough hybrid. He now has an international reputation for the quality of his yellow hybrids.

As Holmes relates it, nearly all of his genetic material is descended from two plants. One plant had originally been collected in 1907 from Karkloof Falls, then maintained and passed on to members of the Dodd family. It was a very prolific grower with flowers on a short stem and most florets facing one direction. Holmes was able to get a small division of the plant in 1976, but it did not flower until two years later. The plant was self-sterile so he needed pollen from another yellow clone. The Dodd clone flowered in August, while the late Willie Olivier's clone flowered in September, and although both were too late for his plant, Holmes saved pollen from his plant in the refrigerator and then borrowed the Olivier plant to receive the stored pollen. As they are wont to do, the individual flowers started to collapse after pollination, and a maid, intent on tidying up, cut off the pollinated inflorescence and threw it away. Holmes had to repeat the entire procedure the following year and fruits were set.

Half of the seedlings from Holmes's original crossing were sent to Japan. Equal quantities of yellow and orange flowers were obtained in the first generation, and when the yellow offspring were intercrossed the numbers of orange-flowered plants dropped to between 5 and 10 percent. After a few generations, the offspring are all now yellow. Holmes calls his plants the New Dawn strain, although most of the world refers to them as Holmes's Yellows. The best plants in the strain yield inflorescences with thirty-eight to thirty-nine flowers in a spherical umbel. The inflorescences have a light vanilla scent. Some plants produce two umbels at one time. There are sometimes rare mutations or combinations of genes that appear in large-scale breeding programs that can be considered breakthroughs. One such rarity is the color green. Holmes has been able to select out two different all-green clones from his yellow breeding program. He has crossed them together, so the potential for an all-green strain has become a real possibility.

I asked Holmes what his goals in breeding involve. He described his ideal plant as being of intermediate size but with broad leaves and a good, full head of flowers on the umbel. Each flower should have broad, overlapping tepals that are flat, not recurved nor cupped. While such individuals appear in his strain, it needs to be line bred and refined so that a much higher percentage of the seedling will have the desired characteristics. Some of the better individuals have been given cultivar epithets and are discussed below. Holmes says he also looks for form as well as color. He is breeding toward dark, rich yellows and pure whites, and of course also sees a need for good reds. Further in the future he sees a place for better cut flowers, which need lighter stems and fewer flowers on them

During the late 1990s, Holmes harvested between ten and twenty thousand seeds each season. Much of that crop is sold directly as seed to overseas middlemen, who in turn resell some to hobbyists. The rest is used to produce nursery stock. While pollinating, collecting, and cleaning seed involves much manual labor, it is still more economical to raise a good stock of seed from high quality parents than to tissue culture a single clone. One should remember, however, that it takes ten to twenty years to build the foundation stock to do this.

YELLOW CLONES AND CULTIVARS

Specially selected yellow clones have high value, so they were given individual clonal and cultivar names. Sometimes they even received more than one name. Hence, there is a much larger number of named yellow clivias compared to the standard orange varieties.

'Aurea'
This is a popular name in common usage all over the world. Even within the same part of the world the name may be used indiscriminately for many different cultivars. One major clone in Australia is called 'Aurea', although there are other yellow clivias in Australia and also in Californian with that name. In other cases, Aurea is used to refer not to cultivars but rather to several entire but different strains of yellow flowers. This has led to considerable confusion about plants labeled as 'Aurea' and is a powerful argument that an official registry needs to be set up for clivias. The Australian clone of 'Aurea' was introduced or bred by a Mr. Dearing of Victoria. He used this plant as a parent crossing it with *improved* orange *Clivia miniata*. The resulting offspring were of course not yellow, but were nevertheless good enough to be named for his children. One cultivar, *Clivia miniata* 'Ailisa Dearing', is said to be a deep apricot color. In the next generation yellow re-emerged.

'Bodnant Yellow' FCC/RHS and 'Bodnant Variety' AM/RHS

Lord Aberconway named two cultivars after his famous garden at Bodnant, and both received Awards of Merit when shown before the Royal Horticultural Society. Later 'Bodnant Yellow' was elevated to a First Class Certificate. The plant I have under the name 'Bodnant' has an interesting history. At the outbreak of the Second World War, the Royal Botanic Gardens, Kew sent some of their most precious plants over to the NYBG for safekeeping. Among them was a clivia plant named *Clivia kewensis* var. 'Bodnant'. I first saw this flowering in the Enid A. Haupt Conservatory at the NYBG in the mid-1980s. As only two of the Bodnant clivias were named, I have always assumed that this flower was, in fact, 'Bodnant Variety' AM/RHS. There were two pots, each with a single growth and an umbel of creamy white flowers. After some discussion with the curator, I learned that since receiving the plant, they had succeeded in only increasing it to three single growths. There followed an intensive negotiation with the result that one clivia plant was exchanged with the UCI Arboretum (where I worked until 1996) for a collection of over two hundred rare African bulbous species for the NYBG. When the plant was brought to southern California, it was placed outside in a shade structure where other clivias were growing. The plant started to flourish, producing many offsets, and it flowered regularly. Under southern Californian conditions, the flowers were creamy yellow rather than the very pale shade that had developed in the conservatory. The UCI Arboretum made pollen freely available to various local clivia enthusiasts for their breeding programs, and Comstock in particular made good use of it.

The famous garden at Bodnant, after which these cultivars are named, is reputed to have bred its stock by combining an original yellow plant from Kew with a good orange cultivar. In fact, the plant that Bodnant received was already the product of that sort of breeding program as implemented by Mr. Raffill of Kew. All of the first generation offspring must have been orange, but further breeding produced other fine yellows and pastel colors. Flowers of 'Bodnant Variety' AM/RHS are a little on the small side but are very shapely,

Clivia miniata 'Charlotte'.

and its progeny readily inherit this good form. It is trumpet shaped with the distal half of the tepals reflexing and lying in the same plane. There is good overlap between the parts, and spacing on the umbel is excellent. Color under southern Californian conditions is a smooth pale cream. Natural spread of individual flowers is 3 inches (7.5 cm) with each petal 1 inch (2.5 cm) at its widest. The sepals are 3/4 inch (2 cm) wide. Tepals are somewhat pointed. The umbel is held low on a 15-inch (37.5-cm) peduncle but displayed between the opposite ranks of leaves. Leaves are 24 inches (62 cm) long and 2 inches (5 cm) wide and gently arched. This has turned out to be a vigorous plant that regularly produces, albeit consecutively, two umbels during the season.

'Cape Butterfly'
Among the cultivars with the largest flowers to emerge from the

Clivia miniata 'Gold Star'.

New Dawn strain of Holmes is one called 'Cape Butterfly'. Individual flowers have a natural spread of nearly 4 inches (10 cm). The petals are very broad and measure about 1½ inches (3.75 cm) across their widest part.

'Cape Snowflake'
Also from Holmes's stable, this is said to be among the whitest flowers to date.

'Charlotte'
One of Conway's yellow clivias, 'Charlotte' has quite narrow tepals with an open flower of cream and a deeper yellow throat. Sepals are narrower than petals but both parts are narrow ovals with rounded tips. The flower is relatively flat and open with almost no overlap between the tepals.

'Citrina'
This name should be reserved for the yellow clone that Watson described as *Clivia miniata citrina* in 1899.

'Col Pitman'
This is a yellow clivia plant that originated in Australia. Kenneth Smith (1993) has related the history of this cultivar. The plant was named for the late Colin Pitman of Civic Trees Nursery, where it was flowered from a block of seed-grown orange clivias. Seed was sown in 1983 and appears to have been very vigorous. By 1989 it was large enough to be divided, resulting in four flowering-sized plants and one smaller division. The divisions have actively formed additional offsets. Flowers are clear yellow with a deeper yellow stain in the throat. The broad, overlapping flowers flare, and they are borne in a large hemispherical umbel.

'Gold Star'
I selected this clone from among several spider seedlings that were flowering for the first time at Solomone's nursery. It has an excellent shape for a spider-shaped clivia plant. The narrow tepals flare out to form a widely spreading flower that does not twist asymmetrically as so often occurs among the spiders. This plant only carried eight flowers on its maiden umbel, but this number should increase as the plant ages. The flowers are widely spaced, showing off its spider form. Each flower has a natural spread of 4 inches (10 cm). Petals are 3/4 inch (2 cm) wide and 3 inches (7.5 cm) long. Sepals have a similar length but are only 1/2 inch (1.25 cm) wide. The creamy tepals each have a yellow-amber streak that stretches from the base to the tip of each sepal giving an overall deeper impression of yellow than that normally found in the yellow spiders. As is common with most spiders, this spider's leaves are narrow—only 1 1/2 inches (3.75 cm) wide—and 20 inches (50 cm) long.

'Green Bird'
Here we have a distinctively different clivia plant from Comstock's, which borders on being a true green spider. The long narrow tepal

parts expand and flare out, but it is the distinct green flush and deeper green throats that catch one's eye. The number of flowers on the umbel could be greater, but this cultivar is an excellent place from which to start breeding greens.

'Green Grace'

Comstock was lucky to find this most unusual and desirable yellow clivia plant at a local nursery. The plant has relatively narrow tepals that all reflex backwards making for a flattened flower with recurved distal portions. I saw a similarly shaped flower at Anna Meyer's, which she referred to as being a *Nerine* type. What make Comstock's flower even more desirable is the emerald-green star that occupies much of the throat, although one can hardly use the term *throat* for such a flat flower.

'Green Scene'

Since the mid-1990s many breeders have started to find yellow clivias with green throats. There is a tendency to call them *Yellow Green Girls,* but that name has already been used for a cultivar and is not admissible. 'Green Scene' is one of Comstock's selections. The flowers open with a distinct green flush in the throat, and while the amount of green tends to fade somewhat as the flower matures, a hint of green remains throughout the life of the flower. The perianth has rounded tips to the tepals, and the cultivar carries a full umbel of well-spaced flowers.

'Howick Yellow' (synonym: 'Mare's Yellow')

This is a famous yellow clone from South Africa for which we have a fairly detailed history, although there is some confusion now about which are divisions of the original plant and which are seed strains derived from that plant. Sometimes the same name is used to desig-nate both. Mrs. Sarah A. Mare settled in Natal, South Africa, in the 1850s. Grace Mare, her daughter, lived in the town of Howick, which is near a famous waterfall of the same name. Grace had a next-door

Clivia miniata 'Green Bird'.

neighbor, an Indian woman, who called upon her one day offering to sell an unusual specimen of *Clivia* that she had found growing below the waterfall. (Today there is no forest below the falls; it was cut away a long time ago.) The year was 1896, and the plant had a yellow flower. Grace bought the plant for half-a-crown (thirty pennies then), probably a fair price at that time. The plant has remained in the family for over one hundred years. Initially Grace and then the family gave suckers of the plant away to many of their friends; occasional divisions were later sold for seven shillings and sixpence each. No one thought about breeding with it—the plant was merely grown as a novelty. This clone does not make particularly shapely blooms, and has in fact been called an ugly strappy flower with long narrow leaves. 'Howick Yellow' produces elongated seedpods.

Clivia miniata 'Green Grace'.

Gert Wiese married into the Mare family but was initially not very interested in their clivias. However, he did like plants, and in 1990 or 1991 obtained a clump of 'Howick Yellow' from a cousin-in-law. The plant arrived with a seedpod containing two seeds. Wiese planted them and was rewarded with one very fine orange seedling. The second plant he recalled being a "miserable little thing" that took six years to flower. It turned out, however, to be yellow. Along the way Wiese became enthused about clivias and joined the ranks of the obsessed. Today he has an enormous collection with thousands of seedlings, many of which carry 'Howick Yellow' genes in their parentage.

This cultivar actually goes by two names. Thurston refers to this clone as 'Mare's Yellow' in her book *The Clivia*. Wiese prefers to use the name 'Howick Yellow', and I found more people in South Africa using that name than 'Mare's Yellow'.

'Kirstenbosch Yellow'
Another well-known clone named after the world-famous South African botanical garden in Cape Town that carries light yellow flowers with a deeper throat. The somewhat narrow tepals open out and reflex slightly. The flowers are strongly fragrant and, according to Duncan (1999) of the National Botanical Institute at Kirstenbosch, reminiscent of azalea scent. Origins of the plant are obscure. Leaves are broader than many other yellows, but one should remember that yellow clivias tend to have much narrower leaves than their modern orange counterparts. 'Kirstenbosch Yellow' was obtained in 1951 from a commercial plant nursery in the Cape. Presumably the color of 'Kirstenbosch Yellow' is due to a mutation or recombination of genes that appeared in cultivated stock. Seedlings bred from this plant have been widely disseminated via Kirstenbosch's novel plant introduction program. The plant breeds true, producing yellow seedlings.

Duncan explained to me why it took him four years to get a good photograph of 'Kirstenbosch Yellow'. During the first attempt at getting a photograph the film had not been correctly loaded into the camera and did not advance. Photographs were successfully taken in the second year, but the film was accidentally left in a pocket and ended up in the laundry. After taking the pictures during the third season, the camera was stolen before the film was removed. In the fourth year all went well and he was able to get his pictures.

'Leiden'
A good feature of this cultivar is the globular cluster of flowers with more than twenty florets in the umbel. Another Conway yellow clivia, 'Leiden' has flowers with relatively undisciplined undulate and twisted tepals with pointed tips. The arrangement of flowers on the umbel is one of its strong features, and the resulting full cluster

Clivia miniata 'Lemon Cloud'.

makes for a very pleasant inflorescence. The tips of the tepals recurve somewhat, so the spaces of the flower sphere tend to be filled in.

'Lemon Chiffon'
This is a very fine ycllow offered by Conway with nicely formed flowers that have an excellent shape and broad overlapping tepals. It is among the original clones that Dave Conway found in the court-yard of a parking garage (see chapter 5). The tips of the tepals are pointed, and they open outward to form a classic trumpet shape. The umbel carries up to twenty flowers on the umbel. The flowers are somewhat crowded and form a hemispherical mass.

'Lemon Cloud'
This is a very fine mid-yellow clivia plant produced by Comstock. It was bred from the orange 'Adam' by the yellow 'Bodnant

Variety'AM/RHS and shows many of the good qualities of each parent. I particularly like the flaring, almost flat flowers with their rounded tepal tips. The golden-yellow stamen filaments help give the impression of a deep golden throat. This choice cultivar should be useful for further breeding.

'Lessa'

A deeper yellow example from Conway that has relatively narrow flower parts. The sepals have somewhat pointed tips, while those of the petals are more rounded. The florets do not open as widely as 'Charlotte', giving a more traditional flower shape. Heads contain some sixteen to twenty flowers.

'Megan'

Another of the better Conway yellows in terms of the shape of individual florets, which have broader overlapping tepals with rounded tips. The widely flaring flowers are evenly arranged on a hemispherical umbel. They are spaced so no gaps appear between the flowers of the umbel, a feature that many hybridizers strive to obtain. There are less than twenty florets on the umbel, and perhaps this can be bred to other flowers with a higher flower count so that the yellows are brought closer to perfection.

'Mvuma Yellow'

This is a curious clone that was found near the Tongaat River in Natal in approximately 1980. It produces a very shapely flower but on a not very dense head. Flowers open with a greenish tinge that fades to a yellow flower. There is a faint scent. What is unusual about this plant is that its berries have a faint orange tinge, suggesting the formation of some anthocyanin in the plant instead of the pure yellow fruits normally found on yellow clivias. In addition, this is a clone that does not breed true, producing orange flowers even when self-pollinated. The anthocyanin pigment in clivia berries (cyanidin) is different from that coloring the flowers (pelargonidin). This difference suggests that the mutation causing the yellow flower occurs after the branch point in the chain of reactions producing cyanidin (see chapter 6). Why selfing of the clone should result in a conversion to orange flowers is not well understood.

'Natal Yellow'
Cynthia Giddy operated a plant nursery in Natal and was globally renowned, primarily for her work with cycads, but she was also involved in propagating clivias. She called one of her widely disseminated yellow clones 'Natal Yellow'. This clone has shapely florets with overlapping tepal bases. The tepals reflex slightly. It opens quite green and then fades to yellow. The clone is self-sterile and does not produce yellows when mated with most other yellows, suggesting that it contains a mutant allele at a different locus from that in most other yellows. 'Natal Yellow' is a vigorous plant, producing lots of offsets, and it has been vegetatively propagated.

'San Diego Yellow'
This flower has good shape and arrangement of its flaring creamy flowers. The sepals are narrow and quite pointed, whereas the petals are substantially broader. One might prefer a little more overlap between the various parts. It is another Conway selection, but not of his own breeding.

'Sir John Thouron'
Among the largest and most respected spring flower shows is the Philadelphia Flower Show run by the Pennsylvania Horticultural Society each spring. One plant has been a repeat winner for many years, a large, pale yellow clivia called 'Sir John Thouron.' Two enormous clumps are usually displayed each year at the show. The plants are about 42 inches (105 cm) tall, including the pot. As many as ten umbels of flowers may be present on each plant. The head is well filled with trumpet-shaped flowers. Color is a very soft butter yellow with the throat shaded a deeper yellow.

Sir John was a British man who settled in Pennsylvania, and this clivia plant came from his collection. Divisions of the plant were offered by White Flower Farm, a famous American nursery and mail-order company, at the astounding price of U.S. $950 for a flowering-sized division. It is rumored that over thirty plants were sold at that price. Another rumor is that a movie star purchased the plant, flying all the way to Connecticut to the nursery to pick it up. This cultivar was bred in England and seems reminiscent of the Bodnant varieties. While it is a very fine flower, similar quality varieties are often available in the various yellow strains that currently appear in southern Californian nurseries at much lower prices.

'Supernova'
In this cultivar narrow tepals start to approach the shape of a spider flower. There is almost no overlap between the tepals, and they flare to display the gaps between their perianth parts. Tepals are pointed. The flowers are cream, merging to a deeper yellow at the tepal bases. Flowers are nicely arranged in the umbel. The wider spacing shows off the narrow form of the tepals much better than if it were a crowded umbel. This is a Conway introduction.

'Vico Yellow' (synonym: 'Smithers' Yellow')
This is a historic plant as it is among the first tissue-cultured *Clivia* cultivars offered in the general trade. The Miyoshi Company in Yamanashi, Japan, has the distinction of bringing this clone to market. Sir Peter Smithers, better known for his hybridizing work with nerines, magnolias, and lilies also bred this clivia plant. A detailed history of this plant has been published previously and I will review it only briefly here (Smithers 1995). In November 1970, Sir Peter obtained three different clones of the so-called *Clivia* Kewensis group. Pollen from the pale clone called 'Kewensis Cream' was applied to the orange flowers of the other two clones. Seeds were set, but when the plants finally flowered they were—not surprisingly—varying shades of orange. Some seeds from these were discarded under the greenhouse

Clivia miniata 'Vico Yellow'.

bench. They somehow survived, and when they flowered, two turned out to be yellow. The better clone grew well, and an offset was exchanged with Dr. Hirao in Japan. Following Hirao's death, that plant was transferred to Yoshikazu Nakamura in Japan. He was taken with the plant, considering it a "world beater," and he used it in his own breeding program. This plant is regarded as one of the best yellow clivias available. In Japan it is often referred to as 'Smithers' Yellow'.

Under southern Californian conditions, 'Vico Yellow' is a pale creamy flower with a darker yellow throat. The tepals are somewhat pointed but arranged into a well-overlapped, bugle-shaped floret. They are grouped into a relatively dense head on the umbel. Individual flowers of 'Vico Yellow' are somewhat wavy and less disciplined than those of 'Bodnant Variety', with which it probably shares a similar ancestry, but the flower is very much larger. While 'Vico Yellow' is a very fine flower, I have seen many comparable or even better plants in the stud collections of other yellow breeders. This clone has been so widely disseminated all over the world that we can expect it to play an important role in the future breeding of yellow clivias. There is a sister seedling called 'Vico Gold' that may be a much deeper yellow and that could therefore be much more important in the struggle to make deeper yellow colors.

'Watkin's Yellow'
Another well-known South African clone, Watkin's Yellow is a name that is bandied about by many of the clivia specialists. Thurston gives the longer name of 'Watkin's Yellow Glow' and points out that its origins are obscure. This is a much shapelier flower than 'Howick Yellow', and the umbel is well filled with florets. Tepals are broad and overlapping, and flowers tend to be bugle shaped. Plants tend to have shorter leaves and bear rounded berries. It is not clear if 'Watkin's Golden Glow' is the same clone as 'Watkin's Yellow'. Watkin's Yellow is also sometimes used as a strain name.

'Yellow Showers'
I am not sure that I like this cultivar. It is another of the "parking garage yellows." Also a flower with rather narrow spidery tepals, this does not have the charm of 'Supernova'. Individual flowers are not really pendent but twisted at the level of the ovary so that each floret faces either outwards or downwards, leaving a large gap at the top of the umbel. Conway has listed 'Yellow Showers' at his nursery.

The next decade should see yellow clivias taking their place alongside the orange ones, and they should lose their elite position. All of the breeding currently underway should produce newer shapes and both deeper and paler colors, but it will still be some time before strongly colored golden-yellow flowers become available to the hobbyists. Likewise, it may be a long time before one can go to the corner nursery and buy a chartreuse-flowered plant. Tissue culture may, I hope, allow some of these clones wider availability. Until then, set some seeds on your own yellow clivias and see if something novel emerges.

Chapter Ten

Standard *Clivia miniata* Hybrids: Pastel Colors

THE YELLOW CLIVIAS have always been considered the most elite, yet other colors exist that seem to be just as unusual, but those colors have received little attention. Among them are the pink shades. In reality a good pink *Clivia* specimen is far more rare than a good yellow. Perhaps the problem is that there has been a continuum of shades ranging from pale pink to dark orange-red, and the pinks were therefore not as distinctly different as the yellows. This seems to be changing now.

As yellow clivias have become more common, hobbyists have started to look for other novelties. In recent years they have focused on pastel-colored clivias, in particular those tones that range from apricot and peach through to pink. These pastel-colored plants are still very scarce, and we do not really understand much about the production and inheritance of this type of coloration. There may in fact be several quite different forms of color inheritance that give rise to the pastel colors. Some of the soft pastel colors have been found in wild plants, but this type of pigmentation has also appeared spontaneously in several breeding programs scattered around the world. One major focus in this pastel group should be the production of clear baby-pink flowers.

Pink pigmentation is relatively common in standard clivia flowers and is usually visible as the flowers mature. In some *Clivia miniata* there can be striking flowers with pink blotches that develop on the tepals while the border of the petal remains banded with orange-red. Often there is also a strong, central, orange-red stripe. The flowers that produce these color patterns tend to be inconsistent, and flower color is strongly influenced by the weather. The development of color in these flowers is due to the breakdown of carotenoid pigments in those regions of the tepal that develop pink coloration. Presumably the pink color is clarified as the yellow carotenoid pigments fade to ivory or white.

In one pastel flower of *Clivia miniata* 'Morning Light' where Comstock, Griesbach, and I analyzed the anthocyanin pigments, we found a preponderance of pelargonidin-3-rutinoside, whereas pelargonidin-3-glucoside seemed to dominate in the darker orange-red flowers. Whether the pelargonidins in 'Morning Light' are the same and in the same proportions in other pastel flowers is not known. Pink or pinkish forms are also known to occur in the other three species, but those flowers' pigments have not been analyzed.

Flowers in this group form a continuum ranging from apricot to pink, and while it is sometimes difficult to categorize a single bloom, one can generally place the flowers into one of three distinct categories. There is some confusion because the terms apricot, peach, and pink have not been defined before and have been used interchangeably. I would like to suggest that the terms be used separately to encompass the following.

APRICOT. Flowers in this group are those that have a strong base color of creamy yellow with an overlay of pastel orange containing a hint of pink. The flower color looks like a very pale orange-pink with strong tones of amber. Another way of describing apricot is as honey amber with a hint of pink. This is quite a different color from those in the paler pastel oranges found in the standard clivias.

PEACH. In peach flowers the pink is more obvious. Perhaps this is due to decreases in the yellow carotenoid content and increases in the concentrations of pink pigment. There is still some yellow in the background.

OTHER PASTELS. I use this as a relatively loose group to include those flowers that appear to be different from the apricot- and peach-toned flowers. This is where the rare pink clivias and the even rarer mauve-toned flowers fit. Perhaps one day there will be separate pink sections and mauve sections. In this group the flowers have relatively little in the way of yellow carotenoids so that the background color is whitish; with the epithelial overlay, the pink or mauve coloration clearly comes through.

As one might expect, there is a continuum of shades ranging from one group to the next, and even within a group, color may change depending on the season, climatic conditions, and age of the flower. Generally, however, flowers can be assigned quite easily and comfortably to one of the three categories.

There has not been as much effort to understand the basis of pastel colors as there has been trying to understand the yellow clivias. Pastels could be the result of an increased production of pelargonidin-3-rutinoside or simply a blockage of production of pelargonidin-3-glucoside. Perhaps there are several different ways to achieve flowers with these unusual pastel colorings. Pastel shades have originated spontaneously in many different parts of the world. The inheritance of peach coloration must, like yellow, be due to mutations at several different sites along the anthocyanin pathways. Unnamed peach-colored flowers have also appeared in Solomone's program; some in his Charm series have a nice white throat and a few possess relatively clear, pink tepal tips.

Our understanding of the breeding behavior of pastel clivias is not well advanced. Comstock has found that when two of his peach-flowered types were mated that all of the offspring were peach. But when a peach flower was mated with a yellow clivia plant, the offspring were all the normal orange colors. It sounds as if pink color results from the blockage of a pigment pathway and involves homozygous recessive genes, but this explanation is probably an oversimplification. Other peach clivias are known to produce orange offspring when selfed, and some produce a percentage of peach-colored seedlings. Pink and pastel forms also exist for *Clivia caulescens*, *C. gardenii*, and *C. nobilis*. As *C. nobilis* and *C. caulescens* also have cyanidin flavones in their flowers, and as non-miniata species can lurk in the background of some pastel flowers, it is also possible that cyanidin flavones are important for pastel color. Whether the colors in pastel flowers are based on the same pigments is not known. Some of the pictures I have seen of the pink forms of the species show very clear pink coloration with little or no yellow tones in the background. The leaf bases of seedlings from pastel breeding can be a range of different colors; some seedlings have no pigment, and others are quite dark. Generally the plants without pigment will probably yield pastels, but if there is a yellow clivia plant in the background, the flowers could be yellow. It will take some careful study tracing the fate of various seedlings from these breeding programs before generalizations, if any, can be made.

According to Chubb, there were four peach-colored *Clivia miniata* flowers that were originally collected in the wild: 'Ndwedwe Gamma Peach', 'Gail Reed's Peach', 'Naude's Peach', and 'Chubb's Peach'. Many others that are totally unrelated to these four clones have now emerged in various breeding programs. No one knows whether or not pastel colors are due to specific mutations or merely to novel combinations of pre-existing genes.

Relatively few pastels have been named. They are as scarce—if not more so—than the yellow clivias were several decades ago. Growers tend to hold on to them tightly. Hybridizers are still learning how to make them, and it will be several years before they are mass-produced like the yellow varieties are today. Nakamura has shown photographs of some of his excellent pink clivias, but almost nothing else is known of the pinks in Japan.

NAMED PASTEL CLIVIAS

'Angela'
A soft, medium-toned peach with a distinct creamy yellow throat, this is one of Conway's pastels that has shapely flowers with over-lapping segments. Petals are rounded, and the pointed sepals have an obvious mucro. A little low on flower count, umbels average only ten flowers.

'Anna Meyer's Peach'
This is an apricot-colored clone that appeared spontaneously in Meyer's breeding program. The ancestral plant from which most of her clivias have been derived does have considerable pink and pastel coloring combined with the orange. Meyer claims that her first "peach" was achieved by using yellow pollen. She relates that when this plant first flowered, she did not think much of the amber honey color with pink tones until a visitor brought it to her attention. He wanted to buy the plant, offering an exorbitant amount. That offer made her look again, and she kept the plant, which she now regards as something special. It is self-fertile and routinely pollinated, but its breeding capabilities have yet to be explored.

'Avis' Charm'
I found this unusual plant in South Africa at the nursery of Avis Meresman and Danie Nel and was fortunate to be able to purchase it. The size and shape is reminiscent of the Charm series. Its throat is ivory and extends well up the tepal. The pointed tepal tips are a dull salmon-pink. The plant has very narrow leaves.

'Being Peach'
A very fine, pastel-colored clivia plant of Comstock's breeding that comes close to being a true pink. It was bred from 'Morning Light' by 'Tessa', two peach parents. The tepals are relatively narrow and pointed with an apricot throat. The sepals support the very wide,

Clivia miniata 'Anna Meyer's Peach'. Anna Meyer's home, Gauteng Province, South Africa.

Clivia miniata 'Avis' Charm'.

rounded petals. The throat area is very small and ivory-colored. Individual flowers are wide and flaring. Flower count in the umbel is small, which can be forgiven in light of the superior coloration.

'Chubb's Peach'

Thurston relates that this clone was originally found in the Ingwahlume Valley near Eston in KwaZulu-Natal in about 1950. Petals and sepals are relatively narrow, and the sepals are pointed. The plant is self-fertile, and when it is self-pollinated, about one-third of its offspring yield peach colors. Chubb, who owns the plant, has backcrossed the first generation peach seedlings back to the mother plant, and several extremely good and improved peach flowers have already resulted from his work. I grow some of those seedlings, and most have darkly pigmented leaf bases suggesting that many of the seedlings will be orange to red. When 'Chubb's Peach' was crossed with a wild yellow *Clivia miniata* called 'Ndwedwe Alpha Thurston', all the resultant seedlings had darkly pigmented bases. Comstock has made similar

Clivia miniata 'Cynthia Ann'.

observations after putting yellow clivias onto his own peach-colored flowers. 'Chubb's Peach' is vigorous and makes offsets.

'Cynthia Ann'
A very nice flower in large rounded umbels, it opens a soft cream with pink tones. As the flower matures, it rapidly takes on deeper pink tones. In the mature flower, the sepals are more darkly colored than the petals. The petals have a darker midline and may have a slight notch at their apices. The sepals are narrow but have rounded tips. The throat is obvious only in matured flowers and is creamy and quite small. This is a fine Conway selection.

'Dorothy'
One of Conway's introductions, this plant bears soft apricot flowers with pinkish tones. The plant has a somewhat compressed

Clivia miniata 'Ellexa'.

inflorescence. When the flowers open, they are a very pale ivory with pale orange blush. As the flower develops, it gets stronger pink tones in the petals while the pointed sepals deepen to a mid-orange color. Flowers are 2³/₄ inches (7 cm) wide. The petals themselves are just under 1 inch (2.5 cm) wide, and the sepals about ¹/₂ inch (1.25 cm) across. Fruits are bright cerise.

'Ellexa'
One of Conway's pastels that I would classify as typical of the apricot-colored clivias as I define them. This plant produces umbels that can carry more than seventeen flowers. Flowers are arranged in a tight umbel. Individual flowers are narrow trumpets that tend to approach tulip shapes. Petals are broad and well rounded, and the broad sepals acute with a distinct mucro at the tip. Both sepals and petals are the same shade of honey amber with apricot tones. There

is no obvious throat to the flowers. Unlike many other pastel clivias, there is little change in tone with flower maturation.

'Emmie Wittig's Pink'
Some call this 'Wittig's Pink' or 'Emmie Wittig's Peach', but on that flowering as grown by Des Andersson in Pietermaritzburg, South Africa, it was the clearest and truest pink I have ever seen. Flowers of this clone that were just opening at Sean Chubb's Nursery had definite peach tones, but that may just have been because they were younger. This clone is self-fertile but is said to yield orange-red flowers when self-pollinated. It is not clear how big a sample of seed was actually grown, and it is difficult to make predictions based on small samples. Other pastel-flowered clivias such 'Chubb's Peach' yield a percentage of orange flowers too, but they do yield some that are peach.

'Four Marys'
McNeil made this hybrid with its very peculiar color pattern. He considered it his best clivia plant and described it as a "big open head of apple blossom pink flowers." The flowers open widely and are a soft yellow color. As the florets age they take on pink tones, particularly on the reverse of the flower segments, so that a pink flush appears to be shining through the flower. Eventually some pink color also flushes the inner face. As flowers in the umbel mature at different rates, the entire head of flowers presents a patchwork of flowers all at different stages of color development. McNeil recorded that he had crossed pollen of *Crinum powellii* onto a *Clivia miniata* plant. He must have been disappointed that the plant looked just like a clivia because he self-pollinated *C. miniata* 'Four Marys' hoping to see some segregation of *Crinum* characteristics in the second generation. Unfortunately, the next generation of seedlings showed only clivia characteristics. Few believe that McNeil was able to make intergeneric *Clivia* hybrids because the seedlings always resembled the pod parent. He seldom bothered to emasculate or isolate the flowers he pollinated. There is something about the color pattern of *C. miniata*

Clivia miniata 'Emmie Wittig's Pink'.

'Four Marys' though that is reminiscent of *C. nobilis*, where anthocyanins are also often confined only to the outer faces of the tepals.
Despite the flowers that seem to be purely *C. miniata* in shape, it is
possible that *C. nobilis* features in its background. Blackbeard, who
supplied most of McNeil's original material, had made many complicated *Clivia* hybrids that featured *C. nobilis* in their ancestry.

In a letter written in February 1980 to Murphy, McNeil related
how he chose the cultivar name. When it first flowered, the umbel
had only four blossoms, and being a bit of a Scottish nationalist
("rebel" was the word McNeil used), he named it after Mary Queen of
Scots and her three ladies-in-waiting, Mary Beaton, Mary Seton, and
Mary Carmichael. McNeil also had an old flame, a missionary in the
Cameroons, named Mary Carmichael, so the flower commemorated
her as well. For the story of how this plant made its way to California,
see chapter 5.

'Gillian'

A very shapely, apricot toned flower originally from Anderson with a nice flaring shape. It had a reputation for being an almost white flower with a faint pink blush, but the examples I have seen have had darker apricot tones.

'Helen'

'Helen' is among those luscious flowers that are basically a very pale ivory cream painted over with tints of clear pink. The base of the flower is a deeper creamy yellow, but there is no obviously demarcated throat area. The flowers are widely flaring with broad, rounded petals that are sometimes deeply notched and at other times only slightly notched. Young flowers have a hint of green in their base. It ranks among the top flowers of the Conway pinks.

'Louisa'

Best described as a striped pink, 'Louisa' opens as a pale ivory flower that rapidly acquires a pink flush that develops into a full umbel of flaring flowers. The sepals rapidly develop a strong pink flush that is somewhat deeper in tone along the midline of the sepal. The rounded broad petals carry a paler pink petal blade, and there is a distinct, broad, central pink stripe running the length of the petal down to the edge of the small creamy throat. This is a color pattern in clivias that deserves to be developed and more fully explored, and I hope that the flower breeders will give it more attention. 'Louisa' is a great Conway plant.

'Mary Helen'

Another Conway peach-colored flower with widely flared petals that make a fairly flat flower, 'Mary Helen' makes a medium-sized truss of flowers. Florets are well colored when they open and do not seem to change much as the flower ages. The color is a shade of rich mid-peach. The throat is small, ivory-colored, and not clearly demarcated from the rest of the flower.

Clivia miniata 'Helen'.

'Miriam's Picotee'
Not really a picotee in the traditional sense of the word, this is a very interesting flower found by Miriam Metzler in South Africa. The flowers are a pale ivory cream brushed with tints of orange toward their edges.

'Moments of Mauve'
As clivia flowers age, the orange colors often start to fade leaving pink areas on the petals and sepals. In this chance seedling from the Belgian strain, the flowers open soft orange and then quickly start to change color, and for much of the flower's life the tepals carry mauve, lavender, and lilac tones. This is a clone selected from the modern Belgian strain sold in California. The medium-sized flowers themselves are nicely shaped with overlapping rounded segments that flare and are well spaced on the umbel. Leaves are

Clivia miniata 'Moments of Mauve'.

short and arching, about 10 inches (25 cm) in length and nearly 3 inches (7.5 mm) wide. This coloring has also been found in one of Conway's larger flowered seedlings, providing hope that one day hybridizers might be able to develop mauve and purple clivias. Some believe that Anderson may once have had a mauve-toned plant of *Clivia*.

'Morning Light'
This is an early Comstock find that has many good qualities. It blooms very early in the season and is among the more strongly scented clivias. It is also a wonderful parent. The flowers are quite large for a peach-type, and some are about 3 inches (7.5 cm) across. The well-rounded petals are 1 inch (2.5 cm) wide with a slight central notch, while the narrower sepals are 3/4 inch (2 cm) wide with a clearly defined mucro. The pistil is exerted well passed the stamens. Flowers open a clear peach and then change to a warm apricot as

Clivia miniata 'Morning Light'.

they flush with carotenoids. The peduncle is 24 inches (62 cm) tall and carries about twenty-five evenly arranged flowers in the umbel. Leaves are 2½ inches (6.25 cm) broad and 30 inches (75 cm) long. Leaves are more or less erect. Its large, well-formed flowers, as well as it performance as a parent rank it at the top for clivias in the peach to apricot range.

'Ndwedwe Gamma Peach'
The Ndwedwe region of KwaZulu-Natal has yielded two yellow clones in recent years. From a different part of Ndwedwe came this third clone, which was found in 1996. As the first two were called 'Alpha' and 'Beta', the next interesting plant was obviously 'Gamma'. The flowers are spiders. Thurston (1998) described the flower segments as being pale peach with a darker peach midstripe. As the flowers mature, the outer margins fade to pale cream. The throat is yellow. This is a self-fertile clone.

Clivia miniata 'Sunrise Sunset'.

'Pink Perfection'
The name Conway selected for this *Clivia* specimen implies that he was very taken with it. It makes a big umbel of full-shaped flowers with rounded petals and narrow pointed sepals, each tipped with a white mucro. Sepals and petals are a strong, medium pink peach evenly painted over the flower part. Petals flare and are partially reflexed for the distal third of their length. There is a large throat area of contrasting ivory. This plant has a number of good features and deserves to be used for breeding these pastel kinds of flowers.

'Sunrise Sunset'
A yellow flower painted over with hints of orange and pink, this Conway cultivar is aptly named. I would place the plant among the apricot-colored clivias. It is one of those plants that makes me wish

that routine tissue culture could be applied to any clivia plant to make them generally available to the gardening public. The sepals are exceptionally broad and have rounded tips, while the petals are almost diamond shaped, making a rather unusual arrangement for a clivia flower. The inside-facing surfaces of the flower parts are uniformly colored, but the tepal reverses are more deeply pigmented. When the flowers open they are almost all yellow with just a hint of peach. As they mature, they acquire a deep flush of peach. If a plant has two or more umbels of different ages they can look like different clones; thus the name 'Sunrise Sunset'.

'Tessa'
This is a peach-colored clivia plant from Conway He had originally used mixed pollen on yellow and orange flowers, harvesting about one thousand seedlings that he then grew up to flowering. In the group were several peach-colored flowers as well as several clones with various pink tones, one of which was 'Tessa'. This is among the lesser of the Conway pinks because the flower number in the umbel is low and the arrangement is poor. The individual flowers, however, are quite nice. They present a flaring tulip shape with incurved and overlapping floral parts. Sepals are slightly pointed and the petals are rounded. Tepal color is a medium pink peach that slowly fades toward the base. Overall impression is of a smoothly colored flower.

Breeding apricot, peach, and pink clivias will become a very fertile field for future endeavors. Hybridizers are currently in the initial exploratory phase of their breeding activities, and the plants—many of which have interesting patterns and color arrangements—are still considered to be novelties. The emergence of breeders who appear to be concentrating on this type, such as Chubb and Comstock, bodes well for future development. The pastel clivias are still very rare in the Orient but there is much interest in such flowers there too. Japanese clivia enthusiasts now come to California to scout for pastel breeding materials, and Conway's 'Helen' has been featured on the cover of a Chinese book. The demand for this type will increase, and once their seeds become available, the pink and pastel clivias will become widespread, and I expect even more breeding activity to follow.

Chapter Eleven

VARIEGATED CLIVIAS

V ARIEGATION OCCURS when leaves have areas with different
colors. Most commonly, parts of the leaf are green, and
other portions are white, yellow, or even a different shade
of green. There is usually a clear line of demarcation between areas
of different color. Many different kinds of variegation occur in
plants, and while some patterns are reproduced more or less regularly from leaf to leaf, the patchwork in others may be very irregular
and each leaf may have its own pattern. Variegation has been known
in *Clivia* for a long time, and plants with variegated leaves are much
sought after. They are still relatively expensive, although the price
has started to drop now that methods for producing them have been
worked out. A really good variegated clivia plant is quite beautiful,
incredibly expensive, and should be treated with the same respect as
any valuable piece of art. Only in this case it is also a living organism
and it requires a modicum of care.

In some parts of the world, particularly Japan and China, production of variegated clivias is almost an industry. Many nurseries
are involved, and the product is carefully raised and graded according to quality before being admitted to the market place. There has
long been an interest in variegated plants in the Orient, but the current infatuation with variegated clivias is relatively new, dating back
barely a century. Both standard and dwarf clivias have variegated
forms, but most breeders focus on dwarf variegated plants. Japanese

interest in all types of clivias parallels that of Europe, and importation of both *Clivia nobilis* and *C. miniata* occurred soon after their initial discovery. The original variegated dwarf clivia in Japan appears to have been a wide-leafed dwarf plant with narrow yellow striations that was imported from Belgium. This must have occurred at least near the start of the twentieth century because variegated plants were widespread by the 1930s. No one knows if the original variegated plant was imported as such or if it was a variant in a batch of seedlings that an astute plantsman then recognized as being something extraordinary. Variegation does occur repeatedly among clivia seedlings, but there has been continual production and selection of variegated clivia plants in Japan ever since then. This original variegated plant did not have very fine flowers. The peduncle was quite short and the flowers were buried between the leaves. The short peduncle is now a common trait with many of the dwarf clivias derived from Japanese stock. The stems may elongate somewhat after pollination but they never seem to get clear of the foliage.

The first variegated clivia plants were considered an oddity in Europe. In Japan, however, these plants must have been considered especially desirable because they became expensive and were really only affordable to the upper classes. During their imperialistic excursions into Manchuria and Korea, the ruling Japanese authorities took their variegated clivias with them. They were forced to leave some plants behind when they withdrew after being defeated in the Second World War, and the Chinese who acquired them also thought they were exceptional. Clivias were once again reserved for the privileged classes. Then came the Cultural Revolution in China. During this period of upheaval, horticulture was regarded as frivolous, and many plants and nurseries were destroyed. Somehow the variegated clivias survived. The excesses of the revolution were followed by a period of stability, and in the last decades of the twentieth century, horticulture was once again more acceptable.

Production of variegated clivias has expanded so that they are now available to a wider sector of the Chinese population. Today

A collage of variegated *Clivia miniata* leaves showing only some of the range of leaf patterns.

there are hobby groups and special clivia shows where individual breeders vie with each other to produce and exhibit the best plants.

Of course, some of the best plants are still exorbitant in price. Some Chinese hobbyists pay tens of thousands of dollars for extra special plants, but there is enough production so that the plants are not restricted to only the wealthy. The Japanese now visit Manchuria to buy variegated clivias because the best quality plants are said to be grown in Manchurian nurseries.

UNDERSTANDING VARIEGATION

Clivia leaves develop from a ridge of dividing cells produced by the apical meristem, the growing tip of the rhizome. The apical meristem itself produces leaf meristems as it grows. The leaf meristem is a strip of cells behind the shoot apex. Meristems, by their nature, are able to divide, and the leaf meristem starts off making the lamina or blade of the leaf. More cells adjacent to and below the strip later divide, and these cells help to make the sheath that encircles the rhizome. The meristem remains at the base of the lamina, and leaves on clivias elongate by adding more cells at their base.

The nature of the cell budded off from the meristem depends to a large degree on the nature of the cell undergoing the division. When a plant cell divides, it provides each cell with a full complement of nuclear chromosomes and a set of organelles. The number of organelles can vary, but since they are capable of dividing within the new daughter cell, enough can be produced to meet the needs of the cell. The organelles include mitochondria for the production of energy and proplastids that later develop into the chloroplasts necessary for photosynthesis. These two organelles have their own chromosomes and they divide independently of the mother cell. If a mother cell is lacking functional chloroplasts, it will bud off daughter cells that appear white or yellow instead of green; it is those daughter cells that manifest themselves as a white or yellow streak in the leaf. Mother cells do not move laterally, so the section of leaf they produce will be a stripe that runs the length of the leaf. The width of a stripe depends on how many mother cells lacking functional chloroplasts lie adjacent to each

Select Japanese varieties of variegated clivias.
Photograph courtesy of Yoshikazu Nakamura.

other. Because the placement of mother cells along the intercalary meristem occurs purely by chance, the probability of getting leaves that produce symmetrical bands of color centrally or laterally is quite small. Consequently, plants with symmetrical leaves are quite rare and hence much sought after.

Nonfunctional chloroplasts do not make chlorophyll and are not green; as a result they are unable to photosynthesize. They may be able to make other pigments such as carotenoids, however, and the stripes derived from those cells will be yellow. The tissue appears white if carotenoid synthesis is also blocked, so stripes in clivias may be either yellow or white. Carotenoids are sensitive to light and can be bleached to a creamy white color. Young leaves of clivias often display rich yellow stripes and must age before they show their mature creamy or even clear white nature. Although it is possible for yellow plastids to mutate to white ones, thus producing a mixture of yellow, white, and green stripes, this is very rare. Chinese sources have described such a combination, but I have never seen all three colored stripes in the same leaf.

In order to make meristems that produce discrete stripes, nonfunctional chloroplasts must be separated into groups that are distinct from patches of cells that create tissue with functional chloroplasts. When an egg cell is produced in the ovule, the mother plant donates a small number of proplastids to the cytoplasm of the developing egg. The proplastids will develop into chloroplasts when the tissue matures. The pollen parent does not provide any proplastids. If the egg is provided with both functional and nonfunctional proplastids, there is a possibility that when the embryo develops it may have a few cells that lack functional proplastids entirely. During cell division, proplastids are assigned to their various cells purely by chance, but because the total numbers of proplastids in the egg are low, there is a chance that some cells will be totally deficient in functional chloroplasts. As those cells divide, they can give their daughter cells only nonfunctional organelles, which will lead to white or yellow tissue. Some cells may get only functional chloroplasts, and others may get a mixture of the two. Cells with functional proplastids will produce green tissue. Some cells will have both types of tissue that can, purely by chance, produce cells without functional chloroplasts at some future date and thus become a potential source for the re-emergence of variegation. If most or all of the proplastids provided by the mother are nonfunctional, then the seedling may not inherit any functional plastids at all, and it will die following germination. Breeders often get seedlings from variegated parents that are pure yellow or white, but those seedlings usually die. One can often gauge the variety and extent of variegation of a plant by examining its first seedling leaf.

GENERAL CULTURE OF VARIEGATED CLIVIAS

Variegated clivias are too costly and delicate to use in the landscape. Their leaves suffer both sun and wind damage much more easily than standard varieties. Variegated plants that do survive outside often have patches of dead and dying tissue on most of their leaves and tend to look quite ratty and dishevelled. Variegated clivias are ideal, however, as pot plants and have relatively few needs. I recommend that they be used only as container subjects. The compact and dwarfed forms are easier to manage than the larger standard types, and accordingly are more popular. Dwarf variegated forms tend to outsell the standard variegated types when they are available.

For the most part, variegated clivias are so similar to normal clivias that their cultural requirements are the same, and the two sorts can be combined into a mixed collection and given the same conditions. (The reader is referred to the sections on container cultivation and pest management in chapter 4.) However, there are a few provisos. Variegated leaves appear to be even more sensitive to sunlight than normal leaves, and care must be taken to ensure that the plants do not burn. Some growers recommend that the shade cloth used for variegated hybrids be increased by 10 percent, so if you use 70 percent shade cloth for standard varieties, then the variegated plants should be grown under 80 percent shade cloth. Besides offering protection, denser shade also results in the production of more chloroplasts in those regions of the leaf able to produce functional chloroplasts. Such an increase leads to a better color contrast between the white or yellow stripes and the very deep bottle green of the photosynthetic areas. Plants in greater shade appear even more distinctive than those grown under lighter shade. Some light may be needed to bleach the leaves and achieve good contrast, and the amount needed must be determined by trial and error. Remember to avoid placing plants in direct sunlight.

Variegated leaves may also show more sensitivity to phytochemicals than nonvariegated leaves, and if you are using a new insecticide, try it first on a single plant or leaf before making a wholesale application. Of course this is also a sensible precaution to use with nonvariegated plants.

During one season of the year, the sun shining on a windowsill may provide ideal lighting for a potted variegated clivia plant. The arc that the sun travels does change during the year, however, and the light through the window may become too bright as the year proceeds. Even a few minutes in strong sunlight can damage the leaves, so hanging a lace curtain between the windowpane and the plant can go a long way toward avoiding sun damage. To determine if the light is too bright, hold your hand between the leaf and the light source about 1 foot (30 cm) from the leaf. If your hand shows a distinct outline or shadow, the light is too bright. Although it is easy to burn and disfigure the leaves, the plants are quite tough and will recover during the next growing season. They can produce a new set of leaves in a matter of months, so you can minimize the apparent damage with some judicious leaf-tip pruning or even removal of entire leaves.

I too have had to learn the lesson about too much sunlight on my plants. I had been away on a trip for a few days and returned to find all my variegated plants carefully arranged outside on a hot sunny patio. Many of the leaves were sunburned, and the foliage was spoiled for the next twelve months. Who would have thought that the caretaker would have taken the initiative to give my plants their own vacation in the hot California sunshine? I now know to carefully caution the next person who looks after my plants.

Variegated clivias at Joe Solomone's range. Watsonville, California.

Only those parts of the leaves that have functional chloroplasts are able to provide carbohydrates for the plant. Nonfunctional tissue in a plant (the white- or yellow-striped parts) has to be supported by the green tissue. It stands to reason then that plants with a lot of yellow or white tissue will grow considerably slower than siblings with a greater proportion of green tissue. One cannot compensate for this slow growth by providing extra chemical fertilizer because what the plants lack are carbohydrates and not inorganic salts. It is interesting that the fertilizers recommended by Chinese growers are all organic in nature. Some orchids—vanda and ascocenda hybrids, for example—can be sprayed with sugar water at a rate of 1 tsp/1 gal (13 ml/10 l) that they are apparently able to take up through their leaves (Grove 1995). Plants that are sprayed with this solution are supposed to grow more rapidly, withstand transplantation shock, and recover from desiccation more quickly. I wonder if this kind of treatment would speed up the growth of clivia seedlings with variegated leaves. I hope someone will experiment with this theory, but I caution that person to carefully monitor plants to make sure ants and fungi are not taking advantage of the sugar.

When they are mature, variegated clivias will produce offsets around the base just as normal clivias do. The variegation in the offsets is often similar to that of the parent plant, but it can also be quite different depending on the cells present in the area where the bud will be produced. Sometimes the offset will have no stripes at all, and if that is the case, then the all-green portion will grow more vigorously, often outgrowing the variegated portion. It is a good idea to detach nonvariegated pups from the variegated parts, but do not be tempted to detach the variegated pups prematurely. Wait until they are large enough and have their own strongly growing root systems because small offshoots can take many years to reestablish themselves.

People have come up with many reasons for the disappearance of variegation suggesting that it results from incorrect feeding, too much nitrogen, or excessive shading. The most likely reason is that it is due merely to chance, depending only on which tissue is available for forming the new apical meristem for the developing shoot between the old leaf bases.

CHINESE VARIEGATED CLIVIAS

The Manchurians, who seem to grow most of the striped leaf clivias in China, categorize variegated clivias into a large number of discrete types based on leaf width and length as well as on the placement and color of the stripes. Very wide and very short leaves with distinct and symmetrical variegation patterns are most desirable. A recent Chinese booklet on *Variegated Clivia for Commercial Nurserymen* lists eleven distinct categories of variegated clivias based on the length of the leaves (Shiang and Song 1999).

A superb variegated *Clivia* specimen that is similar to the "Dancing Moon Goddess" type. Plant grown by David Conway.

Long leaf types

Shiang and Song enumerate six distinct types in this group, and they are strains rather than named individual clones. All of the long leaf variegated varieties are considered to be older types, but they are relatively stable for their variegated patterns. They usually have acutely pointed leaf tips.

"DANCING MOON GODDESS" has long narrow leaves varying from slightly over 1 to 2 inches (2.5 to 5 cm) wide to 30 inches (75 cm) long. The leaves are basically green with a white margin. The central green section occupies about three-quarters of the width. Leaves are erect at their base, but arch over from halfway along their lengths.

"NARROW CHASM" has leaves of similar dimensions to that of "Dancing Moon Goddess." The color pattern of the leaves is reversed, however, with green margins and a central white or gray-white stripe. The width of the stripe varies depending on the particular clone under consideration.

"MANDARIN DUCK" carries leaves that range from 2 to 3 inches (5 to 7.5 cm) wide and 15 to 28 inches (37.5 to 70 cm) long. Each leaf is divided longitudinally into a white or green section. Once again, variation in the comparative widths of the two parts may occur. These varieties get their name because the two sides of each leaf are as different as the coloration of the two sexes of the mandarin duck.

"JADE INLAID WITH GOLD" refers to standard variegated types that have yellow rather than white stripes.

Another variety, which does not seem to enjoy a specific descriptive name, has either thin white stripes on a broad green field or the reverse—fine green threads of color in a white leaf. The last variety (also without a name) has green leaves with the faintest of almost indistinguishable stripes.

Medium leaf types

These more modern varieties have shorter leaves than the long leaf types, and they make up about 80 percent of current Chinese variegated clivia production. These are quite variable but are characterized by wide leaves that have white or golden-yellow stripes against dark green backgrounds. Where there is a layer of white tissue overlaying normal green, a gray color and gray stripes that coexist with white stripes appear. Leaf tips may be pointed or rounded. Leaves are usually neatly arranged and tend to be erect. The best types have clean, clear white stripes that resemble porcelain, or they might be a bright, rich golden-yellow, and in both instances, the green portions should provide a vivid contrast.

Short leaf types

The leaves in this group are quite short, usually between 4 to 6 inches (10 to 15 cm), and their width is nearly the same dimensions of 3 to 4 inches (7.5 to 10 cm). Leaves tend to be very thick and the tips

The "Narrow Chasm" type of variegation.

are rounded. Stripes may be white or yellow. Among these types is a unique variety called "Five Color Orchid" that has stripes of dark green, white, gray, yellow, and light green.

A leaf of the "Jade Inlaid with Gold" type.

Miniatures

Smaller clivias with wide, very short leaves that are neatly stacked on each other are called miniatures. They tend to have leaves that have dull matte surfaces. They may also be white, yellow, or gray, and the stripes are unevenly distributed. The flower peduncle in this type is extremely short, and flowers are borne between the leaves.

Pygmies

This type has even smaller leaves with pointed tips. The peduncle and pedicels are so short that they appear to be absent in these forms.

JAPANESE VARIEGATED CLIVIAS

The Japanese classify their variegated clivias into four main groups based on the arrangements of leaf color patterns rather than leaf dimensions or conformation (Mori 1990).

"Shima han"

These clivias have leaves with a large number of longitudinal stripes. The position of the stripes and their widths can be quite irregular, but stripes do tend to be relatively narrow.

"Fukurin"

This type has the variegation confined to the edge of the leaf. The pattern is sometimes described as encircling stripes because they form a contrasting margin around the leaf.

In both "Shima han" and "Fukurin" types, the band may be yellow, white, or some shade in between. Where the stripe is laid over green tissue, a gray streak may be produced. As with the Chinese categories, placement of stripes is variable. Every time a new leaf or side shoot is produced, a different pattern may emerge because of the way variegations are produced by a plant.

A dwarf variegated Japanese *Clivia* displayed at the National Botanical Institute at Kirstenbosch, South Africa. Photograph courtesy of Yves Aubry.

"Torazu" (synonym: "Kozu")
A very unusual and rare type of clivia plant, the color variegation is likened to that of a tiger, although in reality a leopard would be more apt. Variegation is in the form of distinct blotches that look like irregular, yellow-bleached areas randomly arranged on the blade of the leaf.

"Akebono"
Another kind of variation that has been recognized in Japan and that has also cropped up independently in other parts of the world displays bands of paler, horizontal color. The emerging leaves appear faded with horizontal bands of pale cream-yellow, green-yellow, or cream-white running at right angles to the length of the leaf. The extent of bandings is variable. Edges of the bands are not distinct but instead quite blurred as they gradually merge into those parts of normal green coloration. At first glance one might mistake the

A "Fukurin" type with a uniform contrasting margin around the leaf.

banding for mild sun damage. The banding might also appear to be due to a physiological or developmental malfunction, but it is genetic and can be inherited. Some hybridizers are now deliberately

Example of "Akebono" leaf banding.

breeding for this type of leaf banding. Comstock finds that these leaf patterns are inherited only from the maternal side. The emerging leaves are a dusky, faded ivory-green or yellow-green, but about one month after it has matured in size, the leaf starts to change to a normal, dark bottle green. Coloring appears at the tip of the leaf, and by the fall the entire leaf can be dark green. Leaves tend to be 3 to 4 inches (7.5 to 10 cm) wide and 14 to 16 inches (35 to 40 cm) long. This variety is said to be very popular in the Kansai and Hiroshima regions of Japan. "Akebono" forms appear from time to time in California, while in South Africa the pattern occurs in second and third generation yellow clivias bred from 'Bodnant Variety'.

Most of the Japanese variegated clivias are dwarf. The Japanese also produce microminiature dwarfs that correspond to the Chinese miniatures and pygmies and that can command high enough prices to place them out of the range of the average gardener. In Japan select clones are given cultivar names, a few of which I describe in this section to give a feel for what has been achieved (Ogasawara 1997). The descriptive term *nishiki*, meaning brocade, is often appended to the clonal name of variegated plants. Other terms such as *chabo*, meaning bantam, refers to the smallest dwarf forms, and *daruma*, meaning wooden doll, refers to dwarf forms with wide leaves.

'Ginga-nishiki'
'Ginga-nishiki' has tulip-shaped scarlet flowers with 3- to 4-inch (7.5- to 10-cm) broad leaves and 18-inches (45-cm) long leaves of a blue-green color with white stripes.

'Issun-boushi'
This should be classed as a pygmy with narrow leaves that are less than 1 inch (1 to 2 cm) wide and that barely reach 6½ inches (16.25 cm) in length. The plant has creamy colored stripes on a dark green background.

'Jouhakuden'

'Jouhakuden' also has scarlet trumpet-shaped flowers, but the leaves in this case have a yellow green stripe when young that matures to a clean white stripe. The plant is considered valuable as a parent for breeding white stripes.

'Kirinzan'

'Kirinzan' has wide leaves approximately 5 inches (12 to 13 cm) in breadth and 20 to 24 inches (50 to 62 cm) in length. Young leaves have greenish yellow stripes that mature to a grayish yellow against a dark green background. The large scarlet flowers are trumpet-shaped.

'Kiyohime'

A miniature plant with leaves that are 2 to $2\frac{1}{2}$ inches (5 to 6.25 cm) wide and 4 to 5 inches (10 to 12.5 cm) long. The leaves form a downward arch. The stripes are a whitish cream. The medium-sized flowers have rounded petals and are dark scarlet.

'Kogane-nishiki'

A medium-sized plant that has a wide yellow stripe on the 10-inch (25-cm) long and 3-inch (7.5-cm) wide leaves. When well grown, this clone apparently has a particularly rich golden color to the stripe. The flowers are scarlet and of medium size.

'Otohime-nishiki'

A smaller plant that bears a comparatively large truss of dark scarlet flowers. The leaves are only 1 to $1\frac{1}{2}$ inches (2.5 to 3.75 cm) wide and 6 to 7 inches (15 to 18 cm) long. They are dark green with white-yellow stripes.

'Suruga-nishiki'

A medium-sized plant that has proved to be a good parent. The stripes are a creamy color against a dark green. Leaves are 2 to $2\frac{1}{2}$

Clivia miniata "Band Ait', showing the banded type of leaf variegation.
Note that this is also a multipetalled specimen.

inches (5 to 6.25 cm) wide and 12 inches (31 cm) long. The large flowers are dark scarlet and have rounded tepals.

'Wada-nishiki'
'Wada-nishiki' has some of the broadest leaves, reaching 5 inches
(12.5 cm) in width and 18 inches (45 cm) in length. The stripes are yel-
low-brushed on a dark green background. This plant was bred from
'Ginga-nishiki', and although it also has tulip-shaped flowers, they
are smaller than those of its parent.

Very few variegated clones have been given cultivar names in the
West and I will not describe any here. Comstock has named a few of
his, including 'Band Ait', which is illustrated here. This clone is also

a multipetalled type and carries flowers with eight tepals. 'Variegated Rust' is a rare, variegated type with brick-colored flowers that was named by Conway.

BREEDING VARIEGATED CLIVIAS

As with other special forms of clivia plants, selected types of variegated clivias are outrageously expensive. Nearly all variegated clivia plants will produce variegated seedlings, and breeding your own is among the most interesting and satisfying aspects of clivia horticulture. Leaf patterns are seen upon germination, so you get a sense of achievement without having to wait several years before the plants flower.

To breed variegated clivias you must select the variegated plant as the pod parent. Inspection of the inflorescence peduncle and pedicels of a variegated plant should reveal variegated stripes running up the length of those stalks. Plants with the best and widest clean stripes tend to make the worst parents because the majority of their seeds produce seedlings that are totally albinisitic (they lack all chloroplasts) and that die once all the food reserve from the seed has been used up. The best yields of seedlings are from plants that have many, very fine striations in their leaves. They will produce a variety of leaf patterns ranging from seedlings with broad stripes to those with finer stripes, and a few will have no obvious markings. You might want to reserve seedling plants with finer striations for your own future breeding stock. If the mother plant has only a very few fine stripes, and if there is no obvious variegation in the peduncle, the chances of producing variegated seedlings is markedly reduced. Ideal mother plants have lots of fine stripes rather than broad bands of achlorotic tissue, even though the latter may be the more desirable plant for display. The ripe fruits should also have obvious striations in color.

The male parent does not contribute toward variegation. Proplastids appear to be excluded from either the pollen grains or

Seeds from variegated fruits like these will often produce variegated seedlings.
Photograph courtesy of Yoshikazu Nakamura.

from the sperm cells that are formed in the pollen tube. While the male parent is not important in terms of the kind of variegation produced, it is very important in helping determine the size and shape of the leaves in which the variegation is to be displayed. Very wide and variegated leaves are desirable, and you might want to select the pollen parent for its leaf width characteristics. People are now trying not only to produce variegated plants with yellow flowers, but also to introduce the other species characteristics into variegated plants. Although some variegated yellow clivias have occurred spontaneously, most of them are very poorly striped.

An alternative way of making variegated yellow clivias is to deliberately pollinate a striped clivia plant with yellow pollen. Variegated offspring from this mating will all have orange flowers. If the pollen from the yellow parent is then applied to its variegated offspring (a backcross), a certain percentage of yellow variegated clivias should result. You must be careful to make the backcross with either the exact same yellow parent or with another compatible yellow plant since not all yellow clivias are equivalent in their breeding abilities. (The breeding abilities in yellow clivias are explored more fully in chapter 9.) It is also possible to make peach-colored seedlings with variegations this way.

Fruits of variegated clivias, like the leaves, will be striped, although red anthocyanin pigment will be produced in the skin of the fruit and striping will be pigmented. Fruits and seeds take the same time to mature as regular standard clivias, and they should be harvested, stored, and germinated in the same way.

Variegation will manifest itself in the initial seedling leaf. The amount and type of patterning often changes as more leaves are produced. Occasionally the plant looses its variegation altogether and appears all green. The reverse can happen, and the variegated seedling may produce all yellow or white leaves. If the latter happens the seedling will eventually die. It is inevitable that you will also get a certain percentage of germinating seedlings that are totally albinistic from the start and have no green banding, and these will die. Parent plants with very wide bands of achlorotic tissue in their leaves will produce a higher percentage of those doomed seedlings. Mother plants with many thin stripes will give a higher percentage of survivors, and among those will be seedlings with wide white or yellow stripes. Seedlings that initially have wide bands of color are unlikely to change to a pattern of very fine lines.

Although young clivias grow well in community pots, you might want to sort them by type after the first year. Rates of seedling growth appear to be directly proportional to the amount of photosynthetic tissue found in the seedling leaves. Seedlings with a lot of variegation may have trouble competing with seedlings displaying little or no striping, and they should be separated from their more vigorously growing siblings. One tends to discard the smaller and slower growing seedlings of most other groups of plants, but that is not the case in clivias, particularly if they also have unusual leaf shapes. Clivia growing has been deeply influenced by Japanese horticulture in which even the most dreadfully crippled monsters and aberrations can be grown and treasured for their own sakes. When using a dwarf or miniature as one or both parents, you may find a few seedlings that are a particularly small and much slower growing than their siblings. These microminiature plants are especially desirable. Microminiatures can also occur spontaneously especially where very large quantities of seed are grown, and you should be on the lookout for them among your own seedlings.

VARIEGATES WITH YELLOW FLOWERS

If yellow-flowered standard clivias are considered something special then yellow-flowered clivias with variegated leaves must be considered as something exceptional. Good variegated yellow clivias have appeared spontaneously in several yellow breeding programs but most of the first generation plants have only a few thin yellow or white stripes in their leaves. Breeding with these might one day result in yellow flowers with broader stripes.

FUTURE TRENDS

Future directions for development in variegated clivias are, like any kind of plant, limited only by one's imagination. Interest in *Clivia* is so intense that any really new type will get instant attention. Any

An unnamed but excellent yellow-flowered and strongly variegated *Clivia* specimen grown at Joe Solomone's range. Watsonville, California.

breeder who produced a compact miniature plant with broad variegated leaves and pure yellow flowers would have the world's clivia collectors beating a pathway to his or her door. Comstock has found that he can combine the "Akebono" types with the more usual longitudinal striping but he has yet to make a good checkerboard pattern.

Nearly any of the forms that now occur—with the exception of the wild species—could be produced with variegated leaves, provided that there is a good variegated plant to use as the pod parent. However, unless breeders find variegates of each of the pendent-flowered species, or use mutagens that cause variegation, it is unlikely that variegated species other than *Clivia miniata* will ever exist. Although it is possible to use a plain-leafed *C. nobilis* to make a variegated *C.* Cyrtanthiflora Group by mating it with a variegated *C. miniata* pod parent, there is no way to make variegated *C. nobilis* unless a variegated plant of that species already exists.

Clivia seedlings usually have red-purple pigment at the base of their leaves, and I have seen young plants with leaves that are intensely suffused with these anthocyanins. It should be possible to select for that kind of pigmentation in mature leaves through a breeding program, although no one appears to have done so. If a plant retained its seedling leaf cyanidin into its mature phase, then it might be possible to make variegated clivia leaves with red or pink stripes.

Chapter Twelve

CYRTANTHIFLORA-TYPE CLIVIAS AND RELATED HYBRIDS

I T WAS NOT LONG after *Clivia miniata* had been described that the new species was mated to *C. nobilis*. When van Houtte (1869–70) named this artificial hybrid he thought that the flowers resembled those of the genus *Cyrtanthus*, hence the grex name *Clivia* Cyrtanthiflora. Actually, he named it *Imantophyllum* Cyrtanthiflorum as there was still confusion over which was the correct genus name for the plant. He also described the plants as having long-lasting blooms and being perpetually in flower. I, too, find that these plants are among the first to flower in the season and that they tend to throw additional flowers at irregular intervals throughout the year. Thus they make up for their less spectacular flowers by providing an extended display. There are two important features of these hybrids that would be worth getting into the larger and more standard clivias. The first is the intense red color; the most intense reds I have seen in clivia flowers were in hybrids between *C. miniata* and the other species. The second feature is the distinctly different color (compared to the outside color) that sometimes occurs on the inside of the flower. The inside is pale ivory-cream or bright yellow, while the outside can be a bright orange-red. Either of these color

Clivia Cyrtanthiflora Group from *Flores des Serres*. Photograph courtesy of
Huntington Library.

patterns would be stunning in a standard clivia plant and can be achieved with a large enough breeding program.

Strictly speaking, the name *Clivia* Cyrtanthiflora is an outdated grex name that refers only to those offspring that are the either the result of crossing *C. miniata* with *C. nobilis* or of sibling or selfing plants of *C.* Cyrtanthiflora. Although such grex names are no longer allowed, horticultural taxonomists allow the modification of a grex name to a cultivar group name for convenience sake. The new name of this grex is more properly *Clivia* Cyrtanthiflora Group. Special clones from this group should also be given a cultivar name, such as *C.* [Cyrtanthiflora Group] 'Jamboree'.

The resurgence of interest in clivias has resulted in considerably more active breeding, particularly the mating of the other various species with *Clivia miniata* or *C. nobilis*. Unfortunately, nearly all of the resulting hybrids have also been referred to as *C.* Cyrtanthiflora. This name would be incorrect even if grex names were still valid as the name *C.* Cyrtanthiflora was reserved only for the cross between *C. nobilis* and *C. miniata*. One could, however, refer to all of the hybrids with narrow, somewhat pendent tubular flowers as Cyrtanthiflora-types, and I will use that term here.

In some parts of the world there seems to be considerable confusion between the parent *Clivia nobilis* and *C.* Cyrtanthiflora Group, and the latter is often sold under the former's name. To make matters worse, most beginners cannot distinguish between *C. nobilis*, *C. gardenii*, and *C. caulescens*, and those hybrids also get labeled Cyrtanthiflora irrespective of the actual species in the background. The second-generation hybrids, usually back to *C. miniata*, are often called Cyrtanthiflora as well. All these errors lead to additional perplexity. It is important to keep the pedigrees organized because each of the different species has different breeding behavior and possesses different complements of anthocyanins. For those who have a serious interest in hybridizing and understanding the breeding behavior of their hybrids, keeping track of the actual species in the background of these plants is key. The easiest way to do that is to use group names (modified from the old grex names in most cases) as well as cultivar names. While group names are not used for actual cultivar registrations, the former practice of using grex names for the first few generations past the primary hybrid stage conveyed a great deal of information. I suggested a series of grex names—now more properly group names—in the *Clivia Yearbook* (2000) that follow the rules set up for orchid names. Those names are useful for labeling entire seed batches and keeping track of the genetic potential of the plants involved.

The primary hybrid Cyrtanthiflora-types cannot compete with the standard clivias for making spectacular flower spikes, but they seem to have been grown as *Clivia* variants for a long time and have become widespread in those climates where the plants can be accommodated in the landscape. Even in less clement climates they are often grown as large potted plants. Frikkie Marais told me that divisions of *C.* Cyrtanthiflora Group that were for sale in Hungary had actually been made for the Empress of Austria and Hungary more than one hundred years previously in 1869. In Australia and California, similar plants can be found in the nursery trade, although they are often mislabeled as *C. nobilis* instead of *C.* Cyrtanthiflora Group. It is easy to tell the two apart because *C. nobilis* has individual flowers with narrow tubes and no flaring at the mouth. They are usually strongly pendent and hang perpendicularly downwards. *Clivia nobilis* also has definite green tepal tips that usually last for much of the flower's life. *Clivia* Cyrtanthiflora Group, on the other hand, has florets with curved and somewhat flaring tubes, and although the flowers droop, they are often closer to being horizontal. Any green on the tepal tips usually fades rapidly before or as the flowers open.

The contemporary Cyrtanthiflora-types are destined to play an important role in the development of modern clivias. The other wild species contain combinations of genes that differ from those of *Clivia miniata* and could code for unusual flower colors and forms. *Clivia gardenii* is a fall-blooming species, and it could help widen the flowering season, which is now primarily spring. Rudo and Wessel Lötter in South Africa are flowering a series of second generation hybrids from *C. miniata* by other species and they find that some very usual color combinations segregate out. Another person who has produced some very fine Cyrtanthiflora-type hybrids is Brian Tarr at the Natal National Botanical Garden in Pietermaritzburg, South Africa.

The use of the term *Clivia* Cyrtanthiflora Group for clivia crosses involving any of the other species is invalid, and I recommend using the new group names. Additional group names could be any short descriptor, perhaps even a single word or name. In orchids, where grex names are commonly used, the length of the grex name is usually limited to three words. Latinized words are usually not allowed for modern group names. It is useful but not necessary for breeders making up group names that these reflect the plant's parentage.

Primary hybrids are the results of crosses between two different species. Crosses between primary hybrids and other parents are often called advanced hybrids. One such second generation hybrid between *Clivia* Cyrtanthiflora Group and *C. miniata* appears to have been made several times, and that deserves its own grex name. Below is a list of both new and the old grex names for some of these clivia combinations (Koopowitz 2000).

Group Name	Parentage
Clivia Caulgard Group	*C. gardenii* × *C. caulescens*
Clivia Cyrtanthiflora Group	*C. miniata* × *C. nobilis*
Clivia Minicyrt Group	*C.* [Cyrtanthiflora Group] × *C. miniata*
Clivia Minigard Group	*C. gardenii* × *C. miniata*
Clivia Minilescent Group	*C. miniata* × *C. caulescens*
Clivia Nobilescent Group	*C. nobilis* × *C. caulescens*
Clivia Noble Guard Group	*C. gardenii* × *C. nobilis*

The hybrids between *Clivia miniata* and the other three species all tend to be difficult for the beginner to differentiate, and to a certain extent that is understandable because the plants do vary somewhat depending on the specific clones that were used as the parents. They also tend to have somewhat similarly shaped flowers. Rudo and Wessel Lötter are the world's premier experts on the Cyrtanthiflora-type hybrids, and Rudo kindly provided me with descriptions of their first generation results of crossing *C. miniata* with each of the different species. His descriptions are as follows.

The flowers found in the *Clivia* Minigard Group (*C. gardenii* × *C. miniata*) are more like those of *C. gardenii* in that they are completely orange-red. Some are horizontal while others are upright. This gives the plants an untidy appearance, and they produce a lot of untidy offspring in the F_2 generation, which resemble an inferior *C. miniata*. The flowers are slightly curved, and their mouths are more flaring than those of *C. gardenii*.

Flowers in the *Clivia* Cyrtanthiflora Group (*C. nobilis* × *C. miniata*) are completely tubular and pendulous, and they are as long as those of *C. miniata*. The color is red with green tips. The plants show leaf characteristics of both parents. They grow much faster than *C. nobilis* and are an overall improvement on *C. nobilis*. They produce spectacular F_2 hybrids such as *Clivia* [Cyrtanthiflora Group] 'Chanèl' but they also produce a large percentage of F_2 plants with short, straight, open flowers. Rudo stresses that he finds the short straight flowers undesirable.

The F_1 plants in the *Clivia* Minilescent Group (*C. caulescens* × *C. miniata*) grow very fast and flower in three years. Long peduncles protrude above the plants. All the flowers are semipendulous and nicely arranged in a full circle. They are delicate with flaring mouths, and they all curve—a characteristic that Rudo finds highly desirable. The color of the flowers is a nice pinkish orange. Although Rudo does not know what the F_2 plants will look like, he imagines that, based on the F_1 characteristics, most will be of high quality and a good percentage will be superb.

Rudo has told me what he considers an ideal Cyrtanthiflora-type: semipendulous flowers arranged 360° around the umbel; at least twenty-five flowers; flowers that are long and curved with a mouth

Clivia Cyrtanthiflora Group.

that is as wide and flaring as possible. It should not be a failed *C. miniata*. While I agree with Rudo's suggestions I think that there is also room for noncurved flowers in a typical *C. miniata* arrangement, particularly if the flowers are distinctive and have novel coloring, which is likely to result from mixing all the species genes thoroughly.

There is very little information about some of the other primary hybrids such as *Clivia* Caulgard Group, *C.* Noble Guard Group, or *C.* Nobilescent Group. People have avoided crossing two pendent-flowered species together thinking that there might be little improvement in these types over the parental species. However, hybridizers do know that the various species contain different combinations of flavonoid pigments, as well as other genes that govern their leaves, stems, and physiology. Mixing all of these genes from different species together would be an excellent strategy for creating new types. Hybridizers need to look ahead several generations and not insist on receiving instant gratification. It took only two generations to go from the less desirable Cyrtanthiflora Group to the very desirable flowers of the Minicyrt Group; some very fine and unusual plants have emerged from the *C.* Minicyrt Group, which are the backcrosses of *C.* Cyrtanthiflora Group with *C. miniata*.

It is worth examining some of the older *Clivia* Cyrtanthiflora Group hybrids to see how far this type of breeding has come. One plant of the old *C.* Cyrtanthiflora Group growing in the Huntington Botanical Gardens had narrow pendent tubes of mid to deep orange flowers with almost no flaring at the mouth of the flower. It carried about twenty-five flowers in the umbel.

The following are some of the named cultivars that I have come across. There are many fewer of these than in the various categories of standard clivia plants. Perhaps with the increase in breeding activity around the world and the wide dissemination of all of the species, we will see an increase in hybrids between species and standards.

Clivia [Minicyrt Group] 'Apricot Blush'
Tarr has produced an apricot-colored *Clivia* Cyrtanthiflora Group hybrid at the Natal National Botanical Garden that clearly shows the potential for color development in this group of flowers. The tubular flowers had widely flaring mouths, and the creamy yellow flowers were painted with a blush of soft pink. This plant was developed from a cross of *C. miniata* 'Natal Yellow' by *C.* Cyrtanthiflora Group and should be grouped in with the *C.* Minicyrt Group. When this coloring is transferred to the larger, more complex hybrids, there will be some spectacular flowers. This cultivar is very vigorous and produces many offsets.

Clivia [Minicyrt Group] 'Barbra'
A wonderful peach-colored hybrid from Comstock that shows how fine these hybrids have become. The *Clivia nobilis* species is several generations in the background, and there are no suitable group

Clivia [Minicyrt Group] 'Apricot Blush'.

names for these plants. At least fifteen fairly large flowers are held
on the umbel. They flare nicely and have much of the grace of the
C. Cyrtanthiflora Group hybrids. I would like to see a large collection of seedlings flowering out from a cross of 'Barbra' with a good
peach *C. miniata*.

Clivia [Minicyrt Group] 'Chanèl'
During a visit to South Africa in 1999 to see clivias, I found this to
be the most dramatic and distinctive of all the very interesting

Clivia [Minicyrt Group] 'Barbra'.

flowers that I saw. The flowers have a striking contrast between the sepals and petals. The outer surface of the sepals is a dark rusty red with a strong green contribution that is more apparent at the edges of the sepal where the red fades slightly. The outside of the petal is an ivory cream with a flush of pale green, while the inside of the entire flower is an ivory cream. The sepals are narrow and pointed, and the petals broad and rounded. There is a slight curve to the flower. The truss can carry about twelve to sixteen flowers and produce several umbels each year. A second-generation hybrid, 'Chanèl' demonstrates what can be achieved using the right combination of genes.

Clivia [Minicyrt Group] 'Chanèl'.

Clivia [Minicyrt Group] 'Comstock #3'
I like this hybrid that Comstock produced. The flowers have a nice peachy color with a somewhat darker outer coloration and an inner throat of much paler and softer pinky peach. The curved pendent flowers flare at their opening. This is an exceedingly choice variety with narrower flowers than Comstock's 'Barbra'.

Clivia [Minigard × *C. miniata*] 'Lötter #F2012'
In this second generation Lötter hybrid from *Clivia gardenii*, the *C. miniata* is much more dominant for shape. The widely flaring flowers have an untidy arrangement in the umbel but are a pleasant orange with pinkish highlights.

Clivia [Cyrtanthiflora Group] 'Lötter #F2026'
This is a first generation hybrid that was in flower at the Lötter range. The narrow curving flowers have a deep orange coloration.

Clivia [Minicyrt Group] 'Comstock #3'.

The umbel's flowers are held nearly horizontal and are arranged nicely in a circle around the end of the peduncle.

Clivia [Minigard Group] 'Lötter F2604'
There are only a few pure yellow Cyrtanthiflora-types. This one is from the Lötter stable and was bred from *Clivia gardenii* by a yellow *C. miniata* to make a *C.* Minigard with yellow genes, and then back-crossed to another yellow *C. miniata*. The flowers tend to be curved but are held at a high angle typical of the stance seen in many of the *C.* Minigard Group.

Clivia [Minicyrt Group] 'Goodwill'
This is a hybrid in the *Clivia* Minicyrt Group and hence a second generation, Cyrtanthiflora-type. Made by Comstock, this hybrid holds fifteen attractive flowers in the umbel. The outside surface of the sepals is painted a dark orange, while the petals and inner face of

Clivia [Minigard Group] 'Lötter #F2604'.

the sepals and petals are a soft yellow-orange. The broad overlapping and rounded petals have a nice flare.

Clivia [Minicyrt Group] 'Juliette'
Perhaps the most intriguing of Comstock's clivias from Minicyrt breedings is this advanced hybrid, which is several generations from the species. This cultivar illustrates the wonderful color patterns that can produced. The slightly curved flowers are a rich orange-red with the sepals only slightly darker than the petals. Most of the flower's throat is a similar color, but the flaring edges of the petals are highlighted and brushed with pale pink tones that make the rim of the flower seem to glow.

Clivia [Minicyrt Group] 'Goodwill'.

Clivia [Minicyrt Group] 'Orange Belle'
Another of Tarr's hybrids, this one was on display at the Natal
National Botanical Garden. Also a second-generation hybrid, it is
labeled Cyrtanthiflora × *Clivia miniata*. The outside of the flowers is
a uniform mid-orange while the inside is a softer and paler pastel
orange. The petals flare nicely around the wide mouth of the flower.

Clivia [Group unknown] 'Orange Rain'
I was attracted to this plant from a local nursery, even though it was
mislabeled as *Clivia nobilis*. I bought it and attached the name of
'Orange Drops'. It looks as if it could either be a second generation
C. Cyrtanthiflora Group or the backcross of *C*. Cyrtanthiflora Group

Clivia [Minicyrt Group] 'Juliette'.

with *C. miniata*. There is a slight curvature to the flower, each being nearly 2 inches (5 cm) long and a little less than 1 inch (2.5 cm) across its opening. As with many of the flowers of this type of breeding, the color pattern of the flower is complex with the outside of the tepals a different color from the inner surface. When the buds first mature, the outside of all the tepals is a pale orange-yellow. The outside of the sepals matures to a dark orange and the petals to a paler orange. The tips of the tepals have a green flush that fades as the flowers mature. The inside of the flower opens a uniform, fresh lemon-yellow with a faint orange flush, but it matures to a soft pastel orange. As many as twenty-five flowers are borne in the umbel. The pendent flowers are carried on a peduncle 17 inches (42.5 cm) tall. The leaves are narrow,

Clivia [Minicyrt Group] 'Orange Belle'.

just over 1 inch (2.5 cm) in width and 24 inches (62 cm) long. The leaves arch over and so the umbel is carried above the plant.

Clivia [Group unknown] 'Red Bells'
This is most likely a second or third generation hybrid with *Clivia nobilis* as one original ancestor. Comstock named the cultivar. An acquaintance showed him the flower but was reluctant to share any information about it. Attending a small clivia symposium held at the Huntington Botanical Gardens shortly after this, Comstock found a clump of the same clone growing in the gardens at the Huntington itself. Later, when the gardeners thinned the clump, Comstock was able to beg a small division. The flower is a short flaring bell some 2

Clivia [Group unknown] 'Orange Rain'.

inches (5 cm) long and 1½ inches (3.75 cm) wide at the mouth. There is no curvature to the flower, and each is held at a variety of angles making a full umbel with eighteen flowers on a 16-inch (40-cm) peduncle that is carried just above the foliage. The leaves are 1¾ inches (4.5 cm) wide and 20 inches (50 cm) long. The slight notch at the tip of the leaf gives away it *C. nobilis* ancestry. This clone normally flowers in midwinter before most of the other clivias and it bears very dark red flowers. Additional trusses of flowers produced during warmer summer months are considerably paler. The cultivar is vigorous and makes numerous offsets.

One other hybrid worth noting is Andersson's *Clivia* Minigard Group. In his small, Pietermaritzburg garden Andersson has produced a most unusual hybrid from a cross of a yellow *C. miniata* and a regular *C. gardenii* with a strong green flush. Surprisingly, the result

Clivia [Minicyrt Group] 'Lucinda' showing the absence of throat patterning in this kind of clivia flower.

was a flower with extensive green shadings on the outside of a pale ivory tube, and there was no obvious anthocyanin pigmentation. The inside of the flower also had considerable green color. I surmise that the *C. gardenii* must have had recessive genes for yellow coloring since it normally takes at least two generations to achieve a pure yellow Cyrtanthiflora hybrid following a similar type of mating between a yellow *C. miniata* and *C. nobilis*. Another unusual feature of this clone is its diminutive stature. One would not immediately recognize the plant in flower as being a clivia. This novelty probably deserves a clonal name of its own within the Minigard Group.

The Cyrtanthiflora-type hybrids hold much promise. There are the obvious changes to the shape or color patterns that hybridizers are interested in, particularly since the pigmentation on the outside of the tepals of these hybrids is often much darker than that on the inside surface. In addition, most Cyrtanthiflora-types do not have the distinctive throat patterns found in the orange and pure *Clivia miniata* pastel hybrids, and further breeding may produce standard-shaped flowers with smooth coloring. Yet there are other potential benefits to getting more of the species' genes into the bigger hybrids. For example, *Clivia gardenii* flowers in the fall and not the spring, so the earliest clones of *C. gardenii* could be used to expand the flowering season to at least six months of the year. *Clivia nobilis* grows in dunes along the beaches of eastern South Africa, so it can provide salt tolerant genes for those who must garden under poor water quality conditions.

Chapter Thirteen

NOVELTY CLIVIAS

URING THE NORMAL COURSE of evolution, nature is able to take successful organisms and convert them into myriad forms. Consider all the shapes, forms, and colors that birds now come in—and yet they were all derived from a single ancestral bird. Or ponder the differences and similarities between humans and mouse lemurs, two mammals that share a common ancestor. Artificial selection works much faster than natural selection because the former is more easily directed, so in the course of a few centuries rather than hundreds of millennia, we can take any organism and change it so that it hardly resembles its progenitors. When you think that Chihuahua dogs and Afghan hounds no longer look like wolves, you should not be surprised that clivias can be as pliable as any other organism in the hands of a breeder.

The various novelties can be divided into two broad categories: those concerned with the flowers and those that involve unusual leaves. I will deal with flowers first and then with leaf selections.

NOVELTY FLOWERS

There are many unusual flower forms that still need to be developed or are so rare that they are almost unobtainable.

Clivia miniata 'Hime Chabo', a miniature adult clivia plant of Japanese breeding.
The film box provides a sense of scale.

Multipetals and doubles

Good double flowers are almost nonexistent, although pictures of them appear from time to time, especially in Japanese books on clivias. Horace Anderson was said to have had a double clivia plant by 1975, but it appears to have been lost. There are several *Clivia* strains that have flowers with eight rather than six tepals, and the eight tepal flowers often have additional stamens. Multipetal flowers, however, vary in their consistency of eight-tepal production and will usually produce some six tepal flowers among the eight or doubles. Comstock has a fine, deep orange-red clivia plant he calls *Clivia miniata* 'Radiation' that consistently has eight tepals. The relatively narrow tepals lend an air of distinction to this flower. Other eight-petalled types often have wider petals with good overlap, but they merely look like clivias with larger and rounder flowers. True doubles will have the stamens converted into petals, and the center of the flower can sometimes be filled with these petals. Nakamura has provided me with a photograph of a plant of his that made at least one spectacular doubled flower. His plant has very many narrow petals filling in most of the center of the flower, and it appears to me that many petals result from a flattening of the stamen filaments. Petal edges in this clone bear anthers with good pollen. Seeds from multipetal parents are occasionally offered for sale and will sometimes produce flowers that show variable tendencies to produce doubles.

Hiroshi Mitsuhashi in Japan is famous as a Christmas cactus breeder, but he also has a soft spot for clivias, particularly those that are out of the ordinary. He has amassed a collection of over three hundred orange and yellow double and multipetalled forms, some of which have been made available to American breeders.

I have heard no reports of the pendent species with multipetalled flowers, but one species seedling that I flowered of *Clivia caulescens* did throw doubled flowers on its maiden bloom. It has not flowered again, so I do not know if it will be reliable for this feature. If it is, then a future of double Cyrtanthiflora-types becomes possible. There is no reason why clivia breeders cannot produce good

Clivia miniata 'Radiation' bred by Comstock.

double flowers; after all, consistent doubles have been produced in many other plant groups. There needs to be some cooperation and exchange of pollen between those breeders fortunate enough to

A double *Clivia miniata* flower with an exceptionally large number of petaloids.
Photograph courtesy of Yoshikazu Nakamura.

possess good multipetalled and double flowers. Cooperation rather than a dog in the manger attitude is the way to make rapid progress in flower breeding of any type.

Keeled petals
This is an unusual mutation that has spontaneously appeared several times. In this case there is a ridge that runs along the length of the midline of the inner surface of the petals, tepals, or both. This ridge often clasps the base of the stamen's filament but is not fused to it. Comstock has found these forms in both yellow and orange *Clivia miniata* hybrids. The yellow-flowered plant belongs to a southern California grower, Joe Dana, and is among the more extreme forms that I have seen. (I have also noted a few keeled yellows flowering in

A multipetalled form of *Clivia caulescens.*

Solomone's range and an orange-flowered plant in Comstock's collection). I was in South Africa in 2000 and saw several keeled orange *C. miniata* offered for sale at one show. Line breeding these forms for larger keels could result in flowers that look doubled. Similar ridged and crested tepals have been developed in other flowers such as daylilies and begonias.

Capellini and Frat forms
The petals of Capellini forms are reduced to long, thin segments that make the entire umbel resemble a paintbrush. Several of these flowered in Solomone's range during the 2000 season. Nakamura refers to this type as spaghetti forms, but I prefer to call them *Capellini*, the name for fine angel-hair pasta. Connie Abel in South Africa also has a series of orange clivia seedlings with extremely narrow tepals that she calls Frats. Some clivia flowers from Frat breeding have no petals at all.

Joe Dana's unnamed keeled yellow clivia.

Fringed petal margins

This is another type that appeared in several seedlings flowering for the first time in Solomone's nursery in the spring of 2000. They resulted from yellow breeding and they possess narrow tepals with jagged or pinked edges. The Capellini forms may be related to the fringed petal types and may merely represent an extreme of this fringed form. Breeding these types with standard clivias might result in flowers with crisped, pinked, or fringed margins like those in *Odontoglossum* orchids and carnations.

Foliar tepals

Enthusiasts would like to grow clivias with green flowers. Holmes has two chartreuse flowering clivias from his yellow breeding and has mated them together. Comstock also has yellows with a green cast (see chapter 9). In a number of places, however, one finds

A yellow clivia of the Capellini form.

flowers where it looks as if the tepals have taken over some of the characteristics of leaves, and while parts of the tepals may develop anthocyanins, much of the flower is a dark sage green. While the dark green flower buds may open, they never seem to develop fully and stay small. Nakamura has pointed out that the expression of foliar tepals is not consistent and that they may revert to regular tepals in some seasons. Comstock, however, has one cultivar that is consistent in producing foliar tepals although there is some variation from year to year.

Particolored flowers
Conway uses this name for a series of plants where the flowers open pale and then darken. Very often these flowers are also blotched. Colors seem to involve pinks and creams. Comstock has noted that the position and pattern on each petal and sepal can be

Foliar tepals.

quite different. They can be extremely attractive and often display large amounts of pink coloration. Clivias rarely have petals and sepals displaying irregular and asymmetrical color patterns, but Comstock has one such clone with fifteen flowers to the umbel that he calls *Clivia* 'Proteus'. Individual flowers are quite shapely, and the overall effect is of a lovely, pretty flower. Meyer has a series of similar clivias, and her *C. miniata* 'Tarentaal' has won prizes. In 2000 she flowered a group of seedlings where the flowers' tepals opened white and then produced large blotches of bright orange.

Stripes

A startling and unusual *Clivia* clone has been flowered in Japan with a contrasting central stripe running down the center of each petal. It is amazing what rare genetic combinations continue to emerge as more and more breeding takes place.

Clivia miniata 'Proteus'.

Bleached tepals

It is not unusual to find clones in which portions of the tepals rapidly bleach out to produce flowers that have pale patches on the tepals. This is different from the situation where the carotenoids fade, leaving the red pigments that then look pink. It looks as if the red anthocyanins are being destroyed. Comstock photographed a clone in South Africa belonging to Ernie Hobbs called *Clivia miniata* 'Amanda' that was of this type. There are also many pictures in the Japanese literature on clivias that illustrate these sorts of flowers. Such flowers look sunburned to me, and I find them rather unattractive, but others appreciate them.

A striped *Clivia miniata*. Photograph courtesy of
Yoshikazu Nakamura.

NOVELTY LEAVES

There are two sources of novelty leaves, mutation or a combination
of rare genes. In the wild such plants probably would not survive,
but when selected, succored, and pampered by man, they can give
rise to new and unusual families of clivias. As breeding accelerates
around the world with increased seed production, more and more
unusual forms will emerge. If these are not hastily dismissed but
regarded as potential new avenues to pursue, we increase our
options of hybridizing directions to follow.

Clivia miniata 'Amanda'.

I have already discussed several unusual developments within the *Clivia miniata* line, such as leaf variegation, that led to the development of whole new industries in clivia breeding. Two other mutants that seem to have been capitalized on are wide leaves and dark orange-red flowers, neither of which appears to be known in wild *C. miniata* individuals. Both were recognized as desirable when they first appeared in Europe and were developed further.

Japan's early development of clivias for plant shape and form was independent of flower quality, which was originally considered to be of little importance. The total size of the plants has become reduced to dwarfs and then, below that, to miniature plants. Among the dwarfs are plants with very broad leaves that may be a solid dark glossy green color or variegated. Such plants are sometimes described as chabo or daruma. The leaves in some may even curl downwards to embrace the pot. One additional development from the line of miniature breeding is a series of small stunted plants with rugose leaves. Such oddities are appreciated in Japan, and whereas previously they would have been consigned to the compost heap as monstrous runts in Western horticulture, similar plants among the seedlings of American and South African enthusiasts are also now being tended with care and appreciation.

When the Japanese abandoned their dwarf clivias in China, the plants were bred and selected there according to Chinese sensibilities, and a quite different line of plants emerged. The Chinese seemed to favor plants where the leaves were short, broad, and stacked horizontally above each other in two opposite ranks. The architecture of the leaf surfaces became important, and the leaf veins in particular took on an extra significance (Niou et al. 1999). Clivia plants often have naturally prominent veins, and Chinese breeders have selected for exaggerated veining and set criteria for good vein patterns. The veins may either be sunk below the surface of the leaf or raised. In either case what is important is the regularity of and spacing between the long parallel veins as well as the regularity of cross-vein spacing. The leaf tip is also important; it must be nicely rounded and not pointed, and the even spacing of the veins needs to continue into the tip. In order to make the leaf veins stand out more prominently, Chinese breeders have made additional selections for green veins where choloroplast-containing cells are clustered adjacent to the veins, and greenish yellow tissue fills the areas between the veins. The clearer the yellow and the greater the contrast the better. To the Western eye, these leaves tend to look chlorotic as if they are suffering some sort of nutrient deficiency.

Clivia miniata 'Munchkin', a miniature introduction from Conway.

The criteria for judging these plants were recently codified by the Chinese Association for Clivias. Again, as with the Japanese, the flowers are not as important to the Chinese. Few of these Chinese clivia plants have made it to the West but I must admit that the pictures I have seen show very appealing plants. Now that trade barriers are being lifted with the Chinese, hybridizers expect that seed and even plants of the various Chinese clivias will become available worldwide.

A selection of modern Chinese clivias. Note the "desirable" yellow
background with deeper green veins on the leaves. Photograph courtesy of
Yoshikazu Nakamura.

Each season, Comstock tries to wander through the grounds
of several large plant nurseries that grow clivias looking for the
"runts and weirdoes." As those plants are of no use to the unso-
phisticated retail nursery trade, he is often allowed to purchase
and rescue his finds. This takes perseverance and a good eye—
both of which he has. Solomone has a similar appreciation for the
odd and unusual, so Comstock is usually thwarted during his visits to Solomone's nursery. I have also watched Nakamura scurry
through Holmes's nursery looking for flowers with spaghetti-like
petals, ignoring all the wonderful big trusses of yellows that
Holmes produces.

The list of selected clones here is short and incomplete, but it offers a taste of the kinds of unusual plants that result from rare gene recombinations.

Clivia miniata 'Darth Fader'
Yet another of Comstock's strange mutants, this is a standard-sized plant with leaves 2½ inches (6.25 cm) wide and 24 inches (62 cm) long. The leaves are dark sage green when young, but as they mature the green fades and flushes a pewter gray or silver shade. The pattern is like that in the banded "Akebono" clivias but in reverse. The bands of this clone become obvious as the leaves mature and fade, whereas the bands usually deepen to green in "Akebono" forms. The silver bands on 'Darth Fader' leaves occupy different regions of each leaf.

Clivia miniata 'Dragon's Back'
Another standard-sized clivia plant belonging to Comstock with dark green leaves that are 3½ inches (8.75 cm) wide and 18 inches (45 cm) long. This plant has a checkerboard placement of raised areas on the leaves that is passed on to its progeny. Other clivias with irregular, raised blisters scattered across the upper surface of the leaf are sometimes illustrated in Chinese clivia literature.

Clivia miniata 'Hime Chabo'
This is the smallest of the plants that I have obtained from Japan. It is perhaps a little smaller than *Clivia miniata* 'Munchkin'. The leaves measure 1¾ inches (4.5 cm) wide and 7 inches (18 cm) long. This plant has never flowered but produces offsets readily.

Clivia miniata 'Hime Daruma'
I grow this plant, a typical Japanese dwarf grown primarily for its luscious, dark bottle-green leaves that are 4 inches (10 cm) wide and only 14 inches (35 cm) long. As is common with many Japanese cultivars of this type, the flower peduncle is quite short, and the flowers

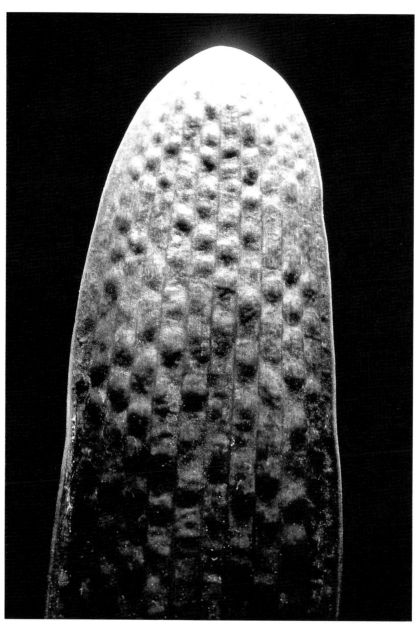

Leaf from *Clivia miniata* 'Dragon's Back'.

barely expose themselves between the leaves. The flowers with their
2½ inches (6.25 cm) natural spread are not noteworthy except that
they often bear seven instead of the normal six tepals. It can be used
as either a pod or pollen parent to breed wide and shapely leaves,
and it appears to be quite dominant for those leaf characteristics.
Even when bred to large Cyrtanthiflora-type clivias, the progeny
appear to be dwarf with wide leaves.

Clivia miniata 'Koh Ryu'
This is a Japanese variety with leaves that bear a number of thickened ridges and longitudinal creases. The thick leaves are rigid and
have lost all flexibility. The kind of leaf folding and corrugations
seen here are sometimes found in the Japanese wide-leaf dwarf and
miniature selections.

Clivia miniata 'Munchkin'
This, the smallest specimen of *Clivia* from the Conway stables, is
a very desirable miniature cultivar. The entire plant in flower is
often less than 7½ inches (18.75 cm) tall. Leaves get to be 7 inches
(18 cm) long and 1¾ inches (4.5 cm) wide. This cultivar carries a
small umbel of six to eight very shapely flowers on a 4-inch (10-cm)
peduncle. Tepals overlap, and the flowers are rounded and full with
a strong mid-orange outer section and a large creamy yellow
throat. Flowers are 1¼ inches (3.1 cm) in diameter, and petals are
less than 1 inch (2.5 cm) wide. The flowers have rather unusual
petals that are rounded but with notched tips, and the sepals are
pointed. My plant does not appear to produce fertile pollen,
although it does produce seed.

Clivia miniata 'Peter Pan'
Another dwarf clivia plant that may be derived from Californian
breeding, this plant is delightful and should be more widely known.
It has many good characteristics, such as the way it holds its large,
well-rounded and green-throated flowers above the foliage.

Clivia miniata 'Silver Lace'
This is among the more curious plants that Comstock rescued from a local hardware store that has a nursery section. The plant has rough, corrugated leaves with a few thick, longitudinal ridges. They are 2½ inches (6.25 cm) wide and 7 inches (18 cm) long. The unusual feature of this plant is a mirrored silver suffusion washed over the leaf's upper surface in a checkerboard pattern, giving it an almost reptilian appearance.

Clivia miniata 'Silver Tiger'
This a new oddity from Mitsuhashi's breeding that he calls "Tiger stripes." The silver cross-banding on the leaves is somewhat irregular, and both the cross-banding and its irregularity are genetic and can be passed on to the offspring. Comstock has one of these plants that he calls 'Silver Tiger'.

Clivia miniata 'Tiny Tim'
For some time this was the only dwarf of American breeding that had been propagated and made available in the American trade. 'Tiny Tim' produces leaves that are only 10 inches (25 cm) long and 2½ inches (6.25 cm) wide. Flowers are carried just above the foliage, and there may be up to fourteen blooms in the umbel. Each flower is 1¾ inches (4.5 cm) wide, and floret length is nearly 2½ inches (6.25 cm). Flowers are tulip-shaped, and petal edges are also incurved. Petals barely reach 1 inch (2.5 cm) in width, and the sepals are slightly over ½ inch (1.25 cm) wide. The flowers are a mid-orange with a large whitish throat. Tepals are rounded. Conway rescued this plant from a local nursery in Santa Barbara and was able to propagate enough divisions to place it on the market. The best offspring from 'Tiny Tim' so far is 'Munchkin', which is a much smaller plant with somewhat smaller flowers. 'Tiny Tim' is self-fertile. It appears to very susceptible to fungal or bacterial problems, and the leaves frequently have dried brown blotches. I have not seen this susceptibility in any of its offspring.

Today's novelties are often tomorrow's commonplace flowers. It is impossible to predict which novelties hybridizers will actively breed and seek out, or what new and unexpected developments are in the future. The one certainty is that we can expect more and more novel combinations of genes to keep cropping up as a result of the accelerated, intensive breeding going on.

Chapter Fourteen

THE FUTURE

THE FUTURE for clivia enthusiasts is bright. Breeding these plants as a hobby is on the increase all over the world, and many more breakthroughs are likely as greater numbers of enthusiasts get involved. The electronic revolution with its attendant e-mail and World Wide Web continues to shrink the world and bring clivia growers together. The electronic interchange of ideas directly facilitates and encourages growers and breeders in a way that was not possible previously. Within a short time of being organized, the e-listing brought several hundred clivia enthusiasts from very different parts of the globe together for a fascinating exchange of ideas. Close and immediate contact between people in disparate parts of the world can only add fuel to the ardor and efforts of those smitten with the clivia bug. There are now clubs, journals, symposia, and even shows devoted to these plants.

The proliferation of clivias is primarily the result of the mass production of seed, so it is possible to find really unusual genetic combinations and very rare mutants that yield unusual varieties. In order to prevent some of the stranger variants being sent to the market place where they will be lost, growers at production nurseries not only need a keen eye but also the ability to recognize and understand a plant's potential. Solomone has been quite astute in keeping and finding these unusual plants. And those are the plants, of course, that create opportunities for new directions in breeding.

It is hard to predict the direction that clivia breeding will take, but there are certainly many areas where hybridizers can improve on the present varieties. Here is my list of some potential improvements:

FLOWER CHARACTERISTICS

Deeper and brighter yellows, golds, and ambers are needed. Most of the current yellow clivias available are washed-out creams with somewhat deeper yellow throats. It is possible to obtain yellows that are evenly colored to the edges of the petals, and with careful selection and breeding, breeders should be able to mass produce those varieties. Similarly, hybridizers might approach creating white clivias by breeding the palest yellows together, although I suspect this would simply yield very pale ivory or cream flowers.

There are a number of clivias with picotee edges. Some of those I described in chapter 8 have clear white throats, and line breeding white-throated varieties and selecting for the narrowest colored margins may eventually lead to clivias that are closer to true white than can be achieved by breeding for paler cream flowers.

Yellow clivias with green throats already exist, and a few of those are nonfading greens. But what about a pure green flower? Green-throated yellows are rare, and I certainly encourage more production of these beauties.

I would like to see deeper reds. Dark orange-red flowers that border on true reds are stunning, but there are so few clones of this type. At least two are available, however, Conway's *Clivia miniata* 'Doris' and Monrovia's *Clivia miniata* Flame™, both of which are in the trade. It should be relatively easy to line breed for deep red coloration. Here is a good direction for a beginning hybridizer.

All the pastels, peaches, apricots, and pinks are in high demand, but the ultimate goal is pure pink. Even among the oranges and reds there are flowers that fade toward pink as they mature. The genes are there, so it is merely a matter of reducing the yellow in the background to purify the pink.

Mauves and purples are still a dream in the hybridizer's mind, but the possibility of working for these colors does exist. It is a matter of being lucky enough to find and recognize those very rare flowers that "blue" as they fade, and then working with those lines.

There needs to be more consistency in both the multipetalled and double types, and a great deal of work is needed to produce umbels in the multipetalled types that consistently bear and breed eight-petalled flowers. There is likewise a long way to go to produce plants that bear symmetrical doubles with increased petal density. Multipetalled and double yellows, peaches, and pastels in variegated and dwarfs are, of course, practically unheard of.

I would also like to see new shapes such as the Capellini types. Unusual mutations appear within most breeding programs, but instead of discarding those as aberrations as they have been in the past, breeders should recognize that those monsters can be tamed. These directions will lead to new dimensions that are limited only by the imagination of the breeder.

Clivias need to better withstand the sun. Like many orange and red flowers, clivias are not sunproof. Selecting and breeding for both leaves and flowers that can take more sunlight without bleaching would be a worthy endeavor.

The rebloom characteristics of clivias can be improved. Clivias that bloom out of season are not unusual, but it would be a definite service to the hobby if someone deliberately found plants that consistently threw several flower stems a year and bred with those to produce a reliably reblooming strain.

Although less glamorous than many of the other lines of breeding I have described, working toward better flower stems on dwarfs is something I regard as necessary. Better growth habits, such as holding umbels above the level of the foliage, are probably just as important as novel flower shapes or color.

PLANT CHARACTERISTICS

I would like to see more broad leaf yellows. Most yellow clivias have relatively narrow leaves, but it should be possible to make broad leaf yellows within two generations of breeding. I would first cross a yellow to an exceptionally broad leaf orange. All of the offspring will have orange flowers. If two of the plants with the widest leaves are crossed, there should be some exceptionally broad leaf yellows among the next generation. I have noticed that in mass breeding programs, such as those of Solomone and Holmes, there appears to be a trend of increasing leaf width among the yellow selections.

Although variegated yellows have started to pop up in various nurseries around the world, there seems to be little effort to deliberately breed yellows, multipetals, Cyrtanthiflora-types, or pastels that have variegated foliage. Variegated leaf plants with the various flower types can be produced in a way that is similar to how the broad leaf yellows can be made. A variegated mother plant should be pollinated with the pollen of the desired flower type, and the offspring with good variegated leaves can be backcrossed to its original, non-variegated parent. The next generation will likely produce some of the desired flower types on plants with variegated leaves. This process is so easy I wonder why not many people have done it.

The Japanese art of horticulture embraces plant forms with novel foliage that clash with many Western ideas. They grow and cherish mutations that include plants with contorted or twisted leaves, as well as leaves that sometimes bear vertical ridges, folds, or even grooves that run through the thick fleshy leaves. To most Western gardeners, these are monstrosities that should be consigned to the shredder or compost heap. But clivia growers in the United States and Africa have been strongly influenced by Japanese ideals and are now open to these new growth forms. Consequently, plants that might have been discarded a generation ago are now coddled. With increased breeding, more of these forms are likely to surface.

There is an emerging role that the Chinese will have in influencing directions of clivia breeding. Their goals regarding leaf shape and texture are somewhat different from those of the Japanese, but as the Chinese clivia industry grows, so will its ideals influence Western clivia growers.

BREEDING AND TECHNOLOGY

Tissue culture
The clivia world is filled with exciting new developments, but traditional methods of multiplication make it unlikely that many of the best clones will ever be widespread in cultivation. It took Monorovia Nurseries (a large wholesale nursery in southern California) nearly forty years of conventional multiplication until it had sufficient stock of *Clivia miniata* Flame™ to introduce. Many of Conway's fine selections number less than ten plants. Perhaps tissue culture is a way around these problems, but it is by no means easy, and even those who have succeeded admit that it is slow. Only two cultivars, Smithers' *Clivia miniata* 'Vico Yellow' and the New Zealand cultivar *C. miniata* 'Redgrove', have been commercially propagated using micropropagation techniques. Tissue culture is unfortunately a double-edged sword. On the one hand it allows for the widespread dissemination of superior clones, which is good. On the other hand, however, such dissemination often causes a decrease in breeding activity because hobbyists and growers become reluctant to spend time and resources on an unproven seedling when they can buy a sure thing instead. If tissue-cultured clivias become commonplace, we can expect a concomitant decrease in the number of hybridizers.

Intergenerics
If true intergeneric hybrids using either *Cryptostephanus* or other related genera such as *Haemanthus* can be produced by embryo rescue, then an entirely new set of doors will open. It should be realized, however, that those first generation hybrids will, in all

likelihood, be sterile and will probably have to be converted into polyploids before they can be used to breed with.

There are a number of purported intergeneric hybrids between *Clivia* and a variety of other amaryllid genera. Some hybrids were reported between such distantly related genera that it seems unlikely they could be true, whereas other crosses have involved somewhat closer relatives. Nevertheless, I have not seen a single purported hybrid that I thought actually showed the true combination between *Clivia* and any other genus.

Among the earliest of these supposed intergeneric hybrids was the cross between *Eucharis* and *Clivia*. McNeil repeated the cross and flowered progeny that looked just like a *Clivia* specimen. He reported that the progeny were scented, and as Eucharis is strongly fragrant, he took this to mean that his hybridization had succeeded. There are, however, naturally fragrant clones of *Clivia*, and the production of scent without other floral or vegetative characteristics from *Eucharis* cannot be used to demonstrate the hybrid nature of those plants.

Another genus that McNeil claimed to have crossed with *Clivia* was *Hippeastrum*. I saw these plants and flowers, and they appeared to me to be pure *Hippeastrum*. It was my impression that even if the pollinated hippeastrum flowers had been emasculated, they had not been isolated from other hippeastrum blossoms. McNeil also claimed that his *C. miniata* 'Four Marys' was bred from *Crinum* pollen onto a clivia, but once again it was pure *Clivia*.

A third more recent case of an apparent intergeneric hybrid involves *Lycoris*. Chinese scientists claimed to have used embryo rescue to get plantlets of the cross Lycoris × *Clivia* and have even marketed mature bulbs as such. All flowers and plants that I have seen of those crosses suggest that the offspring are pure *Lycoris*.

On the face of it the three genera *Eucharis, Hippeastrum*, and *Lycoris* appear to be so far removed from *Clivia*, both geographically and phylogenetically, that it seems unlikely that the actual hybrids could truly exist. They can all be explained away by invoking parthenogenesis, the formation of embryos without fertilization, or poorly controlled pollination. Crosses that would more likely occur are with *Cryptostephanus*, *Clivia*'s sister genus, or with some other fleshy seeded African amaryllids such as *Amaryllis*, *Haemanthus*, and *Nerine*. I did obtain a plant purported to be *Clivia miniata* × *Amaryllis belladonna*, but it looked vegetatively quite similar to Hippeastrum in both the bulbs and leaves. I have not been able to flower that plant yet, and although I was told that it had orange flowers, I am inclined to disbelieve the nature of the hybrid. After hearing about this cross, I tried to remake it. I used frozen *Amaryllis belladonna* pollen from a number of fall-blooming clones on spring-flowering clivias. The first attempt yielded a number of pods filled with good seeds. Upon germination all the seedlings resembled their clivia parent and none produced any sign of bulbs. However, the flowers were not emasculated, and although the flowers were opened indoors and were likely not self-pollinated, that possibility could not be excluded. When pods began forming on that plant I was able to obtain a second plant of the same clone, and I made sure the flowers on the second plant were carefully emasculated before the buds opened. They were also pollinated using frozen *Amaryllis belladonna* pollen, but no ovaries swelled and no fruits were formed. I have found that it is preferable to use the nonbulbous parents as the pod parents when making crosses between bulbous and nonbulbous genera as the formation of bulbs in the progeny reveals their hybrid nature before they flower. If the pod parent is also bulbous, then bulb formation cannot reveal the hybrid nature of those offspring since they could result from self-pollination or parthenogenesis.

Haemanthus species (excluding *Scadoxus*) have many similarities with *Clivia*, including reduced bulbs, leaves in two ranks, large fleshy seeds, and dense umbels of flowers. The molecular data also suggests close affinities to *Clivia*. As long ago as 1837, Herbert suggested that breeders attempt crosses of *Clivia* with *Haemanthus*, but there appear to be no records of such attempts. This cross is an avenue of endeavor that should be attempted because *Haemanthus* is such a diverse assemblage of species that one might be able to incorporate a number of new exciting features into *Clivia*.

There are several reports of attempts to make hybrids between *Clivia* and *Cryptostephanus*. This hybrid might be successful because of the close morphological and molecular affinities between the two taxa, but to date no confirmed hybrids between the two have been produced. My attempts to use embryo rescue techniques to make a cross between *C. miniata* 'Bodnant Variety' and *Cryptostephanus vansonii* have not produced plants, although I did grow large seeds. *Cryptostephanus vansonii* has twenty-four chromosomes compared to the twenty-two of *Clivia* species. If any plantlets originate, they will be dead ends as far as breeding is concerned unless the hybrids are converted into polyploids.

Ploidy conversions
Doubling chromosome numbers is a standard technique in most plant breeding. Tetraploid or polyploid plants usually have larger flowers with heavier substance and more intense coloration, but this is not always the case. Although the large modern hybrids in many flowers are tetraploids, there is no evidence that the large, broad-leafed, modern clivias are tetraploids. Polyploid conversion is not difficult although the active agents are dangerous if mishandled. What the effect of converting clivias into polyploids will be is not known, but it is surprising that so few active attempts at conversion have occurred. This conversion is something that should be attempted in the future because it may be possible to achieve even larger and more spectacular umbels with even larger flowers that last longer. Polyploids have certainly transformed many other garden flowers, such as daffodils, rudbeckias, and gladioli, to the point where interest in older diploid varieties scarcely exists. Only in daylilies, however, have both diploids and tetraploids retained equal popularity. Ploidy conversions are perhaps the most feasible and important techniques that could be used to improve the current clivias.

Mutagens
In an effort to widen flower characteristics (flower color or shape, for example), hybridizers might find it useful to increase the rate at

which novel flower mutations arise. Several decades ago bombarding seeds, bulbs, or other parts of plants with X rays to induce mutations was a popular practice. For the most part the results were disappointing, and few novelties emerged. Nevertheless, the technique is very effective in poinsettia, and it is still used to produce new varieties of that plant. One problem with the technique is that very large numbers of individuals must be used because most of the mutations are either neutral or do not affect floral characteristics. While there has been talk of irradiating clivia seeds or plants, no one has, to my knowledge, actually done so. There are also a series of chemical mutagens that can be used to induce mutations, but the chemicals are dangerous if not handled properly and must be applied under strict laboratory conditions. Again, these techniques have not been applied to clivias.

Gene transfer
There is much activity these days with genetic engineering and the direct transfer of novel genes between plants, sometimes even between animals and plants. On the face of it, genetic engineering would seem the easiest way to change the color of clivias. Most clivia color is anthocyanin-based, so it might not be necessary to transfer the entire constellation of genes responsible for the new pigments but only a subset of those genes. Unfortunately, the process is still prohibitively expensive for anything but a major agricultural crop; it is simply not realistic to expect that genetic manipulation of minor plants such as clivias is likely. This procedure is best carried out in single cells or small clusters of callus growing *in vitro*, so another deterrent to carrying out genetic modification of clivias is the lack of a reliable tissue culture protocol for the plant.

INTERSPECIFIC HYBRIDS

We can expect much more activity using the smaller, pendent-flowered species in the future. These species have different pigments, and as breeders work their way through several generations of inter-specific hybrids, they will likely come across many exciting color combinations and shapes. Second generation hybrids already pro-duced by those doing work like this (Lötter, Nakamura, Comstock, and others) show the very real potential that the species have for creating new color patterns and forms.

CLIVIA POTENTIAL

The future for clivia-growing is very bright. It is a good time to be growing and collecting these plants, especially as they are currently in an active phase of development. Their popularity is expanding exponentially and in diverse parts of the globe. Their popularity has already created several different lines of breeding, each with its own peculiarities and characteristics. It is surprising how much diversity has emerged even where breeders started from an extremely narrow genetic base. The increasing numbers of seed produced to fill the current demand reflects this diversity. Increased seed production has the potential of producing those very rare genetic combinations and mutations that occur very infrequently in nature. Some of these combinations will lead to new lines for development, provided we are able to recognize and retrieve them for future use.

Appendix One

WHO WAS LADY CLIVE?

L ADY CHARLOTTE Florentia Clive, the duchess of Northumberland, was considered a person of influence among the upper ranks of the British aristocracy. She was born in Florence in 1787 to Henrietta Antonia Herbert and Edward Clive, first earl of Powis. Her grandfather was the famous Robert Clive, who helped consolidate British dominion over India, although she never knew him because he had committed suicide in 1774. Charlotte spent part of her early life in India, where her governess, Anna Tonelli, encouraged her to keep a diary. Charlotte became a skilled illustrator, and in 1824 published a book *Castles of Alnwick and Warkworth*, which was illustrated with her own drawings. She also designed an Italian garden at Alnwick castle.

Charlotte wed Hugh, third duke of Northumberland, in 1817. Although she was seven years his senior, their marriage lasted 30 years until his death in 1847. The lady herself lived until 1866. They had no children.

The duke was a model of success. He had been summoned to parliament in 1812 before their marriage, and was later appointed as lord lieutenant of Ireland for the years 1829–30. He eventually became chancellor of Cambridge University, remaining in that august position from 1840 until his death. Lady Clive naturally reflected his social status, but she was also a capable woman in her own right and became one of the most prestigious women of her time. She was a friend of royalty and much sought after.

When the duchess of Kent needed to consolidate support for her daughter, Princess Victoria, (who would become the future queen of England and ruler of the British Empire), she thought the duchess of Northumberland, with her stature and respect among the nobility, should act as her daughter's official governess. At that time Victoria's ascension to the throne was not assured, and the duchess, together with Sir John Conroy, the family steward, thought that Lady Clive's reputation could help support Victoria's case. Victoria's father had died when she was eight months old, and Conroy realized that if Victoria did become queen of England, he might be in a powerful position. For a number of years beginning in 1830, Lady Clive held the position of official governess, although her role was supposed to be purely titular and nominal. Princess Victoria actually had a number of male tutors, and Baroness Lehzen, a member of the household, acted as a real governess.

Although Lady Clive had been selected primarily for her rank and reputation, she did take her role seriously and tried to play an active part in Princess Victoria's education. This was not to the liking of either the duchess of Kent or Conroy, who wanted to limit the influences that any other person might enjoy with the princess. Lady Clive was also concerned about Conroy's authority. In a letter to Lord Liverpool in 1833 she voiced her anxiety that Conroy's bid for power was causing a rift between Victoria and her mother. Neither the duchess nor Conroy was comfortable with Lady Clive, and they looked for an excuse to get rid of her. Their chance came in 1835 when they claimed that Victoria had reached the age of seventeen and no longer required a governess. Such a change needed the approval of the monarch, William IV, but before the request could be acted upon, a confrontation between Lady Clive and the duchess of Kent erupted. The king had sent a letter via Lady Clive to the duchess about Victoria's coming confirmation ceremony. The reply, however, was returned to the king through the archbishop of

Canterbury. (In those days there was a very strict etiquette concerning the proper routes of communication and transmittal of messages. Deviation from these standards was considered a grievous insult.) The implication was, therefore, that the duchess had deliberately slurred Lady Clive. The king was irate for he considered Lady Clive a good friend, and he threatened to delay Victoria's confirmation unless the reply was forwarded through Lady Clive. The princess's mother declined at first, and the king stopped the confirmation. The duchess of Kent eventually gave in and sent the reply through the proper channels. Although relations between the duchess and Lady Clive must have been at their worst, it would have been unseemly to dismiss her as she obviously had the king's ear. Such a brouhaha may seem ridiculous to us today, but it does illustrate the high esteem that the king had for Lady Clive. A year later in 1834 Victoria was named queen, but by then Lady Clive had resigned, presumably of her own accord.

During the years before her intrigues at court began, and without the demands of a family (she had no children of her own), Lady Clive must have turned to other pursuits. There is little detailed information about this period of her life, but she was involved with running Syon House, and it was during this time that the plant that was to be named after her came to be grown in the large conservatory that was built at the estate.

Expansion of the British Empire meant that many regions of the world were for the first time accessible to explorers, and those who were rich enough could indulge themselves in a variety of interests. Natural history was one of those interests, and obtaining collections of tropical plants became very fashionable. In 1828 there had been a large importation of South African plants with strap-shaped leaves. The plants were thought to be a form of *Agapanthus*, a handsome long-leaved plant with umbels of blue flowers, and they were marketed as such. One plant in the duke of Northumberland's collection (he had a conservatory of exotic plants on his estate at Syon House under Mr. Forrest's charge) was the first to flower. It bore an impressive umbel of pendent, tubular, orange flowers with the tips of each petal painted green. Lindley named this new species in honor of Lady Charlotte Florentia Clive, and it became known as *Clivia nobilis*. It was purely happenstance that Lady Clive's plant flowered first and that she is now remembered because of it.

Appendix Two

SOURCES OF INFORMATION

A NOTE ON telephone numbers. For the sake of consistency, I have grouped the numbers into four sets. The first set is the country code. The second set is in parentheses and is the area or city code. When dialing from outside that country, omit the first number (usually the 0 or 1) in the area or city code. The third and fourth set of numbers are the local phone numbers.

THE CLIVIA CLUB

Not only is this a good source of international information about clivias, but it is also a list of sources for seeds and plants. Every four years the Club holds an international symposium devoted to clivias. It publishes the quarterly *Clivia Club Newsletter* and an annual *Clivia Yearbook*. The Clivia Club has several local branches that distribute and sell seed and hold annual shows.

For membership information contact:

Clivia Club
P.O. Box 53219
Kenilworth 7745, South Africa
Tel: 27 (021) 799 8668
Fax: 27 (021) 799 0002
www.clivias.com/Default.htm

Australian contact for the Clivia Club
Kenneth R. Smith
593 Hawkesbury Road
Winmalee
New South Wales 2777
Tel: 61 (024) 754 3287
E-mail: cliviasmith@hotmail.com

Japanese contact for the Clivia Club
Yoshikazu Nakamura
Clivia Breeding Plantation
48-2, Kurodo, Mobara-city, 297-0071
Chiba Prefecture
Tel: 81 (047) 235 5444

United Kingdom contact for the Clivia Club
Michael Jeans
Hugletts Farm
Heathfield
East Sussex TN 21 9BY
Tel: 44 (01435) 662318
E-mail: mjeans@saquet.co.uk

INTERNATIONAL BULB SOCIETY

This is a group that has traditionally maintained an interest in clivias. It produces an annual publication, *Herbertia*, and a quarterly called *Bulbs*. It occasionally publishes articles on clivias. The Society also maintains an international discussion list and e-mail bulb forum that periodically discusses issues related to clivias. It holds an annual symposium and may sponsor local meetings.

For membership and general information contact:

International Bulb Society
Dr. Dave Lehmiller
Membership Director
550 IH-10 South, Suite 201
Beaumont, Texas 77707
United States
E-mail: membership@bulbsociety.org
www.bulbsociety.org

WEB-BASED INFORMATION

Clivia discussion list and chat group
This is a discussion list devoted to clivias that is administered by Rudo Lötter. To join, contact clivia-enthusiast-subscribe@yahoo-groups.com. To post to the mailing list, contact clivia-enthusiast @egroups.com or clivia-enthusiast@yahoogroups.com. To contact the administrator, contact clivia-enthusiast-owner@egroups.com or clivia-enthusiast-owner@yahoogroups.com.

Toshi's page
This is a good source for information and for making contacts about clivias in Japan—much of it is in English.
www.ic-net.or.jp/home/akemi/index1.htm

York Wang's page
A webpage about Chinese clivias.
E-mail: yorkcn@sina.com
http://yorksosoo.net
This is an interesting, English-language page that discusses Chinese clivias.

Appendix Three

SOURCES OF PLANTS

THIS LISTING is not necessarily an endorsement of the nurseries listed. I have not had dealings with many of these nurseries and cannot vouch for all of them.

Australia
David Bearlin
32 McComas Ave
Burwood
Victoria 3125
Tel: 61 (039) 833 3237

Ellison Horticultural
P.O. Box 365
Nowra
New South Wales
Tel: 61 (024) 421 4255
Fax: 61 (024) 423 0859
E-mail: sales@ellisonhort.com.au
www.ellisonhort.com

Pen Henry
Clivia Gardens
120 Caporn Street
Wanneroo
Western Australia 6065
Tel: 61 (089) 405 1027
Fax: 61 (089) 405 1027
E-mail:cliviagdns@optusnet.com.au
Sells seeds. Retail and mail order.

Mainly Amaryllids Garden
6 Waratah Way
Wodonga
Victoria 3690
Daryl (Dash) Geoghegan
Tel: 61 (026) 056 2510
Fax: 61 (026) 056 2510
E-mail: plants_man@bigpond.com
www.users.bigpond.com/plants_man/Home.htm
Sells plants and seeds of various clivias, primarily those that origi-
nate from Japan, China, Africa, and Australia. Mail order sales avail-
able, and retail sales are by appointment only.

Bill Morris
377 Brocklesby Road
Medowie
New South Wales 2318
Tel: 61 (024) 982 8447
Sells seeds and plants for both retail and wholesale. Mail order sales
accepted. Supplies primarily superior yellows, oranges, and reds.
Stocks are very limited and only available in Australia at the moment.

Pine Mountain Nursery
P.O. Box 5016
Brassall
Queensland 4305
Tel: 61 (075) 464 3976
Fax: 61 (075) 464 3700
E-mail: craigie@bigpond.com
Sells *Clivia miniata* cultivars including orange, cream, yellow, peach, gold, and red; Sahin's Twin strains; Belgian strains; *C. caulescens*; *C. gardenii*; *C.* Cyrtanthiflora Group; and various crosses. Wholesale and mail order sales available.

Ken Smith
Clivia Breeder and Collector
593 Hawksbury Road
Winmalee
New South Wales 2777
Tel: 61 (024) 754 3287
E-mail: cliviasmith@hotmail.com
Seed sales only.

Japan
Hiroshi Mitsuhashi
Mitsuhashi Cactus Nursery
893 Shimano
Ichihara City, Chiba-ken 290-0034
Tel: 81 (043) 622 1766
Fax: 81 (043) 623 3634
E-mail: m9489@peach.ocn.ne.jp
This nursery is famous for its epiphytic cactus hybrids, but it also offers clivia plants and has a fine selection of novelty types of clivias, including doubles, species hybrids, and those with unusual leaves.

Yoshikazu Nakamura
Clivia Plantation
48-2, Kuroda Mobara-city
Chiba Prefecture
Tel: 81 (047) 523 5444
Fax: 81 (047) 523 5444
Sells seeds and clivia plants of all kinds. Has an international reputation for clivias with rare and unusual leaf types and flowers.

New Zealand
Peter Goodwin
Kapiti Coast Clivias
29 KoheKohe Road
Waikanae
Tel: 64 (04) 904 7912
Specializes in variegates and yellows. Retail and wholesale in New Zealand, and mail order elsewhere.

Michael L. B. Styles
Clivia Breeder
131 Ruapehu Street
Paraparmu
Tel: 64 (04) 298 8474
E-mail: m.styles@clear.net.nz
http://home.clear.net.nz/pages/s.styles/
Bare root plants and seeds sold via retail and mail order. Specializes in big reds.

South Africa
Connie Abel
89 Brampton Road
Lynwood Manor 0081
Tel: 27 (012) 361 6406
Mature plants and seedlings of *Clivia miniata*, species, multipetals, and others.

Sean Chubb
Thurlow Fish and Flora
P.O. Box 126
Eston 3740
Tel: 27 (031) 781 1978
Fax: 27 (031) 781 1978
E-mail: terric@iafrica.com
Sells seed and plants. Specializes in peaches, pinks, and pastels, as well as in original genetic material, wild originated species, *Clivia miniata* orange-yellow, *C. miniata* peach, *C. gardenii*, and *C. caulescens*.

Welland and Margaret Cowley
Cape Flora
P.O. Box 10556
Linton Grange
Port Elizabeth 6015
Tel: 27 (041) 379 2096
Fax: 27 (041) 379 3188
E-mail: capeflor@iafrica.com
http://users.iafrica.com/c/ca/capeflor
Sells a variety of modern clivias including both seedlings and mature plants. Mail order.

Rodney Ellis
24 Oakhill Road
Vincent
East London 5247
Tel: 27 (043) 726 3463
Sells primarily yellows including banded and variegated leaf plants.

Ken Fargher
The Clivia Store
P.O. Box 1453
Highlands North
Johannesburg 2037
E-mail: info@clivias.com
www.clivias.com
An e-commerce site incorporating the Clivia Store that sells clivia
seed from international clivia hybridizers.

Tino Ferero
P.O. Box 31153
Wonderbloom Park 0033
Tel: 27 (012) 546 8683
Fax: 27 (012) 546 8683
E-mail: fererokp@netactive.co.za
Sells clivia plants and seeds of various kinds.

Pat Gore
669 Killicklaan
Les Marais
Pretoria 0084
Tel: 27 (012) 335 3804
Sells both seeds and plants of a wide variety, though *Clivia miniata* hybrids are predominant.

Jim Holmes
Cape Seed and Bulb
P.O. Box 6363
Stellenbosch 7612
Tel: 27 (021) 887 9418
Fax: 27 (021) 887 0823
E-mail: capeseed@iafrica.com
www.clivia.co.za
A very large operation that sells both seeds and plants. It specializes in yellow- and pastel-colored clivias. Wholesale and retail.

Rudo Lötter
Cyrtanthiflora Breeders
P.O. Box 48570
Hercules
Pretoria 0030
Tel: 27 (012) 694 3774
Fax: 27 (012) 372 1944
E-mail: clivia@iafrica.com
http://users.iafrica.com/c/cl/clivia
Sells seeds and mature plants. Produces wide range of clivias such as *Clivia miniata* yellow, orange, peach, broadleaf, interspecific hybrids, and many more. Wholesale.

Anna Meyer
Safari Nursery
P.O. Box 72244
Lynnwoodrif 0040
Pretoria
This is a general retail nursery that sells a variety of plants including
mixed clivias of Anna Meyer's breeding.

Braam Opperman
P.O. Box 5609
Weltevreden Park 1715
Tel: 27 (011) 475 2586
Fax: 27 (011) 475 2586
Sells seeds and plants of most varieties. Retail and wholesale.

Gert Wiese
12 van der Westhuizen Avenue
Durbanville 7550
Sells plants of various kinds.

United States
Dave Conway
Conway's Clivias
2324 Santa Barbara Street
Santa Barbara, California 93105
Tel: 1 (1 805) 682 7651
Fax: 1 (1 805) 682 7651
E-mail: s.b.conways@worldnet.att.net
Has a number of choice divisions of named clivias of many different
types, including yellows, pale creams, reds, and greens. Retail and
mail order sales available.

Dragon Agro Products
P.O. Box 33
Kendall Park, New Jersey 08824-0033
Tel: 1 (1 732) 619 5817
Fax: 1 (1 732) 297 2829
E-mail: dragon@dragonagro.com
www.dragonagro.com

Monterey Bay Nursery, Inc.
P.O Box 1296
Watsonville, California 95077
Tel: 1 (1 831) 724 6361
Fax: 1 (1 831) 724 8903
E-mail: mbn@montereybaynsy.com
http://montereybaynsy.com
The agent for Solomone hybrids, this nursery sells plants, mainly
yellows and some variegated clivias. Wholesale only.

Plant Horizons
P.O. Box 57
Aromas, California 95004
Fax: 1 (1 831) 726 2018
Distributes for Monterey Bay Nursery. Wholesale only.

Protea Farm of California
P.O. Box 1806
Fallbrook, California 92088
Tel: 1 (1 760) 728 4297

San Marcos Growers
P.O. Box 6827
Santa Barbara, California 93160
Tel: 1 (1 805) 683 1561
Fax: 1 (1 805) 964 1329
E-mail: sales@smgrowers.com
www.smgrowers.com/
Sells plants, particularly yellow clivias, *Clivia miniata*, and *Clivia miniata* 'Aurea'. Wholesale only.

M. and C. Willets
Clivia Growers
P.O. Box 446
Moss Landing, California 95039
Tel: 1 (1 831) 728 2852
E-mail: mandcw@ccnet.com
www.bulbmania.com
Private growers who sell their excess clivias via mail order. Stock includes a yellow hybrid from Gordon McNeil's stock.

GLOSSARY

Akebono. A broad, transverse banding pattern on the leaves of certain clivias that are pale yellow-green or ivory-green when young. The leaves may change to a darker green as they age.

Allele. A gene that occupies a set position or locus on a chromosome. Each plant normally has two genes (alleles) for a certain trait or characteristic, but the alleles are not necessarily the same; for example, for a trait such as the shape of leaf tips, one allele may code for round tips and the other for pointed tips.

Anther. The top portion of the stamen where the pollen is produced.

Anthocyanins. These are water-soluble flavonoid color pigments. They usually produce pink, red, and blue colors and occur in the central vacuole (cavity) of the cell.

Apical meristem. Actively dividing cells at the tip of the rhizome.

Backcross. To make a cross by pollinating an offspring back to one of its parents. It is sometimes used to retrieve parental characters.

Bract. A leaf modified for functions other than photosynthesis.

Callus. Clusters of undifferentiated plants cells. A term often used to refer to cells grown as a mass in tissue culture.

Carotenoids. Chemical pigments that are formed from a long zigzag chain of carbon atoms. Carotenoid pigments are usually yellow to orange. They are not water-soluble and occur inside small granules called plastids in the cell's cytoplasm.

Clones. Genetically identical individuals.

Codominance. Both genes of a pair of alleles are expressed in this situation, and if they are different, intermediate characters are produced.

Cultivar. A contraction of the term *cultivated variety*.

Cyanidin. A group of anthocyanin flavonoids, found in clivia seedling leaf bases, berries, and flowers. They tend to be pink, red, and purple colors.

Dihydrokaempferol. The basic common molecule that can be converted into a wide variety of end products depending on which additional enzymes are present. An important step in anthocyanin synthesis from which a variety of different anthocyanin pigments can be made.

Dominant characters. Features of a parent that invariably emerge in its direct offspring. Orange color is an example of a dominant character. Usually only one allele (copy of the gene) is needed in order for it to be expressed.

Endosperm. The tissue making up the food store of the seed.

Enzymes. The proteins that catalyze reactions, changing the structure of molecules. Each gene codes for an enzyme.

F_1 Hybrids. The progeny in the first generation of a cross.

F_2 Hybrids. The progeny from crosses between F_1 hybrids. Usually F_2 plants will show more variation than F_1.

Filament. The slender stalk that supports the anthers.

Flavonoids. The chemical byproducts of plant cells. Anthocyanins are flavonoids. They are also referred to as flavones.

Grex names. The names used to designate all the progeny of a cross between species. Although once used for clivias, grex names are now used only for orchids.

Group names. Grex names are now designated as group names for clivias. A typical example is Clivia Cyrtanthiflora Group.

Heterosis. A term that refers to hybrid vigor. Often the resulting F_1 hybrid plants are larger and more vigorous growers than either parent.

Hybrid. A plant that is the result of deliberate pollination. Hybrids are the results of a cross between two different parents, either within the same species or between different species.

Inflorescence. A stem with the flowers it bears.

Intercalary meristem. A meristematic layer of dividing cells situated between the leaf blade and sheath. Division of intercalary meristem results in the leaf blade growing and elongating from its base.

Lamina. The blade or main body of the leaf.

Leaf meristem. A strip of dividing cells behind the shoot apex that will develop into a leaf.

Line breeding. Mating parents with similar features together and repeating this through several generations. Line breeding tends to produce more uniform offspring. It can also be oriented toward a goal, such as producing deeper red flowers by mating the two darkest reds together from each generation.

Meristem. Plant tissue containing actively dividing cells. See apical meristem.

Monocot. Plants that have one cotyledon or seed leaf at germination.

Mucro. A small thornlike process or a triangular appendage on the tip of a tepal that is not always present

Outcross. Usually refers to the progeny produced from two parents that are not closely related to each other.

Ovule. The structure bearing the egg cell. The fertilized egg cell will develop into a seed.

Parthenogenesis. The formation of embryos without fertilization.

Pathway. A name given to a chain of chemical reactions that result in a specific end product.

Pedicel. The stalk that attaches the flower to the top of the peduncle.

Peduncle. The stem that supports the entire mass of flowers.

Pelargonidin. Another group of anthocyanin flavonoids of which two feature prominently in clivias. There are two main pelargonidins in *Clivia*, pelargonidin-3-glucoside and pelargonidin-3-rutinoside.

Petals. The three inner colored segments making up the flower.

Phytomelanin. Brown or black pigment in the seed coat of several different kinds of monocotyledonous plants.

Picotee. A flower that has a distinct petal margin of contrasting color.

Plastid. These are small organelles that occur in the cytoplasm of a cell. They usually contain chlorophyll and carotenoids. A chromoplast is a plastid that contains mainly carotenoids, whereas a chloroplast contains primarily chlorophyll. Plastids have their own genetic material but can be influenced by nuclear genes.

Ploidy. This term refers to the number of sets of chromosomes in the plant. Normally plants have two sets of each kind of chromosome and are called diploids. In many garden hybrids such as daylilies or daffodils, there are four sets of chromosomes, and those plants are referred to as tetraploids. Tetraploids are usually larger plants with bigger flowers and thicker tepals. There are no known tetraploids in *Clivia*, and all hybrids and species appear to be diploids. Triploids result from crossing diploids with tetraploids and they tend to be sterile. Clivia breeders are interested in making tetraploid Clivia, but if any have been produced, they have not been well publicized.

Polyploids. Refers to more than two sets of chromosomes.

Proplastid. An undifferentiated plastid that could become either a chromoplast or a chloroplast.

Recessive characters. Genes that are not expressed unless the plant possesses two identical copies of that gene are called recessive. The genes that block anthocyanin synthesis have this characteristic.

Recurved. Bending backwards.

Sepals. The three outer colored segments of a clivia flower. They are usually narrower than the inner petals.

Tepals. The name given to the sepals and petals when they are both colored and when they resemble each other.

Umbel. A distinctive inflorescence in which clusters of flowers appear to all come from a single point on the peduncle or flower stalk.

Variegation. A patterning of the leaves typically involving alternating green and yellow or white stripes of varying thickness.

Velamen. A thick epidermal layer that occurs on clivia roots that is similar to the velamen on roots of orchids.

MAP OF SOUTH AFRICA

References and Additional Reading

Anonymous. 1993. Information about the Bodnant clivias. *Clivia Club Newsletter* 2: 5—7.

Baker, J. G. 1888. *Handbook of the Amaryllidaceae Including the Alstroemerieae and Agaveae*. London: George Bell and Sons.

Bartley, G. E. and P. A. Scolnik. 1995. Plant carotenoids: pigments for photoprotection, visual attraction, and human health. *The Plant Cell* 7: 1027—1038.

Batten, A. and H. Bokelmann. 1966. *Wild Flowers of the Eastern Cape Province*. Cape Town, South Africa: Books of Africa.

Blackbeard, G. I. 1939. *Clivia* breeding. *Herbertia* 6: 190—193.

Brouillard, R. 1988. Flavonoids and flower color. In *The Flavonoids: Advances in Research Since 1980*. Ed. J. B. Harborne. London: Chapman and Hall. 525—538.

Cribb, P. 1979. *Cryptostephanus haemanthoides*. *Curtis's Botanical Magazine* 182: 95—97.

De Coster P. 1998a. History of clivia in Belgium. *Clivia Yearbook* 1998: 31—32.

————. 1998b. Selection and commercial production of *Clivia* in Europe. *Clivia Yearbook* 1998: 32—39.

Drysdale, W. 1990. E. P. Zimmerman, *Clivia* hybridist. *Herbertia* 46: 44.

Duncan, G. D. 1999. *Grow Clivias: A Guide to the Species Cultivation and Propagation of the Genus Clivia*. Cape Town, South Africa: National Botanical Institute.

Dyer, R. A. 1943. *Clivia caulescens*. The Flowering Plants of South Africa 23: t.891. Pretoria, South Africa: J. L. van Schaik.

Forssman, C. 1948. The clivias at Scott's Farm, Grahamstown. *Herbertia* 15: 59—63.

Gouws, J. B. 1949. Karyology of some South African Amaryllidaceae. *Plant Life* 5: 54—81.

Grey-Wilson, C. 1997. *Cyclamen: A Guide for Gardeners, Horticulturists and Botanists*. Portland, Oregon: Timber Press.

Grove, D. L. 1995. *Vandas and Ascocendas and their Combinations with Other Genera*. Portland, Oregon: Timber Press.

Harborne, J. B., H. Baxter, and G. P. Moss. 1999. *Phytochemistry Dictionary: A Handbook of Bioactive Compounds from Plants*. Second edition. London: Taylor and Francis.

Harborne, J. B., and R. J. Grayer. 1988. The anthocyanins. In *The Flavonoids: Advances in Research Since 1980*. Ed. J. B. Harborne. London: Chapman and Hall. 1—20.

Herbert, W. 1837. *Amaryllidaceae; Preceded by an Attempt to Arrange the Monocotyledonous Orders and Followed by a Treatise on Cross-bred Vegetables and Supplement*. London: James Ridgeway and Sons.

Herbert, W. M. 1970. *Amaryllidaceae*. Reprint with an introduction by H. P. Traub. J. Cramer, Hist. Nat. Class. Vol 79. Germany: Verlag von J. Cramer.

Holton, T. A., and E. C. Cornish. 1995. Genetics and biochemistry of anthocyanin biosynthesis. *The Plant Cell* 7: 1071—1083.

Hooker, W. J. 1828. *Imatophyllum Aitoni*: Handsome-flowered *Imatophyllum*. *Curtis's Botanical Magazine* 55: t.2856.

———. 1854. *Imantophyllum ? miniatum*. *Curtis's Botanical Magazine* 80: t.4783.

———. 1856. *Clivia gardeni*. *Curtis's Botanical Magazine* 82: t.4895.

Hutchings, A. 1996. *Zulu Medicinal Plants: An Inventory*. Pietermaritzburg, South Africa: University of Natal Press.

Kington, S. 1998. *The International Daffodil Register and Classified List 1998*. London: Royal Horticultural Society.

Koopowitz, H. 2000. *Clivia* names. *Clivia Yearbook* 2: 30 — 33.

Laing, M. 2000. Bacterial Soft Rot in Clivias. *Clivia Yearbook* 2: 64 — 66.

Lindley, J. 1828. *Clivia nobilis*. Edwards's Botanical Register 14: t.1182.

————. 1854. New Plants *Vallota ? miniata*. *The Gardeners' Chronicle* 8: 119.

McNeil, G. 1963. *Cryptostephanus vansonii*. *Plant Life—The Amaryllis Yearbook* 19: 54.

Matsuno, T., and H. Hirao. 1980. "*Clivia* color pigments" (in Japanese). *Garden Life* 12: 30.

Meerow, A.W., M. F. Fay, G. L. Charles, L. Qin-Bao, Z. Q. Faridah, and M. W. Chase. 1999. Systematics of Amaryllidaceae based on cladistic analysis of plastid sequence data. *American Journal of Botany* 86: 1325 — 1345.

Mori, G. 1990. Kunshi Ran — 12 months (in Japanese). New My Green. Vol. 6. Tokyo: Shufu No Tomo Sha Publisher.

Mullen, R., and J. Munson. 1987. *Victoria: Portrait of a Queen*. London: BBC Books.

Niou, J-q., X-z Liu, et al. 1999. "The evaluation of *Clivia*" (in Chinese). Chang Chun, China: Jiling Science Technology Publications.

Ogasawara, R. 1997. "*Clivia*" (in Japanese). Tokyo: NHK Broadcasting Publication.

Ran, Y., B. G. Murray, and K. R. W. Hammett. 1998. Research in *Clivia* chromosomes. *Clivia Yearbook* 1998: 48 — 55.

Regel, E. 1864. *Clivia miniata* Lindl. *Amaryllideae*. *Gartenflora* 14: 131, t.434.

Schulze, G. M. 1941. "Neue Amaryllidaceen aus Deutsch-Südwest-Afrika" (in German). *Botanische Jahrbeucher feur Systematik Pflanzengeschichte und Planzengeographie* 71: 520 — 525.

Shiang, Q-I, and Y-l. Song. 1999. "Variegated *Clivia*" (in Chinese). Chang Chun, China: Jiling Science Technology Publications.

Smith, K. 1993. Clivia 'Col Pitman'. *Clivia Club Newsletter* 2(3): 8—9.

Smithers, Sir P. 1995. The origins of *Clivia miniata* 'Vico Yellow' and 'Vico Gold'. *Herbertia* 50: 9—12.

Thurston, V. A. 1998. The *Clivia*. Tongaat, South Africa: privately printed.

Van Houtte, L. 1869—70. Imantophyllum (Hybr.) Cyrtanthiflorum. *Flores des Serres et Horticole*. 18: 87 t.1877.

van Huylenbroeck, J. M. 1998. *Clivia miniata* Regel: Control of Plant development and flowering. *Clivia Yearbook* 1998: 13—20.

Verdoon, I. C. 1943. *Cryptostephanus vansonii*. The Flowering Plants of South Africa. 23: Plate 885. Pretoria, South Africa. J. L. van Schaik.

Warren, L. 1999. Plantspeople, Horace and Mary Anderson. *Pacific Horticulture* 60: 20—26.

Woodham-Smith, C. 1972. *Queen Victoria*. New York: Alfred A Knopf.

INDEX OF PLANT NAMES

Page numbers in **boldface** indicate photographs.

Phoenix roeblenii, 100

Raphis, 100

Soleirolia soleirolii, 100
Strelitzia nicolai, 51, 55,100
swamp clivia, 45

Tulbaghia simmerlei, 100

Vallota ? miniata. See *Clivia miniata*
Vallota purpurea. See *Cyrtanthus elatus*
vanda, 281